Shropshire & Downe

Two Landscapes Darwin Held Dear

Shropshire & Downe

Two Landscapes Darwin Held Dear

EWA PROKOP

Front cover: Photograph of ancient woodland near Down House
by Irene Palmer.

Back cover: Photograph 'Heather in Bloom on the Long Mynd'
by Jon Hodgson.

First published 2014 by DB Publishing, an imprint of JMD Media Ltd, Nottingham,
United Kingdom.

ISBN 9781780913605

Copyright © Ewa Prokop 2014.

www.madaboutcharlesdarwin.co.uk

Printed and bound by Copytech (UK) Limited, Peterborough.

Contents

To Nature & Nurture

PREFACE

Charles Darwin (1809–1882) has captured the imagination of millions of people – and I am one of them.

I once worked as a Countryside Officer for the London Borough of Bromley. Its countryside was beautiful, with chalk grasslands full of wildflowers, ancient woodlands full of bluebells, ponds rich in amphibians and dragonflies and hedgerows full of birds. This was no ordinary place either. It included Darwin's countryside. A place he, despite his travels on the 'Beagle', called 'the extreme verge of the world' and where he spent forty years of his life.

After eighteen years working there, I took redundancy and waited fifteen months before being offered another job. This time my role was to be with the Shropshire Hills Area of Outstanding Beauty Partnership, on a river project, on a year's contract. By pure chance, I had ended up working in the county where Darwin had grown up!

When I arrived in Shropshire, I attended a very informative tour around Shrewsbury forming part of the annual 'Darwin Festival'. The tour guide succinctly summarised Darwin's training ground by commenting how his family environment had nurtured his curiosity, his medical profession had helped Darwin develop his knowledge of anatomy, his geological training had taught him the immensity of time and the possibility of change, and his awareness of wildlife diversity and adaptation had been triggered by his travels abroad. Being proud of Darwin's roots in Shrewsbury, I can just about forgive her for failing to highlight the importance of his work at Downe! It left me thinking. What biodiversity could be found in

Shropshire in Darwin's day? How did this compare to species and habitats Darwin came across at Downe (by which I mean 'Darwin's landscape', the landscape broadly around Downe as put forward in 'Darwin's Landscape Laboratory proposed World Heritage Site Nomination Document 2009'[1])?

I started to look at some old publications written about Shropshire and about the Darwins in Shropshire and found that very little had been captured about Darwin's interaction with the natural history of the county. In contrast, much research had been undertaken about Darwin's interaction with the natural history of Downe as part of two World Heritage bids. In an effort to create an image of two of the environments Darwin held dear, I took it upon myself to write this book to capture something of Darwin's Shropshire and Darwin's Downe.

The book starts with the chapter 'An Exceptional Observationist'. This highlights some of Darwin's opinions on observation and some of his influences and possible motivations in developing his skills as an observationist. 'Darwin's Play Settings' takes a look at some of the locations in which Darwin developed his observation skills and his knowledge of natural history. Darwin described his surroundings at Downe in something called 'The General Aspect'; I play on this by presenting briefs of how others and I describe Downe and Shropshire in the chapter 'General Aspects'. The chapters thereafter are mainly based on the biodiversity of Shropshire and Downe and species that Darwin is likely to have encountered or known to have studied. 'Six-Legged Curiosites' focuses on insect species that fascinated Darwin. 'Flight Fantastic' looks at the birds Darwin encounters in 1826 and outlines the range of birds found around Shrewsbury and Shropshire in his day. 'In the Thick of It' looks at trees and hedges of Downe and Shropshire, how he describes them and what species were or can be encountered in them, as well as some of his research. 'A Bit of Botanising' looks at wildflowers around Shrewsbury, including heathland, and then looks at the value of meadows and chalk grassland especially prominent around Downe. It includes some reference to some of the species Darwin studied in Downe. 'Watery Investigations' outlines Darwin's love of fishing and the newts and other pond species of Shropshire and Downe, including some of the investigations Darwin undertook. 'Mammalian and Reptilian Encounters' outlines the mammals and reptiles particularly found in Shropshire and his likelihood of seeing them or his observations of them. 'Under Our Feet' provides brief coverage of Darwin's observations of geology in Downe & Shropshire and his studies on earthworms. 'Brink of Extinction' looks at some threatened species of the Shropshire & Downe landscapes. 'Darwin's Last Years' outlines how Darwin was remembered around the time of his death. 'Landscape Conservationists' summarises the role of conservationists in sustaining and enhancing the quality of the landscapes Darwin held dear.

AN EXCEPTIONAL OBSERVATIONIST

Darwin was an observationist, but other than a couple of quotes from his son Francis[1] 'I used to like to hear him admire the beauty of a flower, it was a kind of gratitude to the flower itself, and a personal love for its form and colour' and 'I seem to remember him gently touching a flower he delighted in; it was the same simple admiration that a child might have', one gets the distinct impression that Darwin's mind could not stop buzzing with questions and that he rarely ever just observed. It turned out better for us that he didn't. His need for answers and his genius of mind gave us a better understanding of the origins, adaptations and diversity of species.

Darwin wrote of himself[2]: 'From my early youth I have had the strongest desire to understand or explain whatever I observed – that is, to group all facts under some general laws...' Francis wrote[3]: 'He often said that no one could be a good observer unless he was an active theoriser...it was as though he were charged with theorizing power ready to flow into any channel on the slightest disturbance; so that no fact, however small, could avoid releasing a stream of theory, and thus the fact became magnified into importance'. Barlow wrote that Emma Darwin used to repeat this saying of Darwin's[4]: 'It is a fatal fault to reason whilst observing, though so necessary beforehand and so useful afterwards'.

What drove Darwin to observe and theorize as he did?
The first driver may be as simple as this. Darwin said of himself 'I was born a naturalist'.[5] Darwin wrote: 'The passion for collecting, which leads a man to be a systematic naturalist...was clearly innate, as none of my sis-

ters or brother every had this taste'[6] Humans are of course born with an innate fascination in the natural world, but there is something to be said for the fact that some people are from a young age exceptionally drawn to the living landscape around them and become a 'sponge', endeavouring to experience nature whenever possible. Natural England reports that: 'it is a recognised fact that contact with nature can play an important role in the educational and social development of children; and that early contact with nature plays an important role in developing pro-environmental values and behaviours'[7]

The second driver may be that Darwin was exposed 'by example' to the benefits of making observations of nature. From an early age, he witnessed his parents' love of nature's variety in the garden of The Mount in Shrewsbury and their care in making records in a garden diary. This probably instilled in him an enhanced awareness of flowers and insects in particular. The Shropshire Archaeological & Natural History Society noted[8] that Darwin said of his father: 'he did not inherit any aptitude for poetry or mechanics, nor did he possess, as I think, a scientific mind. I cannot tell why my fathers mind did not appear to be fitted for advancing science, for he was full of theorizing and was incomparably the most acute observer whom I ever knew. But his powers in this direction were exercised almost wholly in the practice of medicine and the observation of human character.' Various inspirational characters and mentors, would later also influence Darwin in the skills of scientific observation. For example, he wrote of the influence of his brother, Erasmus:

'Towards the end of my school life, my brother worked hard at chemistry and made a fair laboratory with proper apparatus in the toolhouse in the garden, and I was allowed to aid him as a servant in most of his experiments. He made all the gases and many compounds and I read with care several books in chemistry – the subject interested me greatly, and we often used to go on working till rather late at night – it showed me practically the meaning of experimental science'[9].

Darwin also wrote of his time in Cambridge:

'I became well acquainted with Henslow...so I was called by some of the Dons "the man who walks with Henslow". His knowledge was great in botany, entomology, chemistry, mineralogy and geology. His strongest taste was to draw conclusions from long continued minute observations'[10].

The third driver for Darwin may have been the unconscious need for a distraction and focus following the loss of his mother, Susannah. She died at the age of 52, in July 1817, when Darwin was just nine. Bowlby[11] describes under his chapter on 'A vulnerable personality' that Darwin: '...suffered from periods of chronic anxiety and episodes of fairly severe depression... patients who suffer from one or another of this array of symptoms – those of the hyperventilation syndrome, panic attacks, depression – are significantly more likely to have lost their mother in childhood or to have had a chronically difficult relationship with her than are comparable individuals who are healthy...There is a good deal of evidence that an individual who has been prevented, for whatever reason but usually by his family, from expressing feelings of anxiety, sadness or anger during childhood and from recognising the situations that have given rise to them is likely to have considerable problems with certain feelings in later life'. Barlow[12] reported how some mid–20th century doctors had come to the conclusion that Darwin had 'poor nervous heredity on both sides' and that Darwin had 'depressive, obsessional, anxiety and hysterical symptoms'. In modern times, 'recreational pursuits' are prescribed as cognitive therapy for those dealing with mental illness; Darwin may have somehow found 'scientific observation and discovery' to be his own solution. Indeed there has been much written in modern times about the benefits to children's health from contact with nature, including its role in stress reduction.[13]

The fourth driver may have been the 'need to prove himself' by demonstrating that he could concentrate on 'constructive pursuits' such as that provided through scientific observation. Darwin wrote: 'I was considered... by my father as a very ordinary boy, rather below the common standard of intellect'.[14] Darwin's outputs at school were so poor that Darwin's father,

Robert, removed him from school at sixteen saying:[15] 'You care for nothing but shooting, dogs and rat-catching, and you will be a disgrace to yourself and all your family,' to which Darwin later referred to as bringing him 'deep mortification'. There are some conflicting views as to whether Robert Darwin's criticism of Darwin in his youth should be interpreted as harsh or indulgent. Bowlby gives a balanced argument that 'lurking in the back of Charles' mind, ever ready to emerge, was a deep uncertainty. Was he the disgrace to his family his father had so angrily predicted, or had he perhaps made good? On this vital issue, Charles oscillated'. Some go so far as to say that a difficult son-father relationship may have contributed to Darwin's psychiatric symptoms, including 'serious anxiety neurosis'.[16] Receipt of criticism from his sister, Caroline, wouldn't have helped either. Darwin recalled: 'I clearly remember, after this long interval of years, saying to myself when about to enter a room where she was "What will she blame me for now?" and I made myself dogged so as not to care what she might say'[17]. By pursuing his scientific route, was Darwin seeking to impress his family and make them proud of him?

The fifth driver may well be that Darwin had found his natural strength in scientific observation and pursued it to the point of making him a 'workaholic' and 'perfectionist', as has been suggested by some authors.[18] Indeed Darwin wrote[19]: 'A man who dares to waste one hour of time has not discovered the value of life.' 'I am never idle'[20], 'I cannot be idle, much as I wish it, and am never comfortable except when at work'[21] and 'work, which is my sole pleasure in life'[22]. The Shropshire Archaeological & Natural History Society described how Darwin's grandfather, Erasmus Darwin (12 December 1731 – 18 April 1802) had said:[23] 'A fool... you know, is a man who never tried an experiment in his life' The piece continued: 'Charles Darwin was so far removed from his grandfather's definition of a fool that he could spend thirty years over a single experiment and he waited to present his theories to the world until they seemed to be established by the accumulated results of observation and experience'. Some claim that Darwin's delay in publishing the *Origin of Species* may be on account of him seeking 'perfection' in his arguments. It seems that nowadays some see perfectionism as a mental health issue. Optimius Education[24] presents the following differences between perfectionists and high achievers. From this it would appear, from what I have read, that Darwin was, on balance, actually a high achiever, rather than a perfectionist:

Perfectionists
- Are very rarely satisfied with their work
- View mistakes as failures
- Avoid tasks or situations in which they will not excel
- Struggle with constructive criticism and view it as evidence that they are not good enough
- Are set back by 'mistakes' and can feel embarrassed, defensive and ashamed
- Are driven by anxiety and worry that they will not produce a flawless performance or product
- Find it difficult to accept praise and feel they do not deserve it
- Like to follow rules and instructions; are not spontaneous about their learning

Healthy High-Achievers
- Take pride in their work
- View the process of mistakes as a way to grow and learn, take risks and try new things
- Receive and learn from constructive criticism
- Bounce back after a mistake and do not take it personally
- Are driven by the excitement and enjoyment of the task and genuinely enjoy the learning process
- Receive praise happily
- Are very creative, take chances and think out of the box

The sixth driver may well have been his need to shift focus from his debilitating condition, which seemed to manifest itself after Darwin's travels on *The Beagle*. Darwin wrote:[25] 'My chief enjoyment and sole employment throughout life has been scientific work;...the excitement from such work makes me for the time forget, or drivers quite away, my daily discomfort'. Thomson[26] says that his symptoms included lassitude, often accompanied by vomiting and shivering and he had the idea that his condition was part inherited. Indeed recently it has been suggested that Darwin may have carried a mitochondrial DNA mutation commonly associated with the MELAS syndrome[27]. Darwin was 'increasingly distressed by abdominal pain, flatulence, constipation, nausea and headaches...episodes of inflammation of the whole face...joint pains and neural symptoms such as tingling in the fingers and legs, accompanied by fatigue and low fever'[26]. Darwin apparently repeatedly consulted his father, as well as many other doctors; Atkins[28] lists Sir James Clark, Sir Henry Holland, Dr William Brinton, Dr Bence Jones and Sir Andrew Clark. His father, Robert, prescribed calomel or mercurous chloride for him. Darwin's medications also included mercuric chloride, bismuth nitrate, chalk (calcium carbonate) and opium.[29] In addition, Darwin took regular showers using a device erected in Down House's garden and from 1849 visited Malvern for hydropathic treatment. On 22 June 1869, Darwin writes to Hooker from Caerdeon:[30] 'I have hardly crawled half a mile from the house, and then been fearfully fatigued. It is enough to make one wish oneself quiet in a comfortable tomb.' The following letter gives us a glimpse of how Darwin suffered[31].

My dear Hooker, 28th March 1849
Your letter of the 13th of October has remained unanswered till this day! What an ungrateful return for a letter which interested me so much, & which contained so much & curious information. But I have had a bad winter. On the 13th of November my poor dear Father died & no one, who did not know him, would believe that a man above 83 years old, could have retained so tender & affectionate a disposition, with all his sagacity unclouded to the last. I was at the time so unwell that I was unable to travel which added to my misery. Indeed all this winter I have been bad enough, with dreadful vomiting every week,

& my nervous system began to be affected, so that my hands trembled & head was often swimming. I was not able to do anything one day out of three, & was altogether too dispirited to write to you or to do anything but what I was compelled.— I thought I was rapidly going the way of all flesh.

Having heard, accidentally, of two persons who had received much benefit from the Water Cure, I got Dr Gully's book & made further enquiries, & at last started here, with wife, children & all our servants. We have taken a house for two month & have been here a fortnight. I am already a little stronger & now have had no vomiting for 10 days. Dr G. feels pretty sure he can do me good, which most certainly the regular Doctors could not. At present, I am heated by Spirit lamp till I stream with perspiration, & am then suddenly rubbed violently with towels dripping with cold water: have two cold feet-baths, & wear a wet compress all day on my stomach. I eat simply, dine at 1 o'clock & take several short walks daily. Even in first 8 days the treatment brought out an eruption all over my legs. I mention all this to you, as being a medical man, you might possibly like to hear about it.— I feel certain that the Water Cure is no quackery.— How I shall enjoy getting back to Down with renovated health, if such is to be my good fortune, & resuming the beloved Barnacles.— Now I hope that you will forgive me for my negligence in not having sooner answered your letter.'

Lawrence & Nohria[32] state that there are four basic drives embedded in human DNA that motivates us in the choices we make. The drives are said to be independent, interactive and imbalanced. There is said to be a 'drive to acquire' objects and experiences that improve our status relative to others. This relates to more conventional motivations of 'achievement' and 'power'. In relation to Darwin, as already explained, the need for achievement and the respect that comes along with it may well have been a motive. From what I have read about Darwin, there is no real sense that he wanted to see himself as 'better' than anyone else. Financial status can certainly be ignored as a motivator as his family were well-off. The 'drive to bond' relates to establishing long-term relationships that seek cooperation and commitment. In relation to Darwin's work, there does appear to be a good degree of camaraderie with those he shares an interest. This is obviously very important to him, as demonstrated by his letters to fresh and established fellows. The 'drive to learn' to make sense of the world and of ourselves, to satisfy curiosity, to know, to comprehend, to believe, to appreciate, to develop understanding is seen as the third human drive. This, without question, ranks highly in Darwin. The 'drive to defend' ourselves, our loved ones, our beliefs, our resources and our accomplishments from harm, is the last. This perhaps is evident in Darwin on account of his desire to publish more and more works after the publication of 'Origin of Species'. These publications sought to scaffold his theory of evolution by natural selection.

Soon after coming to Shropshire, I decided to keep up my skills in environmental education and chose to help with the Wildlife Trust. There was a short course running called 'Take 5 for Play' which I was able to attend. Here I was given a file comprising course notes and work sheets[33]. The introduction stated:

'Play is the thing that children choose to do when they are not being directed to do other things. It is defined by the fact that it is voluntary, freely chosen, self-motivated and often fun, although not always. Play can take many forms; it can be solitary or with a group; it can be wonderfully creative when children have new ideas; or destructive when children knock things down; it can be physical, emotional, imaginative, fantastical and so much more...Children will play with the environment around them whether it has been designed to be played with or not!...Play spaces should enable children to play freely and allow children to 'be' and develop in their own way. In addition play spaces should enable children to assess and experience acceptable levels of risk...They need spaces that offer opportunities to develop, acquire and practice skills...a good play setting will have a broad range of resources available for children to play with...children...love resources that can be changed and manipulated or moved and transformed. These are 'loose parts', attractive, flexible play materials that children can change and control for themselves'.

When reflecting on Darwin, I could not help but smile at how appropriate this explanation was to Darwin's world of observations and investigations; the word 'children' can so easily be replaced with the word 'Darwin'. His discoveries were indeed 'fantastical'; his imagination couldn't keep still. Darwin did make a choice to study nature; his affluent background made it possible. His 'loose parts' were to be native and exotic plants and animals. His 'playmates' were his family members and correspondents. His 'play settings' or learning grounds were diverse; they came to shape the man and his work. In none of these 'play settings' did Darwin 'switch off' his observation of the natural world.

In relation to Darwin's greatest work, '*On The Origin of Species*', it was at Downe, in particular, where Darwin could get his thoughts together and where intimate studies were made and collated as evidence for his theory. Darwin wrote:[34]

'From September 1854 onwards, I devoted my time to arranging my huge piles of notes, to observing and to experimenting in relation to the transmutation of species...One problem of great importance...is the tendency in organic beings descended from the same stock to diverge in character as they become modified...I can remember the very spot in the road, whilst in my carriage, when to my joy the solution occurred to me; and this was long after I had come to Down.'

The American Museum of Natural History emphasises that before '*On The Origin of Species*' people believed that species were 'unconnected, unrelated and unchanged since the moment of their creation...that...people were not part of the natural world; they were above and outside it.'[35] Darwin's contemporary supporter, Professor Huxley, wrote: 'There is no field of biological enquiry in which the influence of '*On The Origin of Species*' is not traceable'[36]

DARWIN'S PLAY SETTINGS

Some impression can be gained of Darwin's earliest 'play setting' at his former childhood home in Shrewsbury. Perched on the top of some elevated ground is The Mount. His father, Dr Robert Darwin (1766–1848), built it in around 1800 and Darwin was born there on 12 February 1809. This would have been a busy household with a family comprising five other children – Marianne (1798–1858), Caroline Sarah (1800–1888), Susan Elizabeth (1803–1866), Erasmus Alvey (1804–1881) and Emily Catherine (1810–1866). Nowadays, a small tribute by the entrance gate makes reference to Darwin and a tour guide I accompanied assured all attendees that the Land Registry staff that now occupy the building were often 'nice enough to show you the room everyone thought would have been his'.[1]

Francis Darwin wrote of The Mount:[2]

'It is a large, plain square, red-brick house; of which the most attractive feature is the pretty greenhouse, opening out of the morning room...The house is charmingly placed on the top of a steep bank leading down to the Severn. The terraced bank is traversed by a long walk, leading from end to end, still called 'The Doctor's Walk'. At one point in this walk grows a Spanish chestnut, the branches of which bend back parallel to themselves in a curious manner, and this was Charles Darwin's favourite tree as a boy, where he and his sister Catherine had each their special seat'.

The Mount comprised: 'dining room, drawing room, morning room opening into Conservatory, library, fourteen bedrooms with suitable dressing rooms, kitchen and all usual offices, ample cellaring, very extensive Stabling, Coach Houses &c Conservatories, Fernery, Forcing Frames, extensive walled Garden, pleasure grounds and adjoining piece of land...commanding extensive and beautiful scenery, and fit for the immediate reception of any family...'[3] The inventory accompanying the sales particulars also indicated the presence of 'a plant stove', 'vineries', a 'greenhouse', 'tool house' and 'shed', circular parterre with summerhouse and an Ice House. The thick red garden walls that remain nowadays can easily be distinguished within Darwin's Gardens (residential street) and much ivy-leaved toadflax grows upon it.

The existence of a fernery was a sign of the times. Boyd wrote[4]: 'The Victorians had a great passion for ferns...the interest in ferns...really begun in the late 1830s when the British countryside attracted increasing numbers of amateur and professional botanists...they had been little studied compared with flowering plants. Also, they were most diverse and abundant in the wilder, wetter, western and northern parts of Britain...People of many different social backgrounds sought out the species...to grow in their gardens or homes'. An 1878 book on Shrewsbury[5] states the following fern species growing in the area:

Polypodium vulgare Common polypody
Lastrea thelypteris Marsh fern
Lastrea flix mas Common buckler fern or male fern
Lastrea spinulosa Broad prickly buckler fern
Lastrea dilatata Shield fern
Athyrium filix foemina Lady fern
Asplenium trichomanes Maidenhair spleenwort
Asplenium adiantum-nigrum Black spleenwort
Scolopendrium vulgare Harts tongue fern
Blechnum boreale Hard fern
Pteris aquiline Bracken
Botrychium lunaria Moonwort
Ophioglossum vulgatum Southern adders-tongue
Isoetes lacustris Lake quillwort
Pilularia globulifera Pillwort

Equisetum maximum Giant horsetail
Equisetum arvense Common or field horsetail
Equisetum limosum Toad pipe horsetail
Equisetum hyemala Rough horsetail

Thomson[6] says that Robert Darwin: 'gave much energy creating the grounds, hothouse and garden'. Darwin's mother, Susannah, is said to have '...entered zealously into all her husband's pursuits...and their gardens and grounds became noted for the choicest shrubs and flowers'.[7] Francis wrote[8]: 'The Doctor took great pleasure in his garden, planting it with ornamental trees and shrubs, and being especially successful with fruit trees; and this love of plants, was I think, the only taste kindred to Natural History which he possessed'.

Some of this 'green-fingered' behaviour rubbed off onto Charles Darwin. Darwin wrote:[9] 'I tried to make out the names of plants...' and 'I do not remember any mental pursuits excepting those of collecting stones &c. — gardening, & about this time often going with my father in his carriage, telling him of my lessons, & seeing game & other wild birds, which was a great delight to me'. There is a portrait of young Darwin holding what is thought to be a *Lachenalia aloides*, Cape Cowslip, in his lap; a sure sign of his fondness for plants. Darwin wrote in his Autobiography:[10] 'I told another little boy [Leighton]...that I could produce variously coloured Polyanthuses and Primroses by watering them with coloured fluids, which was of course a monstrous fable'. Darwin also told him that his mother had taught him how: 'by looking at the inside of the blossom the name of the plant could be discovered'.[11] A glimpse into how Darwin enjoyed the grounds lies in a letter Susannah wrote to Josiah Wedgwood II in June 1813:[12] 'we are looking very gay, and are in the midst of our hay harvest in the orchard – the Dr and young ones join in'. Darwin refers in his Autobiography[13] about his: 'boldness in climbing a low tree...thinking that people were admiring me, in one instance for perseverance'. His continued interest in the garden is revealed in the following letters sent from his sisters in 1826[14] 'It made me feel quite melancholy the other day looking at your old garden, & the flowers, just coming up which you used to be so happy watching. I think the time when you & Catherine were little children & I was always with you or thinking about you was the happiest part of my life & I dare say will always be'. And also:[15] 'We have all been taking to gardening very vigorously, and shall expect some very elegant compliments from you on its beauty; and I assure you it is very gay, and much admired.'

In 1818, Darwin went to Shrewsbury Grammar School for seven years, until 1825. He summed up his education there as follows[16]: 'Nothing could have been worse for the development of my mind than Dr Butler's school, as it was strictly classical, nothing else being taught, except a little ancient geography and history. The school as a means of education to me was a complete blank'.

Darwin also wrote[17] 'During my school life...I had strong and diversified tastes, much zeal for whatever interested me and a keen pleasure in understanding any complex subject or things'. His interest in the sciences appeared to be highly dependant on his own curiosity rather than in any formal teaching. Emily Darwin writes to him from Maer in June 1823[18] 'My dear Bobby, How does Minerology, Botany, Chemistry and Entomology, go on?'

Glyptis[19] pointed out that 'Visitors to the countryside tend to already live in rural areas or suburbia'. Essentially Darwin was a boy brought up at the edge of a town. The countryside was within grabbing distance and he could explore it whenever he had free time. Here he could 'take nature in sips'. Darwin was very keen on taking walks from a young age. Darwin wrote of his childhood.[20] 'I was in those days a very great story-teller – for the pure pleasure of exciting attention and surprise...I scarcely ever went out walking without saying I had seen a pheasant or some strange bird'.

Darwin frequented two key locations in the Midlands, other than the landscape around Shrewsbury. These were Maer, home of his Wedgwood relatives in Staffordshire, and Woodhouse, home of the Owens at Rednal near Oswestry. So what were these places like?

When Darwin returned from his world trip, he wrote of Maer[21]:

'My visits to Maer during these two and the three succeeding years were quite delightful, independently of the autumnal shooting. Life there was perfectly free; the country was very pleasant for walking or riding; and in the evening there was much very agreeable conversation, not so personal as it generally is in large family parties, together with music. In the summer the whole family used often to sit on the steps of the old portico, with the flower-garden in front, and with the steep wooded bank, opposite the house, reflected in the lake, with here and there a fish rising or a water-bird paddling about.'

Henrietta Litchfield, Darwin's daughter. wrote in 1915[22]: "Round it [Maer Hall] there was a delightful up-and-down sandy walk a mile in length, diversified and well wooded, which made one of the charms of the place. The garden, bright and gay with old-fashioned flowers, lay between the house and the pool, and the little church was just outside the domain. My father [Charles Darwin] used to say that our mother only cared for flowers which had grown at Maer. There was a great deal of wild heath and wood around, and the country is, even now, as rural as ever and quite unspoiled by mines and manufactories."

Bagshaws Directory of Shropshire 1851[23] stated 'Woodhouse is a beautiful mansion of white freestone...delightfully situated on gentle eminence, commanding fine views, and surrounded by park-like grounds beautifully wooded...there is a fine avenue of beech and other trees on the south side of the park'

Later Darwin[24] writes to W.D. Fox in 1828: 'I stayed two days at Maer... and on Monday returned to sweet home. Home is doubtless very sweet, but like all good things one is apt to cloy on it; accordingly I have resolved to go to Woodhouse for a week. This is to me a paradise, about which...I am always thinking...Formerly I used to have two places, Maer and Woodhouse, about which, like a wheel on a pivot I used to revolve. Now I am luckier in having a third...Osmaston'. Osmaston was Fox's home in Derbyshire.

So far, we have got a good idea that Darwin spent much of his time in the middle part of the county, travelling east and west. But how about his exploration of the county, north to south? There is a 'big gap' in our knowledge, here. The Shropshire Museum Service[25] nor the Natural History Museum (London)[26] have any species Darwin collected from Shropshire, which might have given us clues of where he explored. I have only been able to find the following references to places he visited in Shropshire:

'I remember well a walk I took with boy named Ford across some fields to a farmhouse on Church Stretton Road'.[27]

1822 – Tour with sister Caroline 'riding due south from Shrewsbury' where Darwin noted in the 'Fragment', that this was the first occasion he could recollect of 'taking pleasure in scenery, which ever after was to give him vivid delight'[28]

1822 June – Tour with Caroline to Downton[29]

'1822 July – to Montgomery & Bishops Castle with Elizabeth' (probably his cousin Elizabeth Wedgwood)[30]

1831 – Geological tour of the county, 'working like a tiger' at a geological map of Shropshire.[31] His known site visits include Cardeston, Llanymynech, Nescliffe, Meole Brace and Pontesford Hill.[32]

1832 July – Darwin had a holiday at Bishops Castle with sister Susan Elizabeth[33]

1836 – 'Whilst in Shropshire I have some Geology to do. Mr. Murchison has lent me a manuscript map, and has asked me to look at a part of the Country, which he has been describing— It is near Minsterley, a very beautiful scene of very ancient true volcanic phenomenæ.'
Darwin, C. R. to Darwin, C. S. [9 Nov 1836][34]

July 1841 recollection – 'How I should have enjoyed to have followed you about the coral-limestone— I once saw close to Wenlock, something such as you describe, & made a rough drawing'[35]

1863 – Darwin and Emma stayed at Onibury, near Ludlow, home of Emily (Darwin's sister) and Charles Langton.[36]

Other references are more vague, for example Susan wrote[37] to Darwin in 1832: 'I think there is great hope that Charlotte Langton will settle hereafter in Shropshire. Lord Craven has so many livings in this County at his disposal. The one I shd like them to have is Wistanstow very near the Craven Arms in a beautiful situation amongst the Clee Hills.' Does this aim to describe somewhere Darwin doesn't know well or seeks to remind him of somewhere he had previously visited? It's impossible to tell.

The Darwins made regular trips to North Wales. Darwin wrote about his first memory:[38] 'I have heard my Father say that he believed that persons with powerful minds generally had memories extending far back to a very early period of life. This is not my case for my earliest recollection goes back only to when I was a few months over four years old, when we went to near Abergate for seabathing'. This was one of many holidays or 'tours' he would take in the region. As an adult, for example, Darwin wrote:[39] 'During the summer of 1826, I took a long walking tour with two friends with knapsacks on our backs through North Wales. We walked thirty miles most days, including one day the ascent of Snowdon. I also went with my sister Caroline on a riding tour in North Wales, a servant with saddle-bags carrying our clothes.'

In 1825 Darwin was sent to Edinburgh, Robert's former training ground, to study medicine. This followed Darwin's experiences in visiting poor patients in and around Shrewsbury where Darwin 'made notes of his findings so that his father could prescribe the appropriate medicines, which he then dispensed.' Years later the erstwhile student wrote: '...at one time I had at least a dozen patients, and felt a keen interest in the work. My father... declared that I should make a successful physician, meaning, by this, one who got many patients'[40] I was amused to discover on a tour around Darwin's Gardens (residential street), that a house-holder had found a 'bleeding tool' in his garden.[41] This would obviously have been one of the instruments Robert used and perhaps the children 'played with'.

In Edinburgh, Darwin was to hate the sight of blood and the anaesthetic-free operations. He had some regrets in later life, about the absence of training in dissection: 'this has been an irremediable evil, as well as my incapacity to draw.[42]' However, Darwin did gain knowledge of herbal medicines and taxonomy. He also picked up some skills in taxidermy in his spare time from 'a negro [who] lived in Edinburgh...and gained his livelihood by stuffing birds, which he did excellently; he gave me lessons for payment, and I used often to sit with him for he was a very pleasant and intelligent man.'[43]

Darwin wrote:[44] 'After having spent two sessions in Edinburgh, my father percieved or he heard from my sisters, that I did not like the thought of being a physician, so he proposed that I should become a clergyman.' Darwin's studying was now to move to Cambridge University. Darwin called the three and a half years he spent there as 'the most joyful in my happy life; for I was then in excellent health and almost always in high spirits.'[45] Chancellor:[46] says of him that at this time he was 'A most invigorating and attractive person. His contemporaries [spoke] of his pleasant looks, his energy and genialilty, his humour and simplicity, his generous sympathy...and his hatred of anything mean or cruel.'

During his time at Cambridge, Darwin built up his knowledge of botany. Darwin wrote:[47] 'I attended...Henslow's lectures on Botany; and liked them for their extreme clearness and admirable illustrations'. 'A circumstance which influenced my whole career more than any other... This was my friendship with Professour Henslow. Before coming up to Cambridge, I had heard of him from my brother as a man who knew every branch of science, and I was accordingly prepared to reverence him...'[48] Thomson[49] says that: 'Henslow used to take his pupils, including several older members of the university, on field excursions, on foot, or in coaches to distant places or in a barge down the river, and lectured in the rare plants or animals which were observed. These excursions were delightful.'

After Darwin's University life came to an end, at the age of twenty-two, he was given the chance of a lifetime. He wrote:[50] 'I had been wandering about North Wales on a geological tour with Professor Sedgwick when I arrived home on Monday 29th of August. My sisters first informed me of the letters from Prof. Henslow & Mr. Peacock offering to me the place in

The Beagle which I now fill.—I immediately said I would go; but the next morning finding my Father so much averse to the whole plan, I wrote to Mr. Peacock to refuse his offer. On the last day of August I went to Maer, where everything soon bore a different appearance. I found every member of the family so strongly on my side, that I determined to make another effort. In the evening I drew up a list of my Father's objections, to which Uncle Jos wrote his opinion & answer. This we sent off to Shrewsbury early the next morning & I went out shooting. About 10 o'clock Uncle Jos sent me a message to say he intended going to Shrewsbury & offering to take me with him. When we arrived there, all things were settled, & my Father most kindly gave his consent."

Darwin's list of his father's 'principal objections', sent in a letter to Robert on 31 August 1831, included:[51] 'Disreputable to my character as a Clergyman hereafter; A wild scheme; that they must have offered to many others before me, the place of Naturalist; And from its not being accepted there must be some serious objection to the vessel or expedition; that I should never settle down to a steady life thereafter; that my accommodations would be most uncomfortable; That you should consider it as again changing my profession; That it would be a useless undertaking'. Influenced by Josiah Wedgwood, Robert finally agreed to the adventure.

Darwin certainly seems to have been excited by, rather than wary of, the whole opportunity; no wonder – the only other place he had been abroad was on one occasion to France with his uncle, Josiah Wedgwood. He can't have known what a wealth of biodiversity and geodiversity he was to witness on the expedition but he had the confidence to find out. 'As I've got older I have come to realise this to be a sure sign of youth!' Darwin wrote:[52] 'Early in my school days a boy had a copy of the '*Wonders of the World*' which I often read and disputed with other boys about the veracity of some of the statements; and I believe that this book first gave me a wish to travel to remote countries, which was ultimately fulfilled by the voyage of *H.M.S. Beagle*.'

On hearing about Darwin's forthcoming expedition, which then was only scheduled for three years (later extended to five), a friend wrote:[53]

'My dear Darwin, Never did I think so highly of our present Government, as when I heard they had selected Charles Darwin for Gt. naturalist & that he was to be trans-ported (with pleasure of course) for 3 years— Woe unto ye Beetles of South America, woe unto all tropical butterflies—...whilst I, luckless wretch, am rusticating in a country Parsonage & shewing people a road I dont know—to Heaven. One of our friends would say it was "a melancholy fact" that 3 years is a long time & in that long time much may happen both at home & abroad, sorrow sickness or ye grand finale—but if that time passes & finds us both on ye face of "this best of all possible worlds" why then, old boy, what a shake of ye hand we will have, what a bottle of Sherry what excursions, & what stories of wonders seen & dangers past...would be impertinent in an individual like myself to ask a naturalist to waste his time on me but if ever he has nothing to do & would kill a little time he may fancy how glad I should be to hear from him. Hang it I dont half like ending even this quasi-conversation, but it must be some time or other—so we shall dine together again in 3 years. What shall we have for dinner? My best wishes go with you on ye sea & land in ye Old World or New— do sometimes think of happy old times & remember that you've always one sincere friend in | Frederic Watkins.'

The Shrewsbury Journal[54] wrote: '*The Beagle* sailed from England December 27 1831 and returned October 28 1836, having thus been absent nearly five years...Mr. Darwin during the voyage did more for natural history in all its varied departments than any expedition has done since...'

A report of Darwin's journey on his return to The Mount after the *H.M.S. Beagle* voyage, is written in a letter to Fitzroy:[55]

'I am thoroughly ashamed of myself; in what a dead and half alive state, I spent the few last days on board, my only excuse is , that certainly I was not quite well. The first day in the mail tired me but as I drew nearer to Shrewsbury everything looked more beautiful and cheerful – In passing Gloucestershire and Worcestershire I wished much for you to admire the fields, woods and orchards. The stupid people on the coach did not seem to think the fields one bit greener than usual but I am sure, we would have thoroughly agreed, that the wide world does not contain so happy a prospect as the rich cultivated land of England...'

When Darwin returned, Caroline wrote to her cousin Sarah Wedgwood:[56] 'We have had the very happiest morning – poor Charles so full of affection & delight at seeing my father looking so well and being with us all again – his hatred of the sea is as intense as even I can wish'.

Darwin wrote:[57]
'From my return to England Oct. 2, 1836 to my marriage Jan. 29, 1839, these two years three months were the most active ones which I ever spent, though I was occasionally unwell so lost some time. After going backwards forwards several times between Shrewsbury, Maer, Cambridge, London, I settled in lodgings at Cambridge on December 13th, where all my collections were under the care of Henslow'.

After a spell in London, Darwin moved to Down House in September 1842. Emma wrote:[58]

'We...fixed upon a place which had no great charms – a common place looking square house of 3 storeys standing on rather a nice lawn with complete exposure to to the S W in a flat field with some good ashes and beeches on it...At the edge of the table land on which the village and house stand are steep valleys crowned at the top with old hedges & hedgerows very disorderly & picturesque & with enormous clusters of Clematis & blackberries and a great variety of yews, services &c. Under one of these was a flat terrace which made a very pretty walk for pacing & where I used to sit while Charles took several turns. The green valley was crowned on the opposite side with a wood, & also a similar shaw.'

In comparison to The Mount, the grounds of Down House had the bonus of extensive hay meadows and rather than within a town, direct access to nearby countryside and a village a short distance away.

Darwin's Landscape Laboratory Nomination Document[59] listed his key 'play settings', as I now call them, as: Down House Study; Down House Drawing Room; Down House Flower Garden; Down House Garden Frontage; Down House Orchard; Down House Kitchen Garden, Down House Greenhouse; Down House Garden Laboratory; Down House' Great House Meadow; Down House' Sand-Walk Copse; Down House Great Pucklands; Downe Valley; Cudham Valley; Orchis Bank; Hangrove; High Elms Estate; Cudham School Pond; River Ravensbourne and Keston Bog; Keston Common; Holwood; Rural Farmed Landscape with Access.

Darwin used to take a regular walk with his father and brother around a 'thinking path' at the Mount with an objective, according to a visitor tour guide:[60] 'to think about the consequences of their actions on the forthcoming day'. This was a routine he practiced when he finally settled at Downe. According to the instructions in the '*Encyclopaedia of Gardening*', Darwin mixed gravel with 'a sixth part of ferruginous sand to promote its binding' to create a path at Downe, sourcing sand from a pocket of sand in a small clay-pit near the summer house.[61] It is interesting, that the land at the Mount is also sandy. A tour guide suggested that perhaps this is why Darwin called his thinking path at Down House, the Sand Walk – a reflection of his childhood footsteps.[62] To complicate the theory further, there is a sandy walk at Maer that Darwin regularly used too!

Francis wrote about his father's routine at Downe[62]: 'My father's midday walk generally began by a call at the greenhouse, where he looked at any germinating seeds or experimental plants which required a casual examination, but he hardly ever did any serious observing at this time. Then he went on for his constitutional – either round the "Sand-walk", or outside his own grounds in the immediate neighbourhood of the house. The "Sand-walk" was a narrow strip of land 1 ½ acres in extent, with a gravel-walk round it. On one side of it was a broad old shaw with fair-sized oaks in it, which made a sheltered shady walk; the other side was separated from a neighbouring grass field by a low quickset hedge, over which you could look at what view there was, a quiet little valley losing itself in the upland country towards the edge of the Westerham hill, with hazel coppice and larch wood, the remnants of what was once a large wood, stretching away to the Westerham road. I have heard my father say that the charm of this simple little valley helped to make him settle at Down.' One of Darwin's other sons, George, wrote:[63]

'Description of my father's ordinary habits during the latter years of his life...At quarter past seven he was down & then went out & took two turns round the Sand-walk. [After 12.15] he would start for his walk. During the last ten years it was almost invariable that on his way he would stop at the hot-house for 5 minutes or so to examine or perhaps fertilise some experimental plant, and give orders to the gardener on some point. My mother or some of us often joined him in his walk & sometimes we started quite a large party. If he was unwell or if the weather was bad he always went to the Sand-walk but in fine summer weather a favourite walk was to pace to and fro on the "Terrace-Walk", from which there was a charming rural view. Or we would go to Hang-grove wood, to Orchis bank, to the Greenhill (another favourite) or down to the "Big-woods". He very often separated from the rest for the latter part of the walk because talking tired him, & indeed it was only during the last 8 or 9 years that he liked any companion. The walk was not long being about a mile, more or less. He generally at home again by 10 minutes to one, & found the second post awaiting him.'

Rather than travelling, Darwin welcomed letters and visits from others. The Shropshire Archaeological & Natural History Society wrote:[64] 'To Down, occasionally came distinguished men from many lands; and there in later years would sometimes be found the younger generation of scientific students, looking up the great Naturalist with the reverence of disciples, who had experienced his singular modesty, his patient readiness to listen to all opinions, and the winning grace with which he informed their ignorance and corrected their mistakes'

There is no denying that Shrewsbury was Darwin's touchstone. He lived there most of the time until he was sixteen (though also boarding at Shrewsbury School) and he kept coming back to the Mount in between his educational experiences at Edinburgh, Cambridge and on *H.M.S. Beagle* until he was twenty-seven. Even after moving to Downe, effort was still made to make visits to Shrewsbury. His affection for the Mount can be gleaned from a letter he wrote to his sister in 1833, while aboard *H.M.S. Beagle*[65] "I often think of the garden at home as a paradise: on a fine summer's evening, when the birds are singing, how I should like to appear like a ghost amongst you." Darwin last visited in the summer of 1869, three years after the death of his sister. Francis[66] wrote that it: 'left on the mind of his daughter who accompanied him a strong impression of his love for his old home. The then tenant of the Mount showed them over the house, &c., and with mistaken hospitality remained with the party during the whole visit. As they were leaving, Charles Darwin said, with a pathetic look of regret, "If I could have been left alone in that green-house for five minutes, I know I should have been able to see my father in his wheel-chair as vividly as if he had been there before me."

GENERAL ASPECTS

I was brought up in West London. My family home was a Victorian villa. It had a big garden that became our little nature reserve; an oasis in an urban setting and my main exposure to the natural world. I pottered around the garden helping my mother weed, water and plant flowers and vegetables and I was lucky enough to have a good view of the garden and the surrounding swathe of gardens from my bedroom window. It was overlooked by the local church and adorned with Victorian fruit trees. Despite a neighbourhood of shops and a well-used thoroughfare close by, it was sometimes difficult to believe you were in London, being surprisingly quiet.

What did Darwin think of London? There is certainly a case for saying that he oscillated between his love and hatred for it! He had written to his cousin W.D. Fox in June 1828[1] calling it: 'that horrid smoky wilderness, London' and on 26 February 1829: 'Whilst in town I went to the Royal Institution, Linnean Society & Zoological Gardens and many other places where Naturalists are gregarious – If you had but been with me, I think London would be a very delightful place – as things were it was much pleasanter than I could have supposed such a dreary wilderness of houses to be...'

After his voyage on *H.M.S. Beagle* (27 December 1831 – 2 October 1836), Darwin was something of a celebrity; London was the best place to be. Darwin came to live in Great Marlborough Street, from 1837–8. Darwin wrote to W.D. Fox: '...on Tuesday I go into lodgings at 36 Grt Marlborough St. which I have taken for the year. – I am at present in my brothers house no 43. – It is very pleasant our being so near neighbours.'[2]

After marrying on 29 January 1839, Emma and Darwin lived in Upper Gower Street until 1842. They called their dwelling 'Macaw Cottage'. Their son, Francis Darwin, later reported of their experience there[3]: 'The house in which they lived for the first few years of their married life, No. 12 Upper Gower Street, was a small common-place London house, with a drawing-room in the front, and a small room behind, in which they lived for the sake of quietness. In later years my father used to laugh over the surpassing ugliness of the furniture, carpets &c., of the Gower Street house. The only redeeming feature was a better garden than most London houses have, a strip as wide as the house, and thirty yards long. Even this small space of dingy grass made their London house more tolerable to its two country-bred inhabitants.'

Darwin wrote in October 1839 to W.D. Fox[4]: 'We are living a life of extreme quietness: and if one is quiet in London, there is nothing like its quietness – there is a grandeur about its smoky fogs, and the dull distant sounds of cabs and coaches; in fact you may perceive I am becoming a thorough-paced Cockney, and I glory in thoughts that I shall be here for the next six months'.

Like many Londoners, Darwin got fed up with the dust and dirt of the City and longed to move somewhere cleaner and quieter for his new family. His daughter wrote: 'For some time there had been a growing wish on the part of my parents to live in the country. Their health made London undesirable in many ways and they both preferred the freedom and quiet of a country life'[5]. Darwin spent some time searching for houses and settled for an old parsonage in Downe, now within the London Borough of Bromley, but then in the county of Kent. "The choice of Down was rather the result of despair than of actual preference; my father and mother were weary of house-hunting...It had at least one desideratum, namely quietness. Indeed it would have been difficult to find a more retired place so near to London," wrote Francis Darwin.[6]

Francis[7] described the location and character of Down House: 'The house stands a quarter of a mile from the village, and is built, like so many houses of the last century, as near as possible to the road—a narrow lane winding away to the Westerham high-road. In 1842, it was dull and unattractive enough: a square brick building of three storeys, covered with shabby whitewash and hanging tiles. The garden had none of the shrubberies or walls that now give shelter; it was overlooked from the lane, and was open, bleak, and desolate. One of my father's first undertakings was to lower the lane by about two feet, and to build a flint wall along that part of it which bordered the garden. The earth thus excavated was used in making banks and mounds round the lawn: these were planted with evergreens, which now give to the garden its retired and sheltered character.

The house was made to look neater by being covered with stucco, but the chief improvement effected was the building of a large bow extending up through three storeys. This bow became covered with a tangle of creepers, and pleasantly varied the south side of the house. The drawing-room, with its verandah opening into the garden, as well as the study in which my father worked during the later years of his life, were added at subsequent dates.

Eighteen acres of land were sold with the house, of which twelve acres on the south side of the house formed a pleasant field, scattered with fair-sized oaks and ashes. From this field a strip was cut off and converted into a kitchen garden, in which the experimental plot of ground was situated, and where the greenhouses were ultimately put up.'

Darwin was keen to keep his finger on the pulse when it came to scientific discussion and assured people that once he moved to Downe he would regularly come to London. He wrote in a letter to W.D. Fox (1842):[8]

"I hope by going up to town for a night every fortnight or three weeks, to keep up my communication with scientific men and my own zeal, and so not to turn into a complete Kentish hog."

This was an intention he soon failed to live up to as he became content in his environs at Down House. Francis wrote[9]: 'Visits to London of this kind were kept up for some years at the cost of much exertion on his part. I have often heard him speak of the wearisome drives of ten miles to or from Croydon or Sydenham—the nearest stations—with an old gardener acting as coachman, who drove with great caution and slowness up and down the many hills. In later years, all regular scientific intercourse with London became...an impossibility.' A few years later in 1846, Darwin wrote to Captain Fitzroy: "My life goes on like clockwork, and I am fixed on the spot where I shall end it."[10]

Darwin was an avid letter writer and the nineteenth century postal service did him proud as he received and sent letters from within Britain and abroad. Some of his earliest letters on settling in Downe revealed his first impressions of the area, its 'General Aspect'. In a letter sent to his sister Catherine in 1842, Darwin wrote:[11]

...Position: – about 1/4 of a mile from the small village of Down in Kent–16 miles from St. Paul's–8 1/2 miles from station (with many trains) which station is only 10 from London. This is bad, as the drive from [i.e. on account of] the hills is long. I calculate we are two hours going from London Bridge. Village about forty houses with old walnut trees in the middle where stands an old flint church and the lanes meet. Inhabitants very respectable–infant school–grown up people great musicians–all touch their hats as in Wales and sit at their open doors in the evening; no high road leads through the village. The little pot-house where we slept is a grocer's shop, and the landlord is the carpenter–so you may guess the style of the village. There are butcher and baker and post-office. A carrier goes weekly to London and calls anywhere for anything in London and takes anything anywhere. On the road [from London] to the village, on a fine day the scenery is absolutely beautiful: from close to our house the view is very distant and rather beautiful, but the house being situated on a rather high tableland has somewhat of a desolate air. There is a most beautiful old farm-house, with great thatched barns and old stumps of oak trees, like that of Skelton [in Shropshire] one field off. The charm of the place to me is that almost every field is intersected (as alas is ours) by one or more foot-paths. I never saw so many walks in any other county. The country is extraordinarily rural and quiet with narrow lanes and high hedges and hardly any ruts. It is really surprising to think London is only 16 miles off...Our field is 15 acres and flat, looking into flat-bottomed valleys on both sides...House ugly, looks neither old nor new–walls two feet thick–windows rather small–lower story rather low. Capital study 18 x 18. Dining-room 21 x 18. Drawing–room can easily be added to: is 21 x 15. Three stories, plenty of bedrooms...House in good repair.

The 'Account of Down' in Darwin's papers states[12]: 'The valleys on this platform sloping northward, but exceedingly even, generally run north and south; their sides near the summits generally become suddenly more abrupt, and are fringed with narrow strips, or, as they are here called, "shaws" of wood, sometimes merely by hedgerows run wild...Nearly all the land is ploughed, and is often left fallow, which gives the country a naked red look, or not unfrequently white, from a covering of chalk laid on by the farmers. Nobody seems at all aware on what principle fresh chalk laid on land abounding with lime does it any good. This, however, is said to have been the practice of the country ever since the period of the Romans, and at present the many white pits on the hill sides, which so frequently afford a picturesque contrast with the overhanging yew trees, are all quarried for this purpose...There are large tracts of woodland, [cut down] about once every ten years; some of these enclosures seem to be very ancient...Larks abound here, and their songs sound most agreeably on all sides; nightingales are common. Judging from an odd cooing note, something like the purring of a cat, doves are very common in the woods.'

Darwin wrote to W.D. Fox in March 1843[13]:
'I forgot whether I ever described this place: it is a good, very ugly house with 18 acres; situated on a chalk-flat, 560 ft above sea - There are peeps of far-distant country & the scenery is moderately pretty; its chief merit is its extreme rurality; I think I was never in a more perfectly quiet country: Three miles south of us the great chalk escarpment quite cuts us off from the low country of Kent, & between us & the escarpment, there is not a

village or gents: house, but only great woods & arable fields (the later in sadly preponderant numbers), so that we are absolutely at extreme verge of world. – The whole country is intersected by foot-paths; but the surface over the chalk is clayey & sticky, which is worst feature in our purchase. –The dingles & banks often remind me of Cambridgeshire & walking with you to Cherry Hinton, & other places, though the general aspect of the country is very different.'

Gwen Raverat, Darwin's grand-daughter, reported:[14] 'Every day at Down my father used to take us for the most romantic walks, telling us stories about the place as we went: up the steep hill to Cudham Church; or to look for orchids at Orchis Bank, or along a legendary smuggler's track, or to the Big Woods where Uncle William had been lost as a child. The sudden valleys, the red, red earth full of strangely shaped flints, the great lonely woods, the sense of remoteness, made it different from any other place we knew'.

Looking back on my time in Bromley, I wondered whether I could coin the delights of the area within a few sentences. My description of Downe as I know it can be summarised as follows:

'A Borough that considers itself in Kent rather than part of London. A Borough of two halves; urban in the north, hilly and rural in the south. Darwin's landscape nestles in the latter. In many ways a time capsule. Small villages, with churches and other buildings often created from local flint. Hidden valleys, only accessible from a few winding, narrow, sunken lanes, that cut across them; their remainder having to be explored on foot. A place you can surprisingly walk for miles and not come across anyone. When you do get a view point through the trees, as the valley sides drop away, it is one worth waiting for, giving you a peaceful sense of utter satis-faction. There are species rich woodlands, whether ancient or secondary, often connected to fantastic hedges, most shaped from former woodland. You regularly come across foxes and deer walking with determination across the valley bottoms and sometimes you're high enough to be above the speculating birds and hawking dragonflies. Extra treats, such as stoats, appear out of the corner of your eye. Hidden jewels of chalk grasslands are interspersed with arable land, horse paddocks, sheep pasture, golf courses, youth camp sites and remnant parkland estates, one of which is not occupied by a popular Country Park. In quiet corners there are rare ponds, enormous trees, woodland banks and overgrown chalk pits filled with leaves. A landscape, in its north, that oozes with springs, one of which marking the start of the River Ravensbourne. A fragment of remnant heathland, lurking amongst birch, pine and gorse bushes, is an unexpected bonus, at Keston. An extra pride in the area created when a 'new' plant or animal has been spotted by fellow naturalists.'

We don't know how Darwin would have captured the essence of Shrewsbury and Shropshire in a couple of paragraphs. The closest we come to getting a real impression of his love for his county was in a letter he sent to his sister whilst on his travels on *H.M.S. Beagle*[15]: 'I feel inclined to write about nothing else, but to tell you over & over again, how I long to be quietly seated amongst you.—How beautiful Shropshire will look, if we can but cross the wide Atlantic, before the end of October. You cannot imagine how curious I am to behold some of the old views, & to compare former with new impressions. I am determined & feel sure, that the scenery of England is ten times more beautiful than any we have seen.—What reasonable person can wish for great ill proportioned mountains, two and three miles high? No, no; give me the Brythen or some such compact little hill.—And then as for your boundless plains & impenetrable forests, who would compare them with the green fields & oak woods of England?'

In trying to uncover something of nineteenth century Shropshire, as Darwin would have known it, I found a description by Forrest[16]. He states:

'Within this compass we have plateaus and plains, hills and vales, boggy flats and heathery moors, cornlands and pastures, wooded slopes and barren crags, meres and ponds, streams big and little...there is one internal division so natural and well-marked...This may be seen at a glance: the division of the County by the river Severn into two portions...The part that lies to the S.W. is hilly or wooded, while that to the N.E., is comparatively flat and contains numerous pools and some tracts of boggy moors...The whole district is more or less mountainous. The highest hill is Brown Clee...The following are some of the principal heights...Titterstone Clee...Stiperstones...Long mynd...Clun Forest...Wrekin...Wenlock Edge. Almost all these high lands belong to the older geological formations; they consist of hard rocks, and are barren or of a heathy character. The open moorland on the Longmynd is the resort of many kinds of birds which are seldom met with elsewhere in Shropshire. Ravens used to reside there, and here we still find such birds as the Twite, Snow Bunting, Grouse, and Curlew, whilst the intervening wooded valleys teem with a variety of birds and animals that love sheltered places. Across the Severn the country is very different. With the exeption of the isolated Wrekin...the land being open and most of it cultivated. There are no extensive woods and the country is a plain...Whixall, Baggy Moor and the Weald Moors , are peaty or wet bogs, the haunt of wading birds and amphibians, whilst at Ellesmere, Whitchurch and around Baschurch and Berrington, are many meres and pools attractive to water-fowls...The Severn is very liable to floods, whenever there are heavy rains on the Montgomeryshire hills, particularly since improved land-drainage has caused rain-water to find its way more speedily into the river. At such times the water is turbid from the quantities of find mud washed into it from the surface of the plain...'

A later reference about Shropshire is made in 1939 by Watts,[17] who states:

'Its surface is in part hilly, even mountainous and in part a plain diversified by gentle slopes and broad valleys. Its soil, mostly fertile but in places barren, supports ample woodlands dotted among its arable and pasture. It is well watered by abundant streams and rivers...inhabited by a peace-loving and landed population...Thus we find that the county is made up of two distinct parts about equal in size, the Upland and the Plain. The Severn may be taken as the approximate boundary between the two, for the Upland only three times transgresses its

line; once towards Oswestry next where the northnend of the Longmynd cross the Haughmond Hill near Shrewsbury and once again, at
out feet, where Wenlock Edge crosses the river at the Gorge between
Buildwas and Ironbridge, flanked by the Wrekin range on the west
and the uplands of Coalfield on the east...The Northern Plain is a land
of gentle slopes, broad valleys and sluggish streams, with meres and
marshes...The northern rivers have a very gentle gradient from source
to outfall into the Severn...we have found it convenient to divide the
Upland into three parts, the Main Upland, including the Western
Hills of Oswestry and of Clun Forest, the Southern Plateau and the
Peninsula or Coalfield area, the only considerable part of the Upland
which crosses the Severn...Shropshire is a well-wooded country...This,
however is only a relic of the primeval forest with which about two-
thirds of the surface was covered in the time of the Saxons, and not less
than half in Norman times. These forests were mainly situated in the
south of the county, and particularly in the Upland and the Southern
Plateau. Of Clun Forest much still remains in the S.W. corner of the
county...In the fields at their proper season are to be found abundance
of daffodils, cowslips, violets, birds foot trefoil, oxeye and purple or
spotted orchis, harebell and the beautiful meadow saffron. On plough-
land the scarlet pimpernel grows freely. The ground in the woods may
be white with wood anemone, yellow with celandine or St. John's wort,
blue with bluebell or forget-me-not, or a sobern green with a carpet of
the male or lady fern, the prickly shield or the hard fern, or more rarely
with the beech fern. A stiff soil will yield the centaury and the willow
herb; bogs the asphodel and bog myrtle, cotton grass, the royal fern,
the yellow flag and the sundew; and limestone ground the lady's-finger
vetch, traveller's joy, the scabious and hound's tongue, spurge laurel,
bee or butterfly orchids, and such ferns as the polypody. In ponds we
meet with the water violet, the bulrush and the horsetail; on the sides
of brooks are hartstongue and liverwort, garlic, meadow sweet and
butter-bur; while on walls or rock we find the wallflower, the wall-rue,
the black and maiden-hair spleenworts and more rarely the oak fern...

On the drier hills the yellow pansy and the sweet wild thyme grow freely, and at times the field gentian, maiden pink and great mullein; at great heights we meet with ling and heather, bilberries, crowberries and cranberries, and in places the stag's-horn moss. Gorse, bracken and boorm are everywhere when not kept back by cultivation.'

What of my 'general aspect' of Shropshire?

'Apparently the largest land-locked county in England. Cities absent. A lot of creativity resides in the district, with local foods and crafts adorning stalls, shop windows and homes. When on the borders with Herefordshire, the area north of Shrewsbury feels distant. You are very aware that Wales is 'there' and the string of castle ruins and Offa's Dyke reminds you of a troubled past. It includes a hilly district with outcrops with distinctive shapes all harbouring fantastic views. From Stiperstones and Clee Hill, I had my first gasp of Shropshire. The moorland gives a sense of wilderness and is lush with rushes and purple with heathers. A pastoral landscape of sheep, sometimes treated with beet, and cows. Arable elements of the landscape include wheat, maize, rapeseed and potatoes. In spring, a kaleidoscope of rust, hazelnut and green fields cascade into one another. There are farms that don't want to be found; devoid of signs introducing their name. There are soaring buzzards everywhere often accompanied by their comforting cry. The countryside is full of hedges. Trees grow in riverside ribbons, copses and old woodlands. Larger expanses of conifer plantations occur such as at Mortimer Forest. A multitude of ditches, streams and rivers provide a glisten to the landscape. Winter floods transform the fields into calm lakes. The meres in the north sit calmly in flatter countryside, sometimes hidden by a skirting of wet woodland and featuring aquatic delights, such as the pink amphibious bistort. Tractors are a regular feature of the roads and traffic lights are rare. Pancakes of hedgehogs, rabbits and pheasants litter the roads in abundance; a sure sign of their frequency, or in the case of hedgehogs, their decline. There is no escape from the mud in the winter. Gangs of house sparrows line the roadsides, unphased by the oncoming traffic.

The roads are deserted and the locals are snug inside their houses by the time it's dark. The night sky is pitch black so you can see the glory of the stars. '

SIX LEGGED CURIOSITIES

Darwin wrote of his childhood:[1] 'I...collected all sorts of things, shells, seals, franks, coins and minerals. The passion for collecting...was very strong in me...' I must have observed insects with some little care, for when ten years old [1819] I went for three weeks to Plas Edwards on the sea coast in Wales, I was very much interested and surprised at seeing a large black and scarlet Hemipterous insect, many moths (Zygaena) and Cicindele, which are not found in Shropshire. I almost made up my mind to begin collecting all the insects which I could find dead, for on consulting my sister, I concluded that it was not right to kill insects for the sake of making a collection'

From this, Darwin gives us a clue that he observed moths, amongst other insects, in Shropshire, but how would he have done this and what would he have come across? I can only presume that he found moths that were disturbed from vegetation in the daytime or that he he held a lantern to the window or went out at night with a lantern to attract moths. 'Sugaring' for moths was only first recorded in Victorian times in 1831.[2] We can get some idea of which macromoths were recorded in Victorian times in Shropshire from a 1908 account (where it states 'Shropshire, from an entomological point of view, compares very favourably with other counties'), with some additions from Riley[3]:

Ghost swift	Common throughout
Orange swift	Not uncommon
Gold swift	In and near damp woods

Common swift	Abundant everywhere
Map-winged Swift	Very common in the hilly parts among bracken
Leopard Moth	Bomere
Goat Moth	Prees, Ellemere, Borsely, Shrewsbury, Little Stretton
The Forester	Very local
Six spot Burnet	Wenlock Edge, Church Stretton
Narrow–bordered Five spot Burnet	Widely distributed and fairly common
Hornet moth	Ellesmere, Church Stretton, Shrewsbury
Lunar Hornet Moth	Very common around Market Drayton, Church Stretton
Currant Clearwing	Fairly common in gardens
Yellow-legged Clearwing	Wyre Forest, Church Stretton
White barred Clearwing	Wyre Forest
Large Red–belted Clearwing	Caynton, Wyre Forest, Market Drayton, Pendlebury, Church Stretton
December Moth	Generally distributed; common around Church Stretton, Market Drayton
Pale Eggar	By no means common; Shrewsbury, Market Drayton, Church Stretton, Wyre Forest
Small Eggar	Very common around Calverhall, Market Drayton, Church Stretton
The Lackey	Not common; Ragleth Woods
Oak Eggar	Probably found in all flat parts of the county; Church Stretton, Market Drayton, Ellesmere
Whixall Moss Northern Eggar	Occurs commonly on the high moorlands of the county

Fox Moth	*Frequent* Where there is either rough, unbroken ground or moorland; Ellesmere, Longmynd
The Drinker	Common in larval state where there are damp hedgebanks and ditches
Small Lappet	Larval state on the Longmynd on bilberry
The Lappet	Larvae at Church Stretton
Emperor Moth	Of universal distribution; especially common whre there are large tracts of heather
Kentish Glory	Wyre Forest
Scalloped Hook-tip	Occurs freely where birches abound
Oak Hook-tip	Church Stretton, Market Drayton
Barred Hook-tip	Frequent in beech woods around Church Stretton and probably throughout the county
Pebble Hook-tip	Widespread
Chinese Character	Reported from nearly all parts of the county
Peach Blossom	Generally distributed but not abundant
Buff Arches	Generally distributed but not abundant; Market Drayton
Figure of Eighty	Broseley, Wyre
Poplar Lutestring	Recorded infrequently from Ragleth, Church Stretton, Wyre
Satin Lutestring	Wyre, Ragleth Wood
Common Lutestring	Not at all rare
Oak Lutestring	Generally distributed. Larvae often obtained
Yellow-horned	Common among birch

Orange Underwing	Common at Shrewsbury, Wyre Forest, Market Drayton, Church Stretton; Calverhall
Light Orange	Underwing Frequent at Market Drayton
March Moth	Fairly common throughout
Grass Emerald	Infrequent at Market Drayton and Church Stretton
Large Emerald	Fairly common at Market Drayton and Church Stretton; Wyre Forest
Blotched Emerald	Wyre Forest
Common Emerald	Scarce around Market Drayton
Little Emerald	Fairly common
The Mocha	In the vicinity of maple at Church Stretton
Birch Mocha	Wyre Forest; not uncommon around Market Drayton and Church Stretton
False Mocha	Wyre Forest, Markey Drayton
Maiden's Blush	Fairly common at Market Drayton
Blood Vein	Occasional Calverhall; rare Market Drayton; once Cloverley
Small Blood-vein	Scarce at Market Drayton
Lesser Cream Wave	Very common around Market Drayton
Cream Wave frequent	Generally distributed and fairly in meadows
Smoky Wave	Fairly common in Market Drayton
Small Fan-footed Wave	Generally distributed throughout the county
Small Dusty Wave	Common around knotgrass at Church Stretton
Single-dotted Wave	Common

Riband Wave	Found over the whole of the county; very common in damp places
Oblique Carpet	Meole Brace, Market Drayton, Church Stretton
Flame Carpet	Generally distributed but not abundant
Red Twin-Spot Carpet	Uncommon
Dark-barred Twin-Spot Carpet	Common throughout
Silver-ground Carpet	Universal and common
Garden Carpet	Abundant throughout
Shaded Broad-bar	Common throughout The Belle Common on Longmynd (including Lead Belle and July Belle) and the valleys where broom present
Small Argent and Sable	Church Stretton mainly in the Longmynd; Wyre Forest
Common Carpet	Common throughout Wood Carpet Shrewsbury, Oswestry
Galium Carpet	Church Stretton among Lady's Bedstraw
Yellow Shell	Common and widespread
Grey Mountain Carpet	Found amongst heather on the Longmynd
The Mallow Common	in Market Drayton; Church Stretton; Oswestry
Shoulder-stripe	Well distributed and common
The Streamer	Calverhill, Market Drayton, Church Stretton
Beautiful Carpet	Broseley and woods around Church Stretton
Dark Spinach	Scarce; Market Drayton
Water Carpet	Generally distributed and fairly common

Purple Bar	Market Drayton; Church Stretton
The Phoenix	Market Drayton scarce; Church Stretton not uncommon
The Chevron	Common throughout among poplars and sallows
Northern Spinach	Fairly common in Church Stretton and around Market Drayton
The Spinach	Market Drayton fairly common
Barred Straw	Universal
Red-green Carpet	Not uncommon near woods and in lanes near Church Stretton
Dark Marbled Carpet	Frequent in Church Stretton area
Common Marbled Carpet	Common throughout
Barred Yellow	Found wherever wild rose is found
Blue-bordered Carpet	Not uncommon in Ragleth Woods amongst alder; Twemlows, Calverhall, Market Drayton
Pine Carpet	Generally distributed
Grey Pine Carpet	Generally distributed and common
Broken-barred Carpet	Common at Calverhall and Church Stretton
Beech-green Carpet	Frequent amongst Galium in Church Stretton
Mottled Grey	Wyre Forest, Wrekin, Market Drayton, fairly common in Church Stretton
Green Carpet	Found throughout wherever heath bedstraw or hedge bedstraw
July Highflyer	Apparently generally distributed and abundant in some places
May Highflyer	Generally distributed, with the exception of Market Drayton

Argent and Sable	Wyre Forest; occasionally in forests around Church Stretton
Scarce Tissue	Market Drayton locally common; Calverhall
The Tissue	Fairly common throughout
Sharp-angled Carpet	Oswestry
November Moth	Generally distributed
Small Autumnal Moth	Frequent amongst bilberry and heath on the Longmynd; Oswestry
Winter Moth	Only too common
Northern Winter Moth	Larvae from Church Stretton; Benthall Edge
The Rivulet	Fairly common at Church Stretton; Calverhill
Small Rivulet	Generally distributed and fairly common
Barred Rivulet	Wyre Forest
Grass Rivulet	Very local but common where it occurs. Market Drayton, Prees Road, Twemlows
Sandy Carpet	Locally common
Twin-spot Carpet	Common at Claverhall; frequent around Church Stretton
Slender Pug	Very local species; Shavington
Toadflax Pug	Not uncommon
Foxglove Pug	Generally common
Mottled Pug	Fairly common throughout
Valerian Pug	Larvae at Moreton Say and Cloverley
Netted Pug	Scarce and local; Shrewsbury, Benthall, Market Drayton, Church Stretton
Lime-speck Pug	Generally distributed and common

Wormwood Pug	Frequent
Ling Pug	Shrewsbury
Currant Pug	Market Drayton, common
Common Pug	Common throughout
White-spotted Pug	Fairly common around Market Drayton
Campanula Pug	Benthall
Grey Pug	Generally distributed and common
Tawny-speckled Pug	Market Drayton, Calverhall
Ochreous Pug	Very local though abundant at Twemlows
Narrow-winged Pug	Commmon on the Longmynd among heather
Ash Pug	Calverhall
Brindled Pug	Church Stretton, Calverhall
Large Pug	Cloverley Park, Twemlows
Green Pug	Fairly common in orchards
Bilberry Pug	Abundant in Market Drayton
The Streak	Generally distributed
Broom-tip	Market Drayton
Treble-bar	Church Stretton
Chimney Sweeper	Quite common around Church Stretton; Wenlock Edge
Blomer's Rivulet	Common on the Wrekin; Benthall
Welsh Wave	Fairly common in Market Drayton
Dingy Shell	Market Drayton
Small White Wave	Church Stretton, Shavington
Small Yellow Wave	Frequent at Church Stretton
Waved Carpet	Not rare in woods planted with alders around Church Stretton; Market Drayton

Drab Looper	Wyre Forest
Early Tooth-striped	Abundant at Market Drayton and Benthall
Small Serphim	Not uncommon in Church Stretton
Yellow-barred Brindle	Wyre Forest
The Magpie	Abundant everywhere
Clouded Magpie	Farily Common around Church Stretton and the Wrekin; abundant near Staley's Cottage; Bridgnorth, Farley Dingle, Market Drayton
Clouded Border	Common in Church Stretton
Scorched Carpet	Shrewsbury, Benthall
Peacock	Market Drayton
Tawny-barred Angle	Not uncommon at Twemlows; frequent around Church Stretton; Shirlett
Latticed Heath	Common at Church Stretton
V-Moth	Generally distributed
Little Thorn	Wyre Forest
Brown Silver-lines	Hawkstone, Twemlows, Shavington, Wyre Forest
Barred Umber	Claverhall, Prees; not infrequent around Church Stretton
Scorced Wing	Wyre Forest
Brimstone	Abudnant everywhere
Bordered Beauty	Common everywhere
Speckled Yellow	Ellesmere, Church Stretton abundant
Lilac Beauty	Generally distributed
August Thorn	Calverhill occasional, Church Stretton, not uncommon
Canary-shouldered Thorn	Frequent around Church Stretton

Dusky Thorn	Sparingly around Church Stretton
September Thorn	Church Stretton, scarce at Market Drayton and Oswestry
Early Thorn	Frequent throughout
Lunar Thorn	Church Stretton, Benthall Edge
Scalloped Hazel	Very common throughout
Scalloped Oak	Common with apparent exception of Market Drayton area
Swallow-tailed Moth	Common throughout
Feathered Thorn	Well distributed and common
Orange Moth	Wyre Forest
Small Brindled Beauty	Rare at Cloverley Park, uncommon at Church Stretton
Pale Brindled Beauty	Frequent
Brindled Beauty	Occasionally at Helmeth and Ragleth Woods
Oak Beauty	Found sparingly throughout
Peppered Moth	Frequent throughout
Spring Usher	Frequent over greater part of county
Scarce Umber	Very common in and near woods around Church Stretton
Dotted Border	Generally distributed and common
Mottled Umber	Common throughout
Waved Umber	Common at Calverhill and Church Stretton, scarce at Market Drayton
Willow Beauty	Common in most larger gardens
Mottled Beauty	Very common over the greater part of the county
Great Oak Beauty	Wyre Forest, Helmeth, Ragleth Woods, Church Stretton

Brussel's Lace	Not scarce, often at rest on lichen covered trees
The Engrailed	Calverhall, Twemlows
Small Engrailed	Fairly plentiful in woods around Church Stretton
Grey Birch	Occasional in woods around Church Stretton
Common Heath	Common on unbroken wasteground throughout the county
Bordered White	Generally distributed, found in fir woods
Common White	Wave Common throughout
Common Wave	Frequent throughout
Clouded Silver	Common at Helmeth and Ragleth Woods
Early Moth	Common throughout
Light Emerald	Calverhall occasional; Church Stretton common
Barred Red	Infrequently at Twemlows and Church Stretton
The Annulet	Wyre Forest, Church Stretton
Grey-Scalloped Bar	Whixall Moss, Longmynd on heather
Grass Wave	Wyre Forest
Convolvulus Hawk-moth	Bridgnorth, Coalport, Ellesmere, Baschurch, Church Stretton
Deaths Head Hawkmoth	Occurs in favourable years all over county
Privet Hawkmoth	Apparently quite rare; Coalport, Church Stretton, Wyre Forest
Lime Hawkmoth	Rare; Broseley
Eyed Hawkmoth	Fairly common

Poplar Hawkmoth	Common throughout county
Narrow-bordered Bee Hawkmoth	Scarce in Market Drayton and Wyre Forest
Broad-bordered Bee	Wyre Forest
Humming-bird Hawkmoth	Found throughout
Elephant Hawkmoth	Fairly common throughout
Small Elephant Hawkmoth	Ellesmere, Calverhall, Whixall Moss, Whattall Moss, Market Drayton, Church Stretton
Silver-striped Hawkmoth	Broseley
Buff-tip	Abundant throughout
Puss Moth	Common everywhere
Alder Kitten	Market Drayton scarce; Church Stretton occasionally
Sallow Kitten	Church Stretton
Poplar Kitten	Market Drayton occasional, Broseley, Lyth Hall, Church Stretton
Lobster Moth	Wyre Forest
Iron Prominent	Generally distributed
Pebble Prominent	Fairly common at Calverhall, Market Drayton, Church Stretton
Great Prominent	Infrequently around Church Stretton; Market Drayton; Shrewsbury
Lesser Swallow Prominent	Market Drayton frequent; Broseley and Church Stretton frequent
Swallow Prominent	Fairly common among poplars in most parts of the county
Coxcomb Prominent	Generally distributed and common
Pale Prominent	Twemblows, Calverhall; Broseley common; Church Stretton
Marbled Brown	Church Stretton occasional; Wyre Forest

Lunar Marbled Brown	Sparingly Church Stretton
Small Chocolate-tip	Not rare around Church Stretton
Chocolate-tip	Church Stretton
Figure of Eight	Abundant and universal
Scarce Vapourer	Wyre Forest
The Vapourer	Common but not abundant throughout county
Pale Tussock	Shavington; common Market Drayton and Church Stretton
Brown-tail	Broseley, Ellemere, Caynton (near Newport)
Yellow-tail	Fairly common throughout
White Satin	Not uncommon; larvae on poplar
Round-winged Muslin	Shrewsbury, Market Drayton
Muslin Footman	Church Stretton not uncommon, Shrewsbury
Red-necked Footman	Not common; clinging to grass in old pasture
Four-dotted Footman	Wyre Forest
Dingy Footman	Wyre Forest
Scarce Footman	Church Stretton, Caradoc, Staley's Cottage, Benthall, Shrewsbury
Common Footman	Generally distributed and common
Speckled Footman	Rare; Wyre Forest
Wood Tiger	Moorland of the county; abundant on Longmynd
Garden Tiger	Fairly common
Clouded Buff	Regular at Whixall Moss, Wyre Forest, Ragleth Wood near Church Stretton
White Ermine	Common throughout

Buff Ermine	Common throughout
Water Ermine	Near World's End; 1900 sightings
Muslin Moth	Common around Shrewsbury; sparingly around Church Stretton and Wyre Forest
Ruby Tiger	Market Drayton occasional; Ercall Heath near Newport; Longmynd frequent
Cinnabar Moth	Fairly common
Short-cloaked Moth	Calverhall regular; Market Drayton district frequent; Church Stretton
Least Black Arches	
Square-spot Dart	Church Stretton
White-line Dart	Market Drayton scarce; Wellington
Garden Dart	Infrequent at Shrewsbury; Brosely, Church Stretton, Wyre Forest
Light-feathered Rustic	Occasional in Wyre Forest
Turnip Moth	Common throughout
Heart and Club	Infrequent but generally distributed
Heart and Dart	Abundant everywhere
Dark Sword-grass	Scarce or uncommon throughout
The Flame	Shrewsbury, Market Drayton scarce, Wyre Forest
Portland Moth	Shrewsbury
Flame Shoulder	Common everywhere
Plain Clay	Infrequent at Church Stretton
Northern Rustic	Church Stretton
Large Yellow Underwing	Common everywhere
Lunar Yellow Underwing	A few on the Longmynd among heather
Lesser Yellow Underwing	Common everywhere

Broad-bordered Yellow Underwing	Calverhall, Market Drayton common, Church Stretton infrequent, Wyre Forest
Lesser Broad-bordered Yellow Underwing	Calverhall common; Market Drayton scarce; Church Stretton infrequent
Least Yellow-underwing	Scarce at Market Drayton, Church Stretton and Broseley; Shrewsbury and Wyre Forest
Stout Dart	Occurs sparingly throughout the county
Double Dart	Generally distributed
Autumnal Rustic	Market Drayton, Church Stretton
True-lovers Knot	Common at Church Stretton, Market Drayton and Whixall Moss; Shrewsbury
Pearly Underwing	Generally distributed but scarce
Ingrailed Clay	Common
Barred Chestnut	Common at Market Drayton; Wyre Forest; infrequent at Church Stretton
Purple Clay	Common at Broseley and Church Stretton and Market Drayton
Small Square-spot	Common
Setaceous Hebrew Character	Common at Market Drayton, occasional at Calverhall, frequent at Church Stretton and Broseley
Double Square-spot	Calverhall infrequent; Market Drayton frequent; Church Stretton
Dotted Clay	Generally common
Square-spotted Clay	Church Stretton
Neglected Rustic	Not uncommon at Market Drayton and on Long Mynd
Six-striped Rustic	Common
Square-spot Rustic	Common throughout

The Gothic	Frequent at Market Drayton and Church Stretton
Great Brocade	Church Stretton
Green Arches	Occasional at Church Stretton and Wyre Forest
Red Chestnut	Frequent or common throughout
White-marked	Wyre Forest; Church Stretton
Beautiful Yellow Underwing	Wherever there are large tracts of heather; very common on the Longmynd
The Nutmeg	Church Stretton
The Shears	Generally distributed and common
Pale Shining Brown	Wyre Forest
Silvery Arches	Wyre Forest; Market Drayton
Grey Arches	Generally distributed and frequent
White Colon	Ragleth Hill
Bordered Gothic	Church Stretton, Wyre Forest
Cabbage Moth	Common throughout
Dot Moth	Calverhall; Market Drayton scarce; Church Stretton very scarce
Beautiful Brocade	Wyre Forest, Church Stretton
Light Brocade	Church Stretton, Broseley, Wyre Forest
Pale-shouldered Brocade	Apparenlty frequent throughout
Dog's Tooth	Shrewsbury, Wyre Forest, Calverhall
Bright-line Brown-eye	Generally distributed and common
Glaucous Shears	Shrewsbury, Church Stretton
Broom Moth	Generally distributed and common
Broad-barred White	Shrewsbury, Wyre Forest; Church Stretton common
Campion	Frequent at Church Stretton; Broseley

Tawny Shears	Occasional at Church Stretton
Marbled Coronet	Scarce at Market Drayton
Lychnis	Generally distributed and frequent
Antler Moth	Common at Calverhall and Church Stretton
Hedge Rustic	Generally distributed but uncommon, though frequent at Church Stretton and Market Drayton
Feathered Gothic	Shrewsbury, Calverhall common, Market Drayton common, Church Stretton frequent
Pine Beauty	Twemlows, Church Stretton in fir plantations
Small Quaker	Common throughout
Blossom Underwing	Church Stretton, Wyre Forest
Northern Drab	Wyre Forest, Church Stretton
Lead-coloured Drab	Shrewsbury, Church Stretton
Powdered Quaker	Calverhall occasional, Market Drayton frequent, Wyre Forest
Common Quaker	Common throughout
Clouded Drab	Common throughout
Twin-spotted Quaker	Fairly common throughout
Hebrew Character	Common throughout
Brown-line Bright Eye	Common at Church Stretton
Clay Wainscot	Common
Smoky Wainscot	Common flying in damp meadows
Common Wainscot	Generally abundant, flying in damp meadows
Shoulder-striped Wainscot	Common
Chamomile Shark	Common at Market Drayton

The Shark	Generally common
The Mullein	Wyre Forest, Church Stretton, Benthall
Minor Shoulder-knot	Generally distributed
The Sprawler	Shrewsbury, Botyville
Deep-brown Dart	Wyre Forest
Goldenrod Brindle	Occasional at Church Stretton
Pale Pinion	Wyre Forest
Grey Shoulder-knot	Frequent at Church Stretton; Shrewsbury
Red Sword-grass	Not rare in damp marshy localities around Church Stretton; Shrewsbury; Benthall
Sword-grass	Shrewsbury; Church Stretton fairly common; Broseley, Calverhall, Market Drayton
Early Grey	Shrewsbury; frequent at Church Stretton; common at Market Drayton; Cloverley Park, Calverhall
Green Brindled Crescent	Common throughout
Merveille du Jour	Common throughout
Brindled Green	Generally distributed and common
Dark Brocade	Market Drayton, Calverhall, Church Stretton
Grey Chi	Universal and frequent
The Satellite	Common throughout
Orange Upperwing	Wyre Forest
The Chestnut	Common throughout
Dark Chestnut	Frequent throughout
The Brick	Generally distributed and common
Red-line Quaker	Generally but not common

Yellow-line Quaker	Broseley; scarce at Market Drayton; very common at Church Stretton
Flounced Chestnut	Calverhall, Church Stretton, Market Drayton, Wyre Forest
Brown-spot Pinion	General and common
Beaded Chestnut	Common throughout
Centre-barred Sallow	Calverhall, Shrewsbury, Church Stretton occasional
Lunar Underwing	Very common at Shrewsbury; frequent in Church Stretton
Orange Sallow	Fairly common in north-east; abundant in Church Stretton
Barred Sallow	Church Stretton
Pink-barred Sallow	Common at Market Drayton; occasional at Whitchurch and Church Stretton; Shrewsbury
The Sallow	Shavington uncommon; Market Drayton common; Church Stretton frequent
Dusky Lemon Sallow	Generally distributed; Shrewsbury, Calverhall frequent; Market Drayton rare, Church Stretton
Poplar Grey	Fairly common at Market Drayton; frequent at Church Stretton
The Miller	Northern shropshire; Wyre Forest; Church Stretton
Alder Moth	Generally rare; more frequent in south-west and south-east
Dark Dagger	Shrewsbury, Calverhall, Church Stretton
Grey Dagger	Generally distributed
Light Knot Grass	Shrewsbury; boggy parts of Longmynd; not common

Knot Grass	Frequent, especially in central Shropshire
The Coronet	Uncommon at Church Stretton; Wyre Forest
Marbled Beauty	Common in most parts of the county
Marbled Green	1901 sighting, Market Drayton
Copper Underwing & Svensson's Copper Underwing	Church Stretton
Mouse Moth	Very common throughout
Old Lady	Scarce in Market Drayton and Calverhall; common at Church Stretton
Bird's Wing	Wyre Forest, Market Drayton
Brown Rustic	Generally distributed and common
Straw Underwing	Church Stretton not uncommon
Small Angle Shades	Frequent throughout
Angle Shades	Common throughout
Double Kidney	Church Stretton
The Olive	Frequent at Church Stretton; Benthall
The Suspected	Common at Market Drayton; Pendlebury; Benthall Edge
Dingy Shears	Frequent in damp places at Church Stretton; Shrewsbury; Benthall
Lesser-spotted Pinion	Common at Shrewsbury; rare at Church Stretton; Calverhall
White-spotted Pinion	Occasional Church Stretton
The Dun-bar	Generally common
Lunar-spotted Pinion	Shrewsbury, Ragleth Wood
Dark Arches	Common throughout
Light Arches	Generally distributed and fairly common

Reddish Light Arches	Not common; Broseley, Enthall, Wyre Forest
Clouded-bordered Brindle	Frequent and general
Clouded Brindle	Uncommon and local; Calverhall, Church Stretton, Broseley, Wyre Forest
The Confused	Broseley, Wyre Forest, Longmynd
Dusky Brocade	Calverhall, Market Drayton, Broseley, Church Stretton
Small Clouded Brindle	Calverhall, Church Stretton
Union Rustic	Church Stretton
Large Nutmeg	Occasional at Church Stretton, scarce at Market Drayton, Wyre Forest
Rustic Shoulder-knot	Calverhall abundant; Broseley, Church Stretton frequent
Slender Brindle	Generally rare and local; Church Stretton woods
Marbled Minor	Common throughout county
Middle-barred Minor	Common throughout
Cloaked Minor	Frequent throughout
Rosy Minor	Frequent throughout
Common Rustic	Common throughout
Small Dotted Buff	Generally frequent
Small Wainscot	Common but local around Market Drayton and Ragleth Wood, Church Stretton.
Dusky Sallow	Occasionally at Church Stretton
Flounced Rustic	Common throughout
Ear Moth	Abundant at Calverhall, frequent at Church Stretton; Broseley

Rosy Rustic	Shrewsbury; common at Calverhall; frequent at Market Drayton and Church Stretton
Frosted Orange	Shrewsbury; scarce at Market Drayton; not rare around Church Stretton
Haworth's Minor	Scarce at Market Drayton; Oswestry; Longmynd
The Crescent	Calverhall
Bulrush Wainscot	Calverhall, Soudley Pools, Church Stretton
Small Rufous	Calverhall
Treble-lines	Fairly common at Shrewsbury; Ford; Calverhall; Market Drayton; Broseley; Church Stretton
The Uncertain	Scarce at Market Drayton, otherwise common
The Rustic	Market Drayton scarce; Broseley frequent; Church Stretton
Mottled Rustic	Shrewsbury; scarce at Market Drayton; frequent at Church Stretton
Pale Mottled Willow	Infrequent throughout
Small Yellow Underwing	Generally distributed
Marbled White Spot	Wyre Forest
Scarce Silver-lines	Cloverley Park; Market Drayton; Church Stretton
Nut-tree Tussock	Church Stretton
Burnished Brass	Common everywhere
Gold Spot	General and occasional
Silver Y	Common throughout
Beautiful Golden Y	General and frequent
Plain Golden Y	General and frequent

Gold Spangle	Benthall Edge; Shrewsbury
Scarce Silver Y	Church Stretton; Shrewsbury
Dark Spectacle	Generally distributed
The Spectacle	Generally distributed
Red Underwing	Wyre Forest
Mother Shipton	Common around Church Stretton; Wyre Forest
Burnet Companion	Frequent in western parts; Wyre Forest
The Herald	Generally common
Small Purple-barred	Calverhall common; Market Drayton frequent; Church Stretton common; Ragleth Woods
Beautiful Snout	Market Drayton
The Snout	General and common
Buttoned Snout	Wyre Forest
Pinion-streaked Snout	Local; Market Drayton
The Fan-foot	Not rare at Market Drayton
Small Fan-foot	Common in many damp woods

In recent times the following moths have been recorded in the tetrad in which The Mount occurs[4]:

Bright-line Brown Eye	(*Lacanobia oleracea*)
Brimstone Moth	(*Opisthograptis luteolata*)
Buff Arches	(*Habrosyne pyritoides*)
Common Emerald	(*Hemithea aestivaria*)
Common Wainscot	(*Mythimna pallens*)
Dark Arches	(*Apamea monoglypha*)
Flame	(*Axylia putris*)
Flame Carpet	(*Xanthorhoe designata*)

Flame Shoulder	(*Ochropleura plecta*)
Garden Carpet	(*Xanthorhoe fluctuata fluctuata*)
Heart and Dart	(*Agrotis exclamationis*)
Herald	(*Scoliopteryx libatrix*)
Lime Hawk-moth	(*Mimas tiliae*)
Poplar Hawk-moth	(*Laothoe populi*)
Red Twin-spot Carpet	(*Xanthorhoe spadicearia*)
Small Fan-footed Wave	(*Idaea biselata*)
Swallow-tailed Moth	(*Ourapteryx sambucaria*)
Uncertain	(*Hoplodrina alsines*)

It's interesting that later, as part of his scientific studies, Darwin references moths and their transformation:[5] 'There is an analogy between caterpillars with respect to moths, & monkeys & men, — each man passes through its caterpillar state. The monkey represents this state.

It has already been casually remarked that certain organs in the individual, which when mature become widely different and serve for different purposes, are in the embryo exactly alike. The embryos, also, of distinct animals within the same class are often strikingly similar: a better proof of this cannot be given, than a circumstance mentioned by Agassiz, namely, that having forgotten to ticket the embryo of some vertebrate animal, he cannot now tell whether it be that of a mammal, bird, or reptile. The vermiform larvæ of moths, flies, beetles, &c., resemble each other much more closely than do the mature insects.'[6]

Darwin gave W. D. Fox, credit for introducing him to serious entomology at Cambridge in 1828. Beetle-collecting was certainly a passion of Darwin's, and very fashionable at this time. He is even cartooned later by a friend, Albert Way, riding a beetle. In his autobiography[7] Darwin wrote in relation to beetles: 'But no pursuit at Cambridge was followed with nearly so much eagerness or gave me so much pleasure as collecting beetles. It was the mere passion for collecting, for I did not dissect them and rarely compared their external characters with published descriptions, but got them named anyhow. I will give a proof of my zeal: one day, on tearing off some old bark, I saw two rare beetles and seized one in each hand; then I saw a third and new kind, which I could not bear to lose, so that I popped the one which I held in my right hand into my mouth. Alas it ejected some intensely acrid fluid, which burnt my tongue so that I was forced to spit the beetle out, which was lost, as well as the third one'...'I am surprised what an indelible impression many of the beetles which I caught in Cambridge have left on my mind. I can remember the exact appearance of certain posts, old trees and banks where I made a good capture'.

Darwin wrote a letter to W.D. Fox at the end of the summer term in 1828 '[I am] dying by inches, from not having anybody to talk to about insects'.[8] Bowdley[9] writes how in 1828, Darwin took a trip to Barmouth. A companion, J.M Herbert (1808–82) recalls that on their afternoon expeditions 'Darwin entomologised most industriously, picking up creatures as he went along...And very soon he armed me with a bottle of alcohol, in which I had to drop any beertle which struck me as not of a common kind'. Another companion, T Butler (1806–86) recalled that Darwin's enthusiasm had inoculated him with a taste for botany which had stuck with him all his life. Darwin writes to W.D. Fox on 29 October 1828:[10] 'My head is quite full of entomology. I long to empty some information out of it into yours. He [Mr. Hope] thinks he can give me 3 or 400 species at Christmas' Later on 25 August 1830, Darwin writes[11] 'I left Shrewsbury this day fortnight ago, & have since that time been working from morning to night in catching fish or beetles. This is literally the first idle day I have had to myself: for on the rainy days I go fishing, on the good ones entomologizing'. Darwin's soft spot for invertebrates is recollected later by his son, George Darwin (1892)[12] in his experiences at Downe: 'We often used to go out with [our father] on his mid-day walk, generally down the hill to Cudham Lodge Woods, the 'big woods', and do a little collecting as we walked. He seemed to know nearly all the beetles and was immensely interested when any of the rarer sort were found...He used to take long walks of three or four miles before breakfast, starting frequently in the dark. I have heard him say that sometimes in the dusk of the morning in the woods he would walk very slowly, just quietly putting down his foot and then waiting before the next step – a habit, he said, which he had practised in the tropical forests of Brazil.' Nowadays the National Biodiversity Network lists 593 species of beetle in hectad TQ46, in which Down House is located.[13]

There is no doubt that Darwin's beetle interest would have spilled out into his time in Shropshire. After all, a naturalist does not switch off his awareness and interest just like that! Indeed there is a record of Darwin catching the following species in Shropshire[14]: *Ptomaphagus anisotomoides (Nargus anisotomoides), Ptomaphagus wilkinnii (Nargus wilkini), Catops serceus (Ptomaphagus medius)* and *Nitidula punctatissima (Soronia punctatissima).* As for the other species of beetle present in the county, the only list I have been able to find is that recounted in *Victoria History of Shropshire* (with updated names provided by Barclay)[15], written in 1908, where it states: 'The county is probably very rich in Coleoptera'. Interestingly, two of Darwin's species do not appear in the list.

Cicindela campestris	*Cicindela campestris*	Carabidae	
Bychrus rostratus	*Cychrus caraboides*	Carabidae	
Carabus catenulatus	*Carabus problematicus*	Carabidae	
C. convexus	*Carabus convexus*	Carabidae	Only a few old records; probably not a British species
C. violaceus	*Carabus violaceus*	Carabidae	
C. arvensis	*Carabus arvensis*	Carabidae	
Notiophilus substriatus	*Notiophilus substriatus*	Carabidae	
Leistus spinibarbis	*Leistus spinibarbis*	Carabidae	
L. rufescens	*Leistus terminatus*	Carabidae	
Nebria brevicollis	*Nebria brevicollis*	Carabidae	
Elaphrus riparius	*Elaphrus riparius*	Carabidae	
E. cupreus	*Elaphrus cupreus*	Carabidae	
Loricera pilicornis	*Loricera pilicornis*	Carabidae	
Clivina fossor	*Clivina fossor*	Carabidae	
Miscodera arctica	*Miscodera arctica*	Carabidae	Scarce northern and western species, known from the midlands nothwards

Panagaeus crux-major	*Panagaeus cruxmajor*	Carabidae	RDB1 (Endangered); Hyman (1992) gives no Shropshire records
Badister bipustulatus	*Badister bullatus*	Carabidae	
Bradycellus cognatus	*Trichocellus cognatus*	Carabidae	
B. similes	*Bradycellus ruficollis*	Carabidae	
Harpalus ruficornis	*Harpalus (Pseudophonus) rufipes*	Carabidae	
H. latus	*Harpalus latus*	Carabidae	
Sotmis pumicatus	*Stomis pumicatus*	Carabidae	
Platyderus ruficollis	*Platyderus depressus*	Carabidae	
Pterostichus versicolor	*Poecilus versicolor*	Carabidae	
P. vulgaris	*Pterostichus melanarius*	Carabidae	
P. nigrita	*Pterostichus nigrita*	Carabidae	now known to be two species in UK, nigrita and rhaeticus, both likely in Shropshire
P. strenuous	*Pterostichus strenuus*	Carabidae	
P. diligens	*Pterostichus diligens*	Carabidae	
P. vitreus	*Pterostichus adstrictus*	Carabidae	
P. madidus	*Pterostichus madidus*	Carabidae	
P. stiola	*Abax parallelepipedus*	Carabidae	
Amara apicaria	*Amara apricaria*	Carabidae	
A. patricia	*Amara equestris*	Carabidae	
A. tibialis	*Amara tibialis*	Carabidae	
A. lunicollis	*Amara lunicollis*	Carabidae	
A. ovata	*Amara ovata*	Carabidae	
A. sumilata	*Amara similata*	Carabidae	
Calathus flavipes	*Calathus erratus*	Carabidae	
C. mollis	*Calathus mollis*	Carabidae	
C. micropterus	*Calathus micropterus*	Carabidae	
Taphria nivalis	*Synunchus vivalis*	Carabidae	
Prstonychus terricola	*Laemostenus terricola*	Carabidae	
Anchomenus angusticollis	*Platynus assimilis*	Carabidae	
A. viduus	*Agonum viduum*	Carabidae	
A, piceus	*Agonum piceum*	Carabidae	
A, gracilis	*Agonum gracilis*	Carabidae	
A. scitulus	*Agonum scitulum*	Carabidae	Hyman (1992) gives pre-1970 records from Shropshire for this rare species

A. fuliginosus	Agonum fuliginosum	Carabidae	
Olisthopus rotundatus	Olisthopus rotundatus	Carabidae	
Bembidium rufescens	Ocys harpaloides	Carabidae	
B. biguttatum	Bembidion biguttatum	Carabidae	
B. aeneum	Bembidion aeneum	Carabidae	
B. quadrimaculatum	Bembidion quadrimaculatum	Carabidae	
B. lampros	Bembidion lampros	Carabidae	
B. bipunctatum	Bembidion bipunctatum	Carabidae	
B. decorum	Bembidion decorum	Carabidae	
B. monticola	Bembidion monticola	Carabidae	
B. nitidulum	Bembidion deletum	Carabidae	
B. tibiale	Bembidion tibiale	Carabidae	
B. atrocoeruleum	Bembidion atrocaeruleum	Carabidae	
B. saxatile	Bembidion saxatile	Carabidae	
B. femoratum	Bembidion femoratum	Carabidae	
B. bruxellense	Bembidion bruxellense	Carabidae	
B. littorale	Bembidion tetracolum	Carabidae	
B. flammulatum	Bembidion dentellum	Carabidae	
B. varium	Bembidion varium	Carabidae	
B. punctulatum	Bembidion punctulatum	Carabidae	
Tacypus flavipes	Asaphidion curtum	Carabidae	former flavipes has been divided into 3 species, of which A. curtum is the most likely and commonest; but probably at least 2 occur in the county
Perileptus areolatus	Perileptus areolatus	Carabidae	
Trechus longicornis	Thalassophilus longicornis	Carabidae	Hyman (1992) gives pre-1970 records from Shropshire for this rare species
T. minutus	Trechus quadristriatus	Carabidae	
T. obtusus	Trechus obtusus	Carabidae	
Lebia crux-minor	Lebia cruxminor	Carabidae	RDB1: Hyman (1992) gives pre-1970 records from Shropshire for this rare species
L. haemorrhoidalis	Lebia marginata	Carabidae	Considered extinct in UK: no 20th century record: only recorded from Shropshire and Wiltshire

L. cyanocephala	*Lebia cyanocephala*	Carabidae	RDB1: Hyman (1992) gives no records from Shropshire for this rare species
L. chlorocephala	*Lebia chlorocephala*	Carabidae	
Demetrias atricapillus	*Demetrias atricapillus*	Carabidae	
Dromius linearis	*Paradromius linearis*	Carabidae	
D. quadrimaculatus	*Dromius quadrimaculatus*	Carabidae	
D. quadrinotatus	*Dromius spilotus*	Carabidae	
Metabletus foveola	*Syntomus foveatus*	Carabidae	
Haliplus flavicollis	*Haliplus flavicollis*	Haliplidae	
H. variegatus	*Haliplus variegatus*	Haliplidae	
H. lineatocollis	*Haliplus lineatocollis*	Haliplidae	
H. brychius elevatus	*Brychius elevatus*	Haliplidae	
Coelambus decoratus	*Hygrotus (Hygrotus) decoratus*	Dytiscidae	
C. impressopunctatus	*Hygrotus (Coelambus) impressopunctatus*	Dytiscidae	
Hydroporus granularis	*Graptodytes granularis*	Dytiscidae	
H. flavipes	*Graptodytes flavipes*	Dytiscidae	
H. lepidus	*Stictonectes lepidus*	Dytiscidae	
H. rivalis	*Oreodytes sanmarkii*	Dytiscidae	
H. septentrionalis	*Oreodytes septentrionalis*	Dytiscidae	
H. davisi	*Oreodytes davisii*	Dytiscidae	
H. 12-pustulatus	*Stictotarsus duodecimpustulatus*	Dytiscidae	
H. depressus	*Nebrioporus depressus*	Dytiscidae	
H. assimilis	*Nebrioporus assimilis*	Dytiscidae	
H. dorsalis	*Suphrodytes dorsalis*	Dytiscidae	
H. rufifrons	*Hydroporus rufifrons*	Dytiscidae	
H. marginatus	*Hydroporus marginatus*	Dytiscidae	
H. nigrita	*Hydroporus nigrita*	Dytiscidae	
N. tristis	*Hydroporus tristis*	Dytiscidae	
H. umbrosus	*Hydroporus umbrosus*	Dytiscidae	
H. palustris	*Hydroporus palustris*	Dytiscidae	
H. lineatus	*Porhydrus lineatus*	Dytiscidae	
Agabus guttatus	*Agabus guttatus*	Dytiscidae	
A. biguttatus	*Agabus biguttatus*	Dytiscidae	
A. paludosus	*Agabus paludosus*	Dytiscidae	
A. affinis	*Agabus affinis*	Dytiscidae	

A. didymus	*Agabus didymus*	Dytiscidae	
A femoralis	*Agabus labiatus*	Dytiscidae	
A. abbreviatus	*Agabus undulatus*	Dytiscidae	
A. chalconotus	*Ilybius chalconotus*	Dytiscidae	
Platambus maculatus	*Platambus maculatus*	Dytiscidae	
Ilybius guttiger	*Ilybius guttiger*	Dytiscidae	
Copelatus agilis	*Copelatus haemorrhoidalis*	Dytiscidae	
Rhantus exoletus	*Rhantus exsoletus*	Dytiscidae	some confusion over this name
Dytiscus circumcinctus	*Dytiscus circumcinctus*	Dytiscidae	
D. dimidiatus	*Dytiscus dimidiatus*	Dytiscidae	Very rare species; also the absence of the common marginalis is surprising
Hydaticus transversalis	*Hydaticus transversalis*	Dytiscidae	Very rare species
H. seminiger	*Hydaticus seminiger*	Dytiscidae	
Gyrinus minutus	*Gyrinus minutus*	Gyrinidae	the absence of the very common substriatus is surprising
Orectochilus vuillosus	*Orectochilus villosus*	Gyrinidae	
Philhydrus coarctatus	*Enochrus coarctatus*	Hydrophilidae	
Laccobius sinnatus	*Laccobius sinatus*	Hydrophilidae	
L. alutaceus	*Laccobius bipunctatus*	Hydrophilidae	
Limnebius truncatellus	*Limnebius truncatellus*	Hydraenidae	
Chaetarthria seminulum	*Chaetarthria seminulum*	Hydrophilidae	now known to be two species in UK, seminulum and simillima; both possible in Shropshire
Helophorus rugosus	*Helophorus rufipes*	Helophoridae	
Hydrochus brevis	*Hydrochus brevis*	Hydrochidae	
H. elongatus	*Hydrochus elongatus*	Hydrochidae	
H. angustatus	*Hydrochus angustatus*	Hydrochidae	
Henicocerus exsculptus	*Enicocerus exsculptus*	Hydraenidae	
Octhebius margipallens	*Octhebius pusillus*	Hydraenidae	
O. bicolon	*Octhebius dilatatus*	Hydraenidae	
O. rufimarginatus	*Octhebius bicolon*	Hydraenidae	some confusion over this name
O. punctatus	*Octhebius punctatus*	Hydraenidae	
Hydraena riparia	*Hydraena riparia*	Hydraenidae	
H. nigrita	*Hydraena nigrita*	Hydraenidae	
Sphaeridium scarabaeoides	*Sphaeridium scarabaeoides*	Hydrophilidae	
S. bipustulatum	*Sphaeridium bipustulatum*	Hydrophilidae	

Cercyon obsoletus	*Cercyon obsoletus*	Hydrophilidae
C. haemorrhoidalis	*Cercyon haemorrhoidalis*	Hydrophilidae
C. lateralis	*Cercyon lateralis*	Hydrophilidae
C. analis	*Cercyon analis*	Hydrophilidae
Cryptopleurum atomarium	*Cryptopleurum minutum*	Hydrophilidae
Aleochara fuscipes	*Stenus fuscipes*	Staphylinidae
A. bipunctata	*Aleochara intricata*	Staphylinidae
A. maculata	*Aleochara maculata*	Staphylinidae
A. moerens	*Aleochara moerens*	Staphylinidae
A. nitida	*Aleochara bipustulata*	Staphylinidae
Oxypoda spectablis	*Oxypoda spectabilis*	Staphylinidae
O.umbrata	*Oxypoda brevicornis*	Staphylinidae
O. annularis	*Oxypoda annularis*	Staphylinidae
Ocalea latipennis	*Ocalea latipennis*	Staphylinidae
O. badia	*Ocalea badia*	Staphylinidae
Homalota currax	*Aloconota currax*	Staphylinidae
H. insecta	*Aloconota insecta*	Staphylinidae
H. pavens	*Acrotona sulcifrons*	Staphylinidae
H. cambrica	*Aloconota cambrica*	Staphylinidae
H. eximia	*Hydrosmecta eximia*	Staphylinidae
H. fragilis	*Hydrosmecta fragilis*	Staphylinidae
H. longula	*Hydrosmecta longula*	Staphylinidae
H. delicatula	*Hydrosmecta delicatula*	Staphylinidae
H. subtilissima	*Hydrosmecta subtilissima*	Staphylinidae
H. luteipes	*Dilacra luteipes*	Staphylinidae
H. londinensis	*Philhygra gyllenhalii*	Staphylinidae
H. hygrotopora	*Philhygra hygrotopora*	Staphylinidae
H. gregaria	*Aloconota gregaria*	Staphylinidae
H. oblongiuscula	*Liogluta microptera*	Staphylinidae
H. sylvicola	*Atheta hypnorum*	Staphylinidae	this name is for Homalota silvicola; sylvicola may be a misspelling (though there is an Acrotona sylvicola)
H. crassicornis	*Liogluta granigera*	Staphylinidae
H. pagana	*Liogluta pagana*	Staphylinidae
H. monticola	*Bessobia monticola*	Staphylinidae
H. pilicornis	*Atheta pilicornis*	Staphylinidae

H. debilis	*Philhygra debilis*	Staphylinidae	
H. fullaciosa	*Philhygra fallaciosa*	Staphylinidae	
H. erentia	*Boreophilia eremita*	Staphylinidae	This is a guess at what the non-existent (typing error) 'erentia' could be
H. curtipennis	*Schistoglossa curtipennis*	Staphylinidae	
H. decipiens	*Amischa decipiens*	Staphylinidae	
H. exilis	*Meotica filiformis*	Staphylinidae	some confusion over this name
H. pallens	*Meotica anglica*	Staphylinidae	Endemic species to the UK: relatively widespread
H. valida	*Atheta brunneipennis*	Staphylinidae	
H. boletobia	*Atheta nigritula*	Staphylinidae	
H. sodalis	*Alaobia sodalis*	Staphylinidae	
H. humeralis	*Alaobia pallidicornis*	Staphylinidae	
H. gagatina	*Alaobia gagatina*	Staphylinidae	
H. divisa	*Atheta divisa*	Staphylinidae	
H. perxigua	*Microdota minuscula*	Staphylinidae	
H. oblita	*Atheta oblita*	Staphylinidae	
H. subtilis	*Microdota subtilis*	Staphylinidae	
H. indubia	*Microdota indubia*	Staphylinidae	
H. morurorum	*Microdota atricolor*	Staphylinidae	
H. sordidula	*Datomicra sordidula*	Staphylinidae	
H. marcida	*Dimetrota marcida*	Staphylinidae	
H. intermedia	*Microdota indubia*	Staphylinidae	
H. macrocera	*Badura macrocera*	Staphylinidae	
H. cadaverina	*Cadaverota cadaverina*	Staphylinidae	
H. tetudinea	*Coprothassa melanaria*	Staphylinidae	
H. pilosiventris	*Acrotona parvula*	Staphylinidae	
Gnypeta caerulea	*Gnypeta caerulea*	Staphylinidae	
Tachyusa constricta	*Tachyusa constricta*	Staphylinidae	
Autalia impressa	*Autalia impressa*	Staphylinidae	
Encephalus complican	*Encephalus complicans*	Staphylinidae	
Gyrophaena poweri	*Gyrophaena poweri*	Staphylinidae	
G. affinis	*Gyrophaena affinis*	Staphylinidae	
Sipalia ruficollis	*Leptusa ruficollis*	Staphylinidae	
Bolitochara lucida	*Bolitochara lucida*	Staphylinidae	
B. bella	*Bolitochara bella*	Staphylinidae	

B. obliqua	*Bolitochara obliqua*	Staphylinidae	
Myllaena dubia	*Myllaena dubia*	Staphylinidae	
M. elongata	*Myllaena elongata*	Staphylinidae	
M. gracilis	*Myllaena gracilis*	Staphylinidae	
Gymnusa brevicollis	*Gymnusa brevicollis*	Staphylinidae	
G. variegata	*Gymnusa variegata*	Staphylinidae	
Conosoma immaculatum	*Sepedophilus immaculatus*	Staphylinidae	
Tachyporus obtusus	*Tachyporus obtusus*	Staphylinidae	
T. chyrsomelinus	*Tachyporus chrysomelinus*	Staphylinidae	Now known to consist of two species in UK (the other T. dispar); both common
T. hypnorum	*Tachyporus hypnorum*	Staphylinidae	
T. pusillus	*Tachyporus pusillus*	Staphylinidae	
Tachinus humeralis	*Tachinus humeralis*	Staphylinidae	
T. proximus	*Tachinus proximus*	Staphylinidae	
T. rufipes	*Tachinus rufipes*	Staphylinidae	
T. suterraneius	*Tachinus subterraneus*	Staphylinidae	
Megcronus cingulatus	*Bolitobius cingulatus*	Staphylinidae	
M. inclinanas	*Parabolitobius inclinans*	Staphylinidae	
Bolitobius lunulatus	*Lordithon lunulatus*	Staphylinidae	
B. trintatus	*Lordithon trinotatus*	Staphylinidae	
B. pygmaeus	*Lordithon thoracicus*	Staphylinidae	
Mycetoporus lucidus	*Mycetoporus rufescens*	Staphylinidae	
M. punctus	*Mycetoporus punctus*	Staphylinidae	
M longulus	*Mycetoporus longulus*	Staphylinidae	
M clavicornis	*Mycetoporus clavicornis*	Staphylinidae	Now known to consist of two species in UK
Habrocerus capillaricornis	*Habrocerus capillaricornis*	Staphylinidae	
Euryporus picipes	*Euryporus picipes*	Staphylinidae	
Quedius lateralis	*Quedius lateralis*	Staphylinidae	
Q. puncticollis	*Quedius puncticollis*	Staphylinidae	
Q. molochinus	*Quedius molochinus*	Staphylinidae	
Q. fuliginosus	*Quedius fuliginosus*	Staphylinidae	Now known to consist of two species in UK (the other Q. curtipennis); both common
Q. picipes	*Quedius picipes*	Staphylinidae	
Q. nigriceps	*Quedius nigriceps*	Staphylinidae	
Q. fumatus	*Quedius fumatus*	Staphylinidae	

Q. mauroufus	Quedius mauroufus	Staphylinidae	
Q. umbrinus	Quedius umbrinus	Staphylinidae	
Q. rufipes	Quedius semiobscurus	Staphylinidae	
Q. semiaeneius	Quedius semiaeneus	Staphylinidae	
Q attenuatus	Quedius nitipennis	Staphylinidae	
Q. scintillans	Quedius scintillans	Staphylinidae	
Q. auricomus	Quedius auricomus	Staphylinidae	
Ocypus similis	Ocypus nitens	Staphylinidae	uncommon species
Philonthus splendens	Philonthus splendens	Staphylinidae	
P. intermedius	Philonthus intermedius	Staphylinidae	
P. addendus	Philonthus addendus	Staphylinidae	
P. marginatus	Philonthus marginatus	Staphylinidae	
P. sanguinlentus	Philonthus sanguinolentus	Staphylinidae	
P. bipustulatus	Philonthus cruentatus	Staphylinidae	
P. discoideus	Philonthus discoideus	Staphylinidae	
P. fulvipes	Philonthus rubripennis	Staphylinidae	
P. trossulus	Gabrius trossulus	Staphylinidae	
P. nigritulus	Gabrius nigritulus	Staphylinidae	
P. puella	Bisnius puella	Staphylinidae	
Actobius signaticornis	Erichsonius signaticornis	Staphylinidae	
A. prolixus	Neobisnius prolixus	Staphylinidae	
Xantholinus glabratus	Megalinus glabratus	Staphylinidae	
Leptacinus batychrus	Leptacinus batychrus	Staphylinidae	
Lathrobium angusticolle	Lathrobium angusticolle	Staphylinidae	uncommon species
Medon brunneus	Medon brunneus	Staphylinidae	
M. ripicola	Medon ripicola	Staphylinidae	
Scopaeus erchsoni	Scopaeus gracilis	Staphylinidae	
Stilicus affinis	Rugilus orbiculatus	Staphylinidae	
Dianous caerulescens	Dianous caerulescens	Staphylinidae	
Stenus juno	Stenus juno	Staphylinidae	
S. atratulus	Stenus atratulus	Staphylinidae	
S. gynemeria	Stenus guynemeri	Staphylinidae	
S. tempestivus	Stenus nitidiusculus	Staphylinidae	
S. glavipes	Stenus clavipes	Staphylinidae	
S. similus	Stenus similis	Staphylinidae	
S. tarsalis	Stenus tarsalis	Staphylinidae	

Oxytelus inustus	*Anotylus inustus*	Staphylinidae
O. faimairei	*Anotylus fairmairei*	Staphylinidae
Haploderus coelatus	*Aploderus caelatus*	Staphylinidae
Ancyrophorus omalinus	*Octhephilus omalinus*	Staphylinidae
Thinobius linearis	*Thinobius bicolor*	Staphylinidae
T. longipennis	*Thinobius longipennis*	Staphylinidae
Geodromicus nigrita	*Geodromicus nigrita*	Staphylinidae
Lesteva punctata	*Lesteva punctata*	Staphylinidae
Deliphrum tectum	*Deliphrum tectum*	Staphylinidae
Lathrimaeium atrocephalum	*Anthobium atrocephalum*	Staphylinidae
Lathrimaeium unicolor	*Anthobium unicolor*	Staphylinidae
Homalium exiguum	*Omalium exiguum*	Staphylinidae
Hapalarea pygmaea	*Hapalaraea pygmaea*	Staphylinidae
Acrulia inflata	*Acrulia inflata*	Staphylinidae
Anthobium toquatum	*Eusphalerum torquatum*	Staphylinidae
Proteinus ovalis	*Proteinus ovalis*	Staphylinidae
P. atomarius	*Proteinus atomarius*	Staphylinidae
Megrthrus hemipterus	*Megarthrus hemipterus*	Staphylinidae
Leptinus testaceus	*Leptinus testaceus*	Leiodidae
Agathidium laevigatum	*Agathidium laevigatum*	Leiodidae
A. atrum	*Agathidium atrum*	Leiodidae
A seminumlum	*Agathidium seminulum*	Leiodidae
A. globosum	*Agathidium convexum*	Leiodidae
A. nigrinum	*Agathidium nigrinum*	Leiodidae
Amphicyllis globus	*Amphicyllis globus*	Leiodidae
Leiodes humeralis	*Anisotoma humeralis*	Leiodidae
Necrophorus humator	*Nicrophorus humator*	Silphidae
N. vespillo	*Nicrophorus vespillo*	Silphidae
Necrodes littoralis	*Necrodes littoralis*	Silphidae
Silpha thoracica	*Oiceoptoma thoracicum*	Silphidae
S. reticulata	*Aclypea undata*	Silphidae
S. nigrita	*Silpha tyrolensis*	Silphidae
S. atrata	*Silpha atrata*	Silphidae
S. quadripunctata	*Dendroxena quadrimaculata*	Silphidae
Choleva angustata	*Choleva angustata*	Leiodidae
C. intermedia	*Choleva oblonga*	Leiodidae
C. spadicea	*Choleva spadicea*	Leiodidae
C. agilis	*Choleva agilis*	Leiodidae
C. fusca	*Catops fuscus*	Leiodidae
C. coracina	*Catops coracinus*	Leiodidae

C. grandicollis	Catops grandicollis	Leiodidae	
C. kirbyi	Catops kirbii	Leiodidae	
C. chrysomeloides	Catops chrysomeloides	Leiodidae	
C. wilkini	Nargus wilkini	Leiodidae	
C. anisotomoides	Nargus anisotomoides	Leiodidae	
Colon zebei	Colon zebei	Leiodidae	
C. dentipes	Colon dentipes	Leiodidae	
Neuraphes elongatulus	Neuraphes elongatulus	Staphylinidae: Scydmaenidae	
N. sparshalli	Scydmoraphes sparshalli	Staphylinidae: Scydmaenidae	
Scydmaenus scutellaris	Stenichnus scutellaris	Staphylinidae: Scydmaenidae	
Pselaphus heisei	Pselaphus heisei	Staphylinidae: Pselaphinae	
Tychus niger	Tychus niger	Staphylinidae: Pselaphinae	
Bythinus puncticollis	Bryaxis puncticollis	Staphylinidae: Pselaphinae	
B. validus	Bryaxis puncticollis	Staphylinidae: Pselaphinae	no longer regarded as distinct
B. bulbifer	Bryaxis bulbifer	Staphylinidae: Pselaphinae	
B. curtisi	Bryaxis curtisii	Staphylinidae: Pselaphinae	
Bryaxis haematica	Brachygluta haematica	Staphylinidae: Pselaphinae	
Batrisus venustus	Batrisodes venustus	Staphylinidae: Pselaphinae	
Trichony markeli	Amauronyx maerkelii	Staphylinidae: Pselaphinae	
Tirchopteryx thoracica	Acrotrichis thoracica	Ptiliidae	
Phalacrus coruscus	Phalacrus corruscus	Phalacridae	
Olbrus aeneus	Olibrus aeneus	Phalacridae	
Stilbus testceus	Stilbus testaceus	Phalacridae	
Anisosticta 19-punctata	Anisosticta novemdecimpunctata	Coccinellidae	19 spot ladybird
Halyzia 14-guttata	Calvia quattuordecimpunctata	Coccinellidae	Cream spot ladybird
Scymus haemorrhoidalis	Scymnus haemorrhoidalis	Coccinellidae	
Rhizobius litura	Rhyzobius litura	Coccinellidae	
Coccidula rufa	Coccidula rufa	Coccinellidae	
Mycetaea hirta	Mycetaea hirta	Endomychidae	
Dacne rufifrons	Dacne rufifrons	Erotylidae	
Cerylon histeroides	Cerylon histeroides	Cerylonidae	

Hister succicola	*Margarinotus striola succicola*	Histeridae
H. neglectus	*Margarinotus neglectus*	Histeridae
H. carbonarius	*Margarinotus ventralis*	Histeridae
H. stercorarius	*Margarinotus obscurus*	Histeridae
H. bissexstratus	*Hister bissexstratus*	Histeridae
H. 12-stratus	*Atholus duodecimstriatus*	Histeridae
H. bimaculatus	*Atholus bimaculatus*	Histeridae
Myrmetes picens	*Myrmetes paykulli*	Histeridae
Saprinus nitidulus	*Saprinus semistriatus*	Histeridae
S. aeneus	*Saprinus aeneus*	Histeridae
Micropeplus porcatus	*Micropeplus porcatus*	Staphylinidae
M. staphylinoides	*Micropeplus staphylinoides*	Staphylinidae
Cercus pedicularius	*Kateretes pedicularius*	Kateretidae
C. bipustulatus	*Kateretes bipustulatus*	Kateretidae
C. rufilabris	*Kateretes rufilabris*	Kateretidae
Bracypterus urticae	*Brachypterus urticae*	Kateretidae
Meligethes viridescens	*Meligethes viridescens*	Nitidulidae
M. flavipes	*Meligethes ruficornis*	Nitidulidae
M. erythropus	*Meligethes carinulatus*	Nitidulidae
Epuraea aestiva	*Epuraea aestiva*	Nitidulidae
E. obsoleta	*Epuraea biguttata*	Nitidulidae
E. pusilla	*Epuraea marseuli*	Nitidulidae
Micrurula melanocephala	*Epuraea melanocephala*	Nitidulidae
Omosiphora limbata	*Epuraea limbata*	Nitidulidae
Nitidula bipustulata	*Nitidula bipunctata*	Nitidulidae
Omosita depressa	*Omosita depressa*	Nitidulidae
Soronia punctatissima	*Soronia punctatissima*	Nitidulidae
Amphotis marginata	*Amphotis marginata*	Nitidulidae
Pocadius ferrugineus	*Pocadius ferrugineus*	Nitidulidae
Cryptarcha strigata	*Cryptarcha strigata*	Nitidulidae
Rhizophagus depressus	*Rhizophagus depressus*	Monotomidae
R. cribatus	*Rhizophagus cribratus*	Monotomidae
R. perforatus	*Rhizophagus perforatus*	Monotomidae
Monotoma picpes	*Monotoma picipes*	Monotomidae
Coninomus nodifer	*Cartodere nodifer*	Latridiidae
Cartoder ruficollis	*Dienerella ruficollis*	Latridiidae

Corticaria elongata	*Corticaria elongata*	Latridiidae	
Melanophthalma	*Melanophthalma*	Latridiidae	
Laemophloeus ferrugineus	*Cryptolestes ferrugineus*	Laemophloeidae	
Antherophagus pallens	*Antherophagus pallens*	Cryptophagidae	
Cryptophagus lycoperdi	*Cryptophagus lycoperdi*	Cryptophagidae	
C. scanicus	*Cryptophagus scanicus*	Cryptophagidae	
Atomaria fuscipes	*Atomaria fuscipes*	Cryptophagidae	
A. atricapilla	*Atomaria atricapilla*	Cryptophagidae	
Scaphisoma agaricinum	*Scaphisoma agaricinum*	Staphylinidae: Scaphidiidae	
S. boleti	*Scaphisoma boleti*	Staphylinidae: Scaphidiidae	
Scaphidium quadrinmaculatum	*Scaphidium quadrimaculatum*	Staphylinidae: Scaphidiidae	
Typhaea fumata	*Typhaea stercorea*	Mycetophagidae	
Diphyllus lunatus	*Biphyllus lunatus*	Biphyllidae	
Mycetophagus quadripustulatus	*Mycetophagus quadripustulatus*	Mycetophagidae	
M. piceus	*Mycetophagus piceus*	Mycetophagidae	
M. atomarius	*Mycetophagus atomarius*	Mycetophagidae	
M. multipunctatus	*Mycetophagus multipunctatus*	Mycetophagidae	
Triphyllus punctatus	*Triphyllus bicolor*	Mycetophagidae	
T. suturalis	*Pseudotriphyllus suturalis*	Mycetophagidae	
Dermestes murinus	*Dermestes murinus*	Dermestidae	
Attagenus pellio	*Attagenus pellio*	Dermestidae	
Anthrenus claviger	*Anthrenus fuscus*	Dermestidae	
Byrrhus pilula	*Byrrhus pilula*	Byrrhidae	
B. fasciatus	*Byrrhus fasciatus*	Byrrhidae	two species now recognised
Simplocaria semistriata	*Simplocaria semistriata*	Byrrhidae	
Limnius tuberculatus	*Oulimnius tuberculatus*	Elmidae	
Elmis aeneus	*Elmis aenea*	Elmidae	
E. volkmari	*Limnius volckmari*	Elmidae	
E. parallelopipedus	*Esolus parallelepipedus*	Elmidae	
Parnus prolifericornis	*Dryops luridus*	Dryopidae	
P. algiricus	*Dryops striatellus*	Dryopidae	
Heterocerus marginatus	*Heterocerus marginatus*	Heteroceridae	
Lacanus cervus	*Lucanus cervus*	Lucanidae	Stag Beetle
Dorcus parallelopipedus	*Dorcus parallelipipedus*	Lucanidae	Lesser stag beetle

Sinodendron cylindricum	*Sinodendron cylindricum*	Lucanidae	One-horned stag beetle
Onthophagus ovatus	*Onthophagus joannae*	Scarabaeidae	
Aphodius suberraneus	*Aphodius subterraneus*	Scarabaeidae	
A. fossor	*Aphodius fossor*	Scarabaeidae	
A. haemorrhoidalis	*Aphodius haemorrhoidalis*	Scarabaeidae	
A. fimetarius	*Aphodius fimetarius*	Scarabaeidae	
A. ater	*Aphodius ater*	Scarabaeidae	
A. constans	*Aphodius constans*	Scarabaeidae	
A. sticticus	*Aphodius sticticus*	Scarabaeidae	
A. pusillus	*Aphodius pusillus*	Scarabaeidae	
A. merdarius	*Aphodius merdarius*	Scarabaeidae	
A. prodromus	*Aphodius prodromus*	Scarabaeidae	
A, punctato-sulcatus	*Aphodius sphacelatus*	Scarabaeidae	
A. obliteratus	*Aphodius obliteratus*	Scarabaeidae	
A. rufipes	*Aphodius rufipes*	Scarabaeidae	
A. luridus	*Aphodius luridus*	Scarabaeidae	
A. depressus	*Aphodius depressus*	Scarabaeidae	
Geotrupes typhaeus	*Typhaeus typhoeus*	Geotrupidae	Minotaur beetle
G. sylvaticus	*Anoplotrupes stercorosus*	Geotrupidae	
Phyllopertha horticola	*Phyllopertha horticola*	Scarabaeidae	
Agrilus viridis	*Agrilus viridis*	Buprestidae	
Throscus dermestoides	*Trixagus dermestoides*	Throscidae	
Cryptohypnus riparius	*Hypnoidus riparius*	Elateridae	
C. quadripustulatus	*Oedostethus quadripustulatus*	Elateridae	
C. dermestoides	*Zorochros minimus*	Elateridae	
Limonius minutus	*Kibunea minuta*	Elateridae	
Athous niger	*Hemicrepidius hirtus*	Elateridae	
A. haemorrhoidalis	*Athous haemorrhoidalis*	Elateridae	
A. longicollis	*Athous bicolor*	Elateridae	
Corymbites cupreus	*Ctenicera cuprea*	Elateridae	
C. quercus	*Aplotarsus incanus*	Elateridae	
C. holosericeus	*Prosternon tessellatum*	Elateridae	
C. aeneus	*Selatosomus aeneus*	Elateridae	
Ariotes sputator	*Agriotes sputator*	Elateridae	
A. lineatus	*Agriotes lineatus*	Elateridae	
A. obscurus	*Agriotes obscurus*	Elateridae	

Dascillusc cervinus	*Dascillus cervinus*	Dascillidae	
Helodes minuta	*Elodes minuta*	Scirtidae	Now recognised to be several species including several common ones
H. marginata	*Odeles marginata*	Scirtidae	
Microcara livida	*Microcara testacea*	Scirtidae	
Hydrocyphon deflexicollis	*Hydrocyphon deflexicollis*	Scirtidae	
Lampyris noctiluca	*Lampyris noctiluca*	Lampyridae	Glow-worm
Podabrus alpinus	*Podabrus alpinus*	Cantharidae	
Telephorus fuscus	*Cantharis fusca*	Cantharidae	Hyman (1992) gives no records from Shropshire
T. pellucidus	*Cantharis pellucida*	Cantharidae	
T. obscurus	*Cantharis obscura*	Cantharidae	
T. haemorrhoidalis	*Cantharis decipiens*	Cantharidae	
T. flavilabris	*Cantharis nigra*	Cantharidae	
Rhagonycha fulva	*Rhagonycha fulva*	Cantharidae	
R. tetacea	*Rhagonycha testacea*	Cantharidae	
Malthinus fasciatus	*Malthinus seriepunctatus*	Cantharidae	
M. punctatus	*Malthinus flaveolus*	Cantharidae	
Cis boleti	*Cis boleti*	Ciidae	
C. bidentatus	*Cis bidentatus*	Ciidae	
C. fuscatus	*Cis fagi*	Ciidae	
Octotemnus glabriculus	*Octotemnus glabriculus*	Ciidae	
Priobium castaneium	*Grynobius planus*	Ptinidae	
Anobium domesticum	*Anobium punctatum*	Ptinidae	Woodworm beetle
Ernobius mollis	*Ernobius mollis*	Ptinidae	
Dryophilus pusillus	*Dryophilus pusillus*	Ptinidae	
Hedobia imperialis	*Ptinomorphus imperialis*	Ptinidae	
Prionus coriarius	*Prionus coriarius*	Cerambycidae	
Clytus arietis	*Clytus arietis*	Cerambycidae	
Rhagium inquisitor	*Rhagium mordax*	Cerambycidae	
R. indagator	*Rhagium inquisitor*	Cerambycidae	
Toxotus merdianus	*Stenocorus meridianus*	Cerambycidae	
Grammoptera ruficornis	*Grammoptera ruficornis*	Cerambycidae	
Leiopus nebulosus	*Leiopus nebulosus*	Cerambycidae	Two species now recognised, both possible in Shropshire
Pogonochaerus bidentatus	*Pogonocherus hispidulus*	Cerambycidae	
P. dentatus	*Pogonocherus hispidus*	Cerambycidae	
Lema lichenis	*Oulema obscura*	Chrysomelidae	
L. melanopa	*Oulema melanopus*	Chrysomelidae	now two species, both common
Cryptocephalus fulvus	*Cryptocephalus fulvus*	Chrysomelidae	

C. labiatus	*Cryptocephalus labiatus*	Chrysomelidae
Chrysomela varians	*Chrysolina varians*	Chrysomelidae
Phytodecta olivacea	*Gonioctena olivacea*	Chrysomelidae
P. pallida	*Gonioctena pallida*	Chrysomelidae
Phyllodecta vitellinnea	*Phratora vitellinae*	Chrysomelidae
Hydrothassa acta	*Hydrothassa glabra*	Chrysomelidae
H. marginella	*Hydrothassa marginella*	Chrysomelidae
Prasocuris junci	*Prasocuris junci*	Chrysomelidae
Lochmaea suturalis	*Lochmaea suturalis*	Chrysomelidae
Longitarsus melanocephalus	*Longitarsus melanocephalus*	Chrysomelidae
L. pusillus	*Longitarsus pratensis*	Chrysomelidae
L. gracilis	*Longitarsus gracilis*	Chrysomelidae
Phyllotreta cruciferae	*Phyllotreta cruciferae*	Chrysomelidae
P. nemorum	*Phyllotreta nemorum*	Chrysomelidae
P. ochripes	*Phyllotreta ochripes*	Chrysomelidae
P. exclamationis	*Phyllotreta exclamationis*	Chrysomelidae
Aphthona nonstriata	*Aphthona nonstriata*	Chrysomelidae
A. atro-coerulea	*Aphthona atrocoerulea*	Chrysomelidae
Batophila rubi	*Batophila rubi*	Chrysomelidae
B. aerata	*Batophila aerata*	Chrysomelidae
Sphaeroderma testaceum	*Sphaeroderma rubidum*	Chrysomelidae
S. cardui	*Sphaeroderma testaceum*	Chrysomelidae
Crepidodera rufipes	*Derocrepis rufipes*	Chrysomelidae
C. aurata	*Crepidodera aurata*	Chrysomelidae
Chaetocnema hortensis	*Chaetocnema hortensis*	Chrysomelidae
Plectroscelis concinna	*Chaetocnema concinna*	Chrysomelidae now two species, both common
Psylloides napi	*Psylloides napi*	Chrysomelidae
P. affinis	*Psylloides affinis*	Chrysomelidae
Cassida viridis	*Cassida viridis*	Chrysomelidae
Heledona agaricola	*Eledona agricola*	Tenebrionidae
Scapidema aeneium	*Scaphidema metallicum*	Tenebrionidae
Cistela luperus	*Gonodera luperus*	Tenebrionidae
C. murina	*Isomira murina*	Tenebrionidae
Tetratoms fungorum	*Tetratoma fungorum*	Tetratomidae
Abdera quadrifasciata	*Abdera quadrifasciata*	Melandryidae
Rhionosimus planirostris	*Salpingus planirostris*	Salpingidae
Pyrochrea serrticornis	*Pyrochroa serraticornis*	Pyrochroidae
Anaspis fasciata	*Anaspis fasciata*	Scraptiidae
Metaecus paradoxus	*Metoecus paradoxus*	Ripiphoridae
Anthicus floralis	*Omonadus floralis*	Anthicidae
Meloe violaceius	*Meloe violaceus*	Meloidae
Rhynchites uncinatus	*Temnocerus coeruleus*	Rhynchitidae

Apion subulatum	*Oxystoma subulatum*	Apionidae
A. carduorum	*Ceratapion gibbirostre*	Apionidae
A. onopordi	*Ceratapion onopordi*	Apionidae
A. pallipes	*Kalcapion pallipes*	Apionidae
A. seniculum	*Catapion seniculus*	Apionidae
A. rufirostre	*Pseudapion rufirostre*	Apionidae
A. apricans	*Protapion apricans*	Apionidae
A. trifolii	*Protapion trifolii*	Apionidae
A. ebenium	*Synapion ebeninum*	Apionidae
A. punctigerum	*Eutrichapion punctigerum*	Apionidae
A. virens	*Ischnopterapion virens*	Apionidae
A. ervis	*Eutrichapion ervi*	Apionidae
A. violaceium	*Perapion violaceum*	Apionidae
A. hydrolapathis	*Perapion hydrolapathi*	Apionidae
A. humile	*Perapion curtirostre*	Apionidae
Tropiphorus tomentosus	*Tropiphorus terricola*	Curculionidae
Barynotus obscurus	*Barynotus obscurus*	Curculionidae
B. elevatus	*Barynotus moerens*	Curculionidae
Exomias araneiuformis	*Barypeithes araneiformis*	Curculionidae
Brachysomus echinatus	*Brachysomus echinatus*	Curculionidae
Sciaphilus muricatus	*Sciaphilus asperatus*	Curculionidae
Phyllobius calcaratus	*Phyllobius glaucus*	Curculionidae
P. maculicornis	*Phyllobius maculicornis*	Curculionidae
P. oblongus	*Phyllobius oblongus*	Curculionidae
P. viridiaeris	*Phyllobius virideaeris*	Curculionidae
Caenopsis waltoni	*Caenopsis waltoni*	Curculionidae
Otiorrhynchus scbrosus	*Otiorhynchus rugosostriatus*	Curculionidae
O. pcipes	*Otiorhynchus singularis*	Curculionidae
O. muscorum	*Otiorhynchus desertus*	Curculionidae
Sitones cambricus	*Coelositona cambricus*	Curculionidae
S. lineatus	*Sitona lineatus*	Curculionidae
Liosoma ovatulum	*Leiosoma deflexum*	Curculionidae
L. oblongulum	*Leiosoma oblongulum*	Curculionidae
Alophus triguttatus	*Graptus triguttatus*	Curculionidae
Hypera punctata	*Hypera zoilus*	Curculionidae
H. variabilis	*Hypera postica*	Curculionidae
H. polygoni	*Hypera arator*	Curculionidae
H. nigrirostris	*Hypera nigrirostris*	Curculionidae
Grypidius equiseti	*Grypus equiseti*	Erirhinidae
Thryogenes scirrhosus	*Thryogenes scirrhosus*	Erirhinidae
Dorytomus maculatus	*Dorytomus taeniatus*	Curculionidae
D. tortrix	*Dorytomus tortrix*	Curculionidae
Mecinus pyraster	*Mecinus pyraster*	Curculionidae

Anthonomus rubi	*Anthonomus rubi*	Curculionidae
Orchestes fagi	*Orchestes fagi*	Curculionidae
Rhamphus flavicornis	*Rhamphus pulicarius*	Curculionidae
Miccotrogus picirostris	*Tychius picirostris*	Curculionidae
Cionus pulchellus	*Cleopus pulchellus*	Curculionidae
Orobitis cyaneus	*Orobitis cyaneus*	Curculionidae
Caeliodes quercus	*Coeliodes rana*	Curculionidae
C. quadrimaculatus	*Nedyus quadrimaculatus*	Curculionidae
Ceuthorrhynchus erysimi	*Ceutorhynchus erysimi*	Curculionidae
C. contractus	*Ceutorhynchus contractus*	Curculionidae
C. ericae	*Micrelus ericae*	Curculionidae
C. trimaculatus	*Hadroplontus trimaculatus*	Curculionidae
C. asperifoliarum	*Mogulones asperifoliarum*	Curculionidae
C. pollinarius	*Parethelcus pollinarius*	Curculionidae
Phytobius quadrituberculatus	*Pelenomus quadrituberculatus*	Curculionidae
Poophagus sisymbrii	*Poophagus sisymbrii*	Curculionidae
Calndra granaria	*Sitophilus granarius*	Curculionidae
Hylesinus oleiperda	*Hylesinus toranio*	Curculionidae
H. fraxini	*Hylesinus varius*	Curculionidae
Trypodendron domesticum	*Trypodendron domesticum*	Curculionidae

Hyman (1992) relates to Hyman, P. S. (revised Parsons, M. S.) 'A review of the scarce and threatened Coleoptera of Great Britain'. Part 1. U.K. Nature Conservation No. 3. Peterborough: Joint Nature Conservation Committee.

With Darwin's interest in collections, I felt it was appropriate to find out whether Darwin had made a collection of beetles in Shropshire. The Natural History Museum[16] in London stated that it houses: 'about 2000 [insect] specimens presented and, or collected by Darwin', but: 'mainly those accrued from his travels abroad.'[17] Ludlow Local Resources Centre[18] only houses some collections by other entomologists. I visited the collection of Francis Pitt of Bridgnorth, sampled in the late 1910's and 1920's to find out what would have interested collectors in earlier times. I was surprised to find that the species were not all spectacularly coloured of large-ish size, but included minute, plain beetles, such as weevils, too. I had been quite convinced from some of Darwin's reports, that he often spotted his beetles from a distance and therefore presumed they would have been of a larger size and 'striking'. However,

Darwin also stated:[19] 'I was very successful in collecting & invented two new methods; I employed a labourer to scrape during the winter, moss off old trees & place [it] in a large bag, & likewise to collect the rubbish at the bottom of the barges in which reeds are brought from the fens, & thus I got some very rare species. This points out how he was willing to sort through samples of vegetation to find something of interest to him, which he may have otherwise overlooked. There is also a reference to Darwin encouraging W. D. Fox[20] to look more closely for specimens: 'Mr. Hope is gone up to London, so that I shall not be able to get any-more information about the insects we took together...but I trust you have been to the Moor (take your net & sweep), & that you pretty often look over & shake the Fungi'.

The hectad around the Mount (SJ41) has 572 species of beetle listed in present times.[21] The tetrad[22] in which the Mount occurs reveals the follow-ing ladybirds and long-horn beetles residing: Wasp Beetle (*Clytus arietis*), Fourteen-spot ladybird (*Propylea quattuordecimpunctata*), Pine Ladybird (*Exochomus quadripustulatus*), Seven-spot ladybird (*Coccinella septem-punctata*), Harlequin ladybird (*Harmonia axyridis*), Ten-spot ladybird (*Adalia decempunctata*),Twenty-two-spot Ladybird (*Psyllobora vigintidu-opunctata*) and Two-spot Ladybird (*Adalia bipunctata*).

To get a better impression of the type of beetles the area around The Mount may hold nowadays, I discovered that Preston Montford Field Studies Centre held records of beetles collected in its grounds.[23] This site is only three miles from the Mount and the Hall and grounds date back to the 18th century. (St. Chad's Church in Montford is where Darwin's parents are buried). A list is presented below:

Sphaerius acaroids – a mud beetle

Haliplus confinis – a water beetle

Hygrobia hermanni – a screech beetle

Noterus clavicornis – a water beetle

Nebrioporus elegans– a water beetle

Dytiscus marginalis – Great Diving beetle

Acilius sulcatus – a water beetle

Carabus granulatus – a ground beetle

Carabus problematicus – a ground beetle

Carabus violaceus – Violet Ground beetle

Cychrus caraboides – a ground beetle

Leistus rufomarginatus – a ground beetle

Leistus fulvibarbis – a ground beetle

Leistus ferrugineus – a ground beetle

Nebria brevicollis – a ground beetle

Notiophilus biguttatus – a ground beetle

Notiophilus rufipes – a ground beetle

Loricera pilicornis – a ground beetle

Elaphrus riparius – a ground beetle

Clivina collaris – a ground beetle

Trechus quadristriatus– a ground beetle

Asaphidion curtum – a ground beetle

Bembidion biguttatum – a ground beetle

Bembidion punctulatum – a ground beetle

Bembidion lampros – a ground beetle

Bembidion properans – a ground beetle

Bembidion lunatum – a ground beetle

Bembidion illigeri – a ground beetle

Pterostichus madidus – a ground beetle

Pterostichus niger – a ground beetle

Pterostichus melanarius – a ground beetle

Pterostichus rhaeticus – a ground beetle

Pterostichus vernalis – a ground beetle

Pterostichus strenuus – a ground beetle

Abax parallelepipedus – a ground beetle

Calathus piceus – a ground beetle

Calathus rotundicollis – a ground beetle

Calathus erratus – a ground beetle

Calathus fuscipes – a ground beetle

Calathus melanocephalus – a ground beetle

Synuchus nivalis – a ground beetle

Paranchus albipes – a ground beetle

Agonum fuliginosum – a ground beetle

Agonum marginatum – a ground beetle

Agonum muelleri – a ground beetle

Amara plebeja – a ground beetle

Amara aenea – a ground beetle

Amara eurynota– a ground beetle

Amara familiaris – a ground beetle

Amara ovata – a ground beetle

Harpalus affinis – a ground beetle

Harpalus rufipes – a ground beetle

Badister bipustulatus – a ground beetle

Coelostoma orbiculare – a water scavenger beetle

Cercyon haemorrhoidalis – a water beetle

Cercyon lateralis – a water beetle

Cercyon melanocephalus – a water beetle

Cercyon lugubris – a water beetle

Cercyon unipunctatus – a water beetle

Cercyon analis – a water beetle

Megasternum obscurum – a water scavenger beetle

Cryptopleurum minutum – a water scavenger beetle

Onthophilus striatus – a carrion beetle

Margarinotus merdarius – a beetle

Hister bissexstriatus – a beetle

Atholus duodecimstriatus – a beetle

Leiodes polita – a beetle

Ptomaphagus subvillosus – a beetle

Scydmaenus tarsatus – a beetle

Lesteva longoelytrata – a rove beetle

Megarthrus denticollis – a rove beetle

Megarthrus prosseni – a rove beetle

Tachyporus chrysomelinus – a rove beetle

Tachyporus hypnorum – a rove beetle

Tachyporus nitidulus – a rove beetle

Tachyporus pusillus – a rove beetle

Tachinus humeralis – a rove beetle

Tachinus laticollis – a rove beetle

Tachinus rufipes – a rove beetle

Mycetoporus nigricollis – a rove beetle

Mycetoporus splendidus – a rove beetle

Bolitobius analis – a rove beetle

Habrocerus capillaricornis – a rove beetle

Ocalea picata – a rove beetle

Tachyusa constricta – a rove beetle

Nehemitropia lividipennis – a rove beetle

Plataraea brunnea – a rove beetle

Atheta liliputana – a rove beetle

Microdota liliputana – a rove beetle

Atheta basicornis – a rove beetle

Mycetota laticollis – a rove beetle

Chaetida longicornis – a rove beetle

Aleochara bipustulata – a rove beetle

Aleochara intricata – a rove beetle

Aleochara lanuginosa – a rove beetle

Aleochara ruficornis – a rove beetle

Tinotus morion – a rove beetle

Autalia rivularis – a rove beetle

Encephalus complicans – a rove beetle

Scaphidium quadrimaculatum – a rove beetle

Bledius gallicus – a rove beetle

Bledius annae – a rove beetle

Platystethus cornutus – a rove beetle

Oxytelus sculptus – a rove beetle

Anotylus rugosus – a rove beetle

Anotylus sculpturatus – a rove beetle

Anotylus tetracarinatus – a rove beetle

Stenus bimaculatus – a rove beetle

Stenus clavicornis – a rove beetle

Stenus guttula – a rove beetle

Stenus juno – a rove beetle

Stenus similis – a rove beetle

Stenus palustris – a rove beetle

Rugilus orbiculatus – a rove beetle

Rugilus rufipes – a rove beetle

Lithocharis nigriceps – a rove beetle

Lithocharis ochracea – a rove beetle

Lathrobium brunnipes – a rove beetle

Philonthus atratus – a rove beetle

Philonthus varius – a rove beetle

Philonthus cognatus – a rove beetle

Philonthus debilis – a rove beetle

Philonthus intermedius – a rove beetle

Philonthus laminatus – a rove beetle

Philonthus politus – rove beetle

Philonthus sanguinolentus – a rove beetle

Philonthus splendens – a rove beetle

Philonthus tenuicornis – a rove beetle

Philonthus varians – a rove beetle

Gabronthus thermarum – a rove beetle

Bisnius sordidus – a rove beetle

Gabrius piliger– a rove beetle

Ontholestes murinus – a rove beetle

Ontholestes tessellatus – a rove beetle

Platydracus stercorarius – a rove beetle

Ocypus olens – Devil's Coach–horse

Ocypus compressus – a rove beetle

Quedius fuliginosus – a rove beetle

Quedius tristis – a rove beetle

Quedius scintillans – a rove beetle

Othius angustus – a rove beetle

Othius myrmecophilus – a rove beetle

Leptacinus pusillus – a rove beetle

Gyrohypnus fracticornis – a rove beetle

Xantholinus linearis – a rove beetle

Xantholinus longiventris – a rove beetle

Dorcus parallelipipedus – Lesser Stag Beetle

Aphodius rufipes – a dung beetle

Aphodius fimetarius – a dung beetle

Aphodius granarius – a dung beetle

Aphodius prodromus – a dung beetle

Aphodius contaminatus – a dung beetle

Aphodius equestris– a dung beetle

Serica brunnea – Brown Chafer

Clambus punctulum – a beetle

Clambus punctulus – a beetle

Dascillus cervinus – Orchid beetle

Macronychus quadrituberculatus – a water beetle

Athous bicolor – a click beetle

Agriotes acuminatus – a click beetle

Cantharis cryptica – a soldier beetle

Cantharis nigricans – a soldier beetle

Cantharis rufa – a soldier beetle

Cantharis rustica – a soldier beetle

Rhagonycha limbata – a soldier beetle

Rhagonycha fulva – a soldier beetle

Malthodes minimus – a soldier beetle

Brachypterus glaber – a beetle

Kateretes rufilabris – a pollen beetle

Monotoma picipes – a beetle

Pediacus dermestoides – a flat bark beetle

Cryptolestes ferrugineus – a beetle

Atomaria linearis – Pygmy Beetle

Atomaria apicalis – a beetle

Halyzia sedecimguttata – Orange Ladybird

Psyllobora vigintiduopunctata – 22–spot Ladybird

Propylea quattuordecimpunctata – 14–spot Ladybird

Harmonia axyridis – Harlequin Ladybird

Adalia bipunctata – 2–spot Ladybird

Adalia decempunctata – 10–spot Ladybird

Coccinella septempunctata – 7–spot Ladybird

Tytthaspis sedecimpunctata – 16–spot Ladybird

Subcoccinella vigintiquattuorpunctata – 24–spot Ladybird

Enicmus transversus – a beetle

Cartodere bifasciata – a mould beetle

Cartodere nodifer – a mould beetle

Corticaria crenulata – a mould beetle

Corticaria impressa – a mould beetle

Corticaria longicollis – a mould beetle

Corticaria punctulata – a mould beetle

Mycetophagus quadripustulatus – Hairy Fungus Beetle

Alphitophagus bifasciatus –Two–banded Flour Beetle

Oedemera nobilis – Swollen–thighed Beetle

Oedemera lurida – a beetle

Pyrochroa coccinea – Black–headed Cardinal Beetle

Pyrochroa serraticornis – Common Cardinal Beetle

Salpingus planirostris – a beetle

Omonadus floralis – a beetle

Grammoptera ruficornis – a long–horned beetle

Clytus arietis – Wasp Beetle

Anaglyptus mysticus – a long–horned beetle

Bruchus loti – a beetle

Donacia versicolorea – a reed beetle

Cassida rubiginosa – Thistle Tortoise Beetle

Cassida viridis – Green Tortoise Beetle

Chrysolina banksi – a leaf beetle

Chrysolina polita – a leaf beetle

Chrysolina staphylaea – a leaf beetle

Gastrophysa viridula – Green Dock Beetle

Phaedon armoraciae – a leaf beetle

Phaedon tumidulus – Celery Leaf Beetle

Hydrothassa marginella – Buttercup Leaf Beetle

Galerucella lineola – Brown Willow Beetle

Pyrrhalta viburni – Guelder-rose Leaf Beetle

Altica oleracea – a leaf beetle

Neocoenorrhinus aequatus – Apple Fruit Rhynchites

Protapion nigritarse – a weevil

Perapion hydrolapathi – a weevil

Apion frumentarium – a weevil

Apion craccae – a weevil

Eutrichapion ervi – a weevil

Otiorhynchus singularis – Raspberry Weevil

Phyllobius roboretanus – Small Green Nettle Weevil

Phyllobius pyri – Common Leaf Weevil

Phyllobius pomaceus – a weevil

Phyllobius argentatus – Silver-green Leaf Weevil

Barypeithes pellucidus – a weevil

Liophloeus tessulatus – a weevil

Barynotus obscurus – Ground Weevil

Graptus triguttatus – a weevil

Tanymecus palliatus – a weevil

Charagmus griseus – a weevil

Sitona lineatus – a weevil

Sitona puncticollis – a weevil

Sitona striatellus – a weevil

Leiosoma deflexum – a weevil

Dorytomus longimanus – a weevil

Parethelcus pollinarius – a weevil

Ceutorhynchus quadridens – a weevil

Trichosirocalus troglodytes – a weevil

Nedyus quadrimaculatus – Small Nettle Weevil

Rhynchaenus alni – a weevil

I was delighted to come across a paper '*A Beetle's Eye View of the Ice Age*' by the Shropshire Geological Society[24] which merged two of Darwin's passions – beetles and geology. Darwin would have relished reading this scientific study. It stated: 'In ice ages, populations are driven into refuges capable of sustaining only a small population, therefore the selection pressures must be very great. Thus ice ages are likely to produce new, novel species, to speed up the process of evolution...When the ice retreats, vast areas of the country become available for colonization, isolated small populations spread out and in so doing, atypical populations become established. These compete with one another; many will survive to produce new species, and others will become extinct...The number of fossil beetle species is between one and two thousand. During the last million years, there is no evidence of evolution amongst them, neither is there any extinction...Beetles are entomological tanks and, being so strongly built, makes them unique among insects in forming good fossils. An entomologist identifies species on the basis of the exoskeleton. In the case of beetles, the palaeontologist can use exactly the same criteria for differentiating and describing species as the present day biologist...high degree of preservation is vital, since beetle species can only be identified with recognised certainty by the size and structure of the male genitalia and these are also preserved in the fossils...The different types of...beetles...indicate different types of climate and their comings and goings in Britain...an indication of climatic conditions in this very recent geological period...Using biogeographic ranges of different species found in Midland sites, it was shown that...the changing climate [was] polar 50–45,000 years BP; oceanic with temperatures at least as warm as at present 45–40,000BP; continental with cold dry summers 40–25,000 BP, then polar again with maximum ice extension at 18,000 years BP...the beetles indicated that climatic change can be very sudden and that the intensity of change...enormous'. The oldest beetle fossils are from the Lower Permian, about 265 million years old[25].

When arriving in Shropshire, I saw a poster created by Butterfly Conservation called 'South Shropshire – Find out how you can help save our wonderful butterflies'.[26] It stated that the 'geographic position, industrial heritage and underlying geology means that the landscape offers many different places for butterflies to colonise...because traditional farming methods have largely continued, butterflies have survived here while becoming increasingly rare and threatened elsewhere.' It presented a colourful, photographic index of thirty-seven species of butterfly. Most I had seen around Downe and during my lifetime.

The list below outlines butterfly species occurring in Shropshire in Darwin's time[27].

=*+Small Skipper	Common and widespread
=*+Large Skipper	Common and widespread
*+Dingy Skipper	Found on dry banks throughout the county
*+Grizzled Skipper	Local but common where it occurs, Market Drayton, Petton Park, Broseley, Church Stretton, Hopton Wafers, Shrewsbury
Scarce swallowtail	Netley, Longnor
Wood White	Wyre Forest
Pale Clouded	Yellow Westwood
=*+Clouded Yellow	Occurs at times all over Shropshire
=*+Brimstone	Not common, Caradoc, Church Stretton
Black veined	White Wyre Forest
=*+Large White	Generally well distributed and common throughout the county

=*+Small White	Common throughout the county
=*+Green veined	White Common throughout
=*+Orange tip	Common throughout the county
*+Green hairstreak	Common in Millen Heath, Calverhall, Petton Park, Church Stretton, Cross Houses, Caradoc
Brown Hairstreak	Wyre Forest, Petton Park, Ellesmere
Purple Hairstreak	Occurs freely wherever there are oak woods
=*+White Letter Hairstreak	Well distributed
Black Hairstreak	Scarce in the neighbourhood of Petton Park
*+Small Copper	Common all over the county
*Small Blue	Church Stretton, Edge Wood
Silver-studded Blue	Scarce in some dry sandy areas of the Longmynd
*+Brown Argus	Haughmond Hill, Church Stretton, Caradoc
=*+Common Blue	Common throughout
=*+Holly Blue	Widespread and common
Large Blue	Church Stretton
Duke of Burgundy	Church Stretton
*White Admiral	Ragleth Wood, Church Stretton
*Purple Emperor	Ellesmere, Haughmond Hill, Ragleth Woods
=*+Red Admiral	Common most years
=*+Painted lady	Widespread. More common in some years than others
=*+Small tortoiseshell	Common throughout
Large tortoiseshell	Uncommon and erratic Petton Park, Shrewsbury, Ellesmere, Benthall Edge, Church Stretton, Dudgeley

Camberwell Beauty	Rare Ellesmere, Tesmore, Church Stretton, All Stretton, Stapleton
=*+Peacock	Common throughout
=*+Comma	Common in some years and scarce in others
+Small Pearl-bordered Fritillary	Widely distributed Market Drayton, Ellesmere, Church Stretton, Wyre Forest
+Pearl bordered Fritillary	Common in the hills of the county
High Brown Fritillary	Common in Ragleth Woods; Helmeth, Tiger Hall, Wyre Forest, Shrewsbury, Oswestry
*+Dark Green Fritillary	Found in hilly parts of the county, not necessarily in woodlands including Church Stretton, Wyre Forest
*+Silver-washed Fritillary	Common in the wooded hilly parts of the county
Marsh Fritillary	Local and usually scarce; Ragleth, Botvylle, Ticklerton, Wyre Forest, Ludlow, Bomere, Church Stretton
=*+Speckled Wood	Very local and uncommon; Ragleth Wood, Church Stretton, Broseley, Calverhall, Shrewsbury
+Wall	Common throughout
*Marbled White	Ragleth Woods, Ellesmere
+Grayling	Found on the dry stony hills around Church Stretton; Ellesmere
=*+Gatekeeper	Common throughout
=*+Meadow	Brown Common throughout
=*+Small Heath	Common throughout
Large Heath	Common at Whixall Moss, Yetchleys, Ellesmere
=*+Ringlet	Widespread and common in most woodlands

Asterixed * represents species present around Downe in recent times[28]
= represents the butterflies that have been found near the Mount in recent times (tetrad data).[29]
+ represent the butterflies that are at Llanymynech Hill nowadays (a general location we know Darwin visited).[30]

Darwin's excitement at finding an unknown butterfly at the Mount is revealed from a letter he wrote to W. D. Fox in October 1828:[31] 'I want to know the name of a butterfly which you have got, its wings are most wonderfly jagged & of a reddish colour, after an immense chase with all the servants in the house I at last captured it – look over your butterflies and you will soon percieve what I mean.'

An interest in butterflies is further percieved from his comments in 'The Descent of Man and Selection in Relation to Sex' where Darwin writes: 'In the English fritillaries (Argynnis) the lower surface alone is ornamented with shining silver. Nevertheless, as a general rule, the upper surface, which is probably more fully exposed, is coloured more brightly and in a more diversified manner than the lower[32]'

'We may take as an instance the common brimstone butterfly (Gonepteryx), which appears early in the spring before any other kind. The male of this species is of a far more intense yellow than the female, though she is almost equally conspicuous; and in this case it does not seem probable that she specially acquired her pale tints as a protection, though it is probable that the male acquired his bright colours as a sexual attraction. The female of Anthocharis cardamines does not possess the beautiful orange tips to her wings with which the male is ornamented; consequently she closely resembles the white butterflies (Pieris) so common in our gardens; but we have no evidence that this resemblance is beneficial. On the contrary, as she resembles both sexes of several species of the same genus inhabiting various quarters of the world, it is more probable that she has simply retained to a large extent her primordial colours.'[33]

It was in the fields and meadows around Downe that Darwin noted the activity of bees[34]: 'The sainfoin fields are now of the most beautiful pink, &

from the number of Hive Bees frequenting them the humming noise is quite extraordinary. This humming is rather deeper than the humming over head which has been continuous and loud during all the last hot days, over almost every field. The labourers here say it is made of 'air-bees' & one man seeing a wild bee in a flower, different from the Hive kind, remarked: 'that no doubt is a 'air-bee'. This noise is considered as a sign of settled fair weather.'

Darwin undertook bee watching work from 1854–1861. One example of his studies was that Darwin observed bees flying from a hole at the base of an ash tree in the grounds of Down House. He observed that each bee followed a dry ditch, stopping regularly at 'buzzing places'[35] 'I could only follow them along this ditch by making several of my children crawl in, and lie on their tummies, but in this way I was able to track the bees... by stationing five or six of my children each close to a buzzing place, and telling the one farthest away to shout out 'here is a bee' as soon as one was buzzing around'. Darwin found that bees flew at about ten miles an hour and noted that their buzzing places were fixed to within an inch. There were some riddles he was unable to answer. On a page of field notes can be found: 'How on earth do bees coming separately out of the nest discover same place, is it like dogs at cornerstones?'[36]

Darwin was also interested in honey bees. He aimed to show that the honey bees' instinct to build a honeycomb evolved in small steps over a long period of time[37].

'He must be a dull man who can examine the exquisite structure of a comb, so beautifully adapted to its end, without enthusiastic admiration. We hear from mathematicians that bees have practically solved a recondite problem, and have made their cells of the proper shape to hold the greatest possible amount of honey, with the least possible consumption of precious wax in their construction...all this beautiful work can be shown, I think, to follow from a few very simple instincts...At one end of a short series we have humble-bees, which use their old cocoons to hold honey, sometimes adding to them short tubes of wax, and likewise making separate and very irregular rounded cells of wax. At the other end of the series we have the cells of the hive-bee, placed in a double layer: each cell,...an hexagonal prism...Of course the success of any species of bee may be dependent on the number of its parasites or other enemies, or on quite distinct causes, and so be altogether independent of the quantity of honey which the bees could collect. But let us suppose that this latter circumstance determined, as it probably often does determine, the numbers of a humble-bee which could exist in a country; and let us further suppose that the community lived throughout the winter, and consequently required a store of honey: there can in this case be no doubt that it would be an advantage to our humble-bee, if a slight modification of her instinct led her to make her waxen cells near together, so as to intersect a little; for a wall in common even to two adjoining cells, would save some little wax...'

Darwin studied bees visiting violets. Darwin noted their effectiveness at pollination. He wrote[38]: 'I watched 1000s of wild flowers; at last saw on Green Hill one Hive-bee visiting and sucking several. Marked 6 flowers I saw sucked. In one of these 6, 2 set five pods and some others seemed to have been injured'. Elsewhere, he wrote 'Viola canina...saw Bombus hortorum sucking multitude of flowers, and biting holes in nectary...Marked six flowers sucked by black thread and each by stick.'[39]

At Downe the following species of bee have been noted in recent times[40]:

Apis mellifera	House Bee Common
Bombus lapidarius	Red-tailed bumblebee Common
Bombus lucorum	White-tailed bumblebee Common
Bombus pascuorum	Common carder bee Common
Bombus terrestris	Buff-tailed bumblebee Common
Bombus hortorum	Garden bumblebee Common
Bombus rupestris	Nationally Scarce
Bombus humilis	Very local
Bombus vestalis	Common
Bombus hypnorum	Common
Bombus pratorum	Common

Anthophora furcata	Common
Anthophora plumipes	Common
Hylaeus communis	Common
Hylaeus pictipes	Nationally scarce
Hylaeus confusus	Local
Hylaeus cornutus	Nationally scarce
Hylaceus annularis (*H. dilatatus*)	Common
Lasioglossum calceatum	Common
Lasioglossum morio	Common
Lasioglossum xanthopus	Nationally scarce
Lasioglossum fulvicorne	Common
Lasioglossum leucopus	Common
Lasioglossum malachurum	Nationally scarce
Lasioglossum smeathmanellum	Common (but declining)
Osmia bicolor	Nationally scarce
Megachile willughbiella	Common
Megachile versicolor	Common
Megachile ligniseca	Common
Megachile centuncularis	Common
Nomada flavoguttata	Common
Nomada flava	Common
Nomad flavopicta	Common
Melitta tricincta	Common
Sphecodes crassus	Nationally scarce
Sphecodes ferruginatus	Nationally scarce
Sphecodes geofrellus	Local
Sphecodes monilicornis	Local

Sphecodes hyalinatus	Local
Andrena flavipes	Common
Andrena minutula	Common
Andrena bicolor	Common
Andrena dorsata	Common
Andrena semilaevis	Common
Andrena nigroacenea	Common
Andrena fulva	Common
Andrena bicolor	Common
Halictus tumulorum	Common
Anthidium manicatum	Common
Melecta albifrons	Local

Shropshire & Downe: Two Landscapes Darwin Held Dear

FLIGHT FANTASTIC

When I first moved into my cottage, just on the Shropshire borders, I was in doubt whether I would have any birds coming to the feeder as I thought the birds, being 'rural', would not be used to being fed – how wrong I was! As well as a lawn, I had fat balls, seeds and peanuts on offer. In just six months I recorded twenty-one species of bird. They included: song thrushes, red legged partridges, pheasants, blackbirds, coal tits, marsh tits, long tailed tits, great tits, blue tits, gold finches, green finches, bullfinches, crows, great spotted woodpecker, wood pigeons, stock doves, chaffinches, nuthatches, robins, yellowhammers and dunnocks. Later, when I had to move, swallows, jackdaws, magpies, and house sparrows were added to the list. The hooting of an owl also greeted me every night at home, its call coming from a secluded piece of woodland.

Darwin wrote:[1] 'From reading White's '*Selbourne*' I took much pleasure in watching the habits of birds, and even made notes on the subject. In my simplicity I remember wondering why every gentleman did not become an ornithologist'. When I arrived in Shropshire, I found there were no less than three active birds groups in the County – Darwin would have been impressed! In an attempt to learn more about birds, I attended a monthly jaunt with the South Shropshire RSPB group, primed with my binoculars, and later also attended an ornithology course. It is typical for 'birders' to be happy to share their knowledge with others; and this is something from which I benefited as part of these pursuits. I expect Darwin would have done the same; sharing his sightings with his family or co-walkers.

What sort of account of birds do we have for Shropshire in Darwin's time? In 1899, Forrest[2] states: 'we cite the great increase in the numbers of hawfinches and crossbills; both of the birds used to be looked upon as rarities, where now the former has become so numerous in some localities that is does serious damage in gardens; .. The Nightingale is slowly increasing, both in numbers and in the area of its range. On the other hand most of the birds of prey are getting extremely rare on account of the incessant war waged against them by man, and human agency is also responsible for the marked diminution in the number of Goldfinches'...'The boom of the Bittern would resound from the swamps, and the Kite and Buzzard be seen daily sailing overhead in graceful gyrations...The birds mentioned above are still with us, though in greatly diminished numbers...' Forrest also points out that Eyton, one of the contributors to his book, was a Salopian who had extensive knowledge of birds and that he was great friends with Darwin.

A summary of birds present in Shropshire can also be found in a later account by Watts (1939)[3]. He wrote: 'Shropshire abounds in birds, and it is only possible to name a few of the more important. The nightingale occurs regularly in the southern Severn Valley, the goldfinch or 'seven-coloured linnet' is still found where there is thistledown for it to feed on, and the bullfinch is at time very destructive to fruit buds. The raven is a very rare bird, and the carrion crow is diminishing; the swift or 'jack-squealer' is locally common during its short season, but its relative, the nightjar, is much less frequently seen. The buzzard is getting rare, and the white-tailed eagle occurs as a wanderer...Five species of owl are known from the county, but the kestrel and sparrow-hawk are the commonest birds of prey. Black-game still occur in Clun Forest and the red grouse inhabits the Longmynd, the Clees, and Clun. Waterfowls are plentiful on the meres and polls, including the greater and lesser grebe, the heron, the mute swan, the shoveller and tufted duck; and gulls of many kinds pass up and down the Severn Valley.'

One of Darwin's extracurricular activities involved shooting. Darwin wrote:[4] 'In the latter part of my school life I became passionately fond of shooting...and I do not believe that anyone could have shown more zeal for the most holy cause than I did for shooting birds...This taste long continued and I became a very good shot'. Thomson[5] points out that his cousin Bessy Galton recorded that when Darwin first went out with his father 'the birds sat upon the tree and laughed at him'. One year at Maer, Darwin recorded[6] 'fifty-five partridges, three hares, and a rabbit in the first week'. Partridges formed a good proportion of Darwin's shoots in the references I can find. Between 1870–1930, two million grey partridges were being shot in Britain each year.[7] Nowadays, the story is very different; there are believed to be only around 75,000 pairs[8].

It was a common pastime for Victorian gentlemen to shoot birds and so it was very much the case of 'specimens obtained' when you look at accounts of Darwin's time. Forrest[9] states: '...our County owes much to the two taxidermists – William Franklin and Harry Shaw – whose skill and originality were so universally recognized that Shrewsbury became the 'Mecca of Ornithologists' and their services were sought by collectors and sportsmen from all parts of the kingdom'. Darwin writes to W.D. Fox in 1829[10] 'I shot whilst in Shrewsbury, a Dundiver (a female Goosander as I suppose you know). Shaw has stuffed it...' Darwin wrote in his autobiography 'How well I remember killing my first snipe, and my excitement was so great that I had much difficulty in reloading my gun from the trembling of my hands'[11]. The Ludlow Museum Resources Centre[12] nor the Natural History Museum[13] in London have any British specimens of birds collected by Darwin, other than domesticated forms. The only wild exhibits that do exist of Darwin's, are those he accrued on his Beagle voyage, including his famous finches. Ironically, a letter of Darwin's reveals that he himself sent British specimens to museums, namely to Osmaston Museum.[14] 'I think I mentioned that I had a few stuffed birds, & as they would be of much more use to you than to me, I have taken the liberty of sending them to the "Osmaston Museum" & hope they will arrive safe.'

We can get a glimpse of 'A year in the life of' Darwin's experiences in birdwatching – and bird shooting – from a diary 'The Edinburgh Ladies & Gentlemans Pocket Souvenir for 1826'[15] which is possibly Darwin's earliest surviving notebook on field observations. Here are extracts of the notes relating to birds. It is interesting to see how he questions his identification skills and how he poses questions about the behaviour of the birds he sees.

18 January 1826 Saw a Hedge Sparrow late in the evening creep into a hole in a tree; where do most birds roost in winter?

19 January Yellow & grey Wagtail, Diagnosis consists in the former having black legs & in being more brilliantly coloured.—

24 Feb Bought a Ptarmigan

7 March Saw three Snow Buntings shot. They were flying in small flocks about the shore. One of them a great deal whiter & more beautiful than the rest. Is this the Cock or Hen?

1 April Partridges seemed to be pairing were very noisy & running flying after each other

8 April Hedge Sparrow was singing & making that peculiar motion with its wings. — they seemed to be paired.—Heard a lark crying out 20' past 7 o'clock & three bats at 1/2 8 oclock saw a humble bee

10 April Heard Kitty Wren singing

11 April Saw large flock of Wheatears on Arthurs seat.—

13 April Saw two yellow water Wagtails or rather grey??

20 April The nails of the white owl are set at right angles to the toes so that their grasp must be exceeding firm.— their ears also are very capacious & evidently can be closed at the will of the bird by an overlapping skin.—Saw also a red-throated diver the legs are plainly placed on its back. that is to say when held by the beak perpendicularly their origin was behind the tail—

25 April No swallows or rather the genus Hirundo have appeared in or near Edinburgh

26 April Saw Chimney swallows 90 miles South & redstart. also saw a great many Water Ouzels their flight is much similar to a Kingfisher but more undulating.—

28 April Chimney Swallows. Martens. Sand Martens. Willow Wrens are now pretty plentiful. & Sandpipers at Shrewsbury.—

1 May Susan heard a Cuckoo

2 May I believe I saw a swift late in the Evening but am not sure.

6 May Heard several Cuckoos.

8-10 May Swifts seen to have come altogether last night or the night before.
  Blackcaps seem to be very plentiful

15-17 May 1826 A Corncrake was shot & given to me.— Creepers have young ones.

19 May Very few Sand marten have appeared
  Swifts seem to be very plentiful

20 May Kitty Wrens have eggs.—
  Sunday Saw a flycatcher

22-24 May Killed a Red-backed Shrike.—

N.B. the White throat is a very common bird. with brilliant patch of white on its throat. rather a long tail. sings on the wing.— Lark night jar has white spot on the outermost tail feather
  The Tit lark early in the Spring rises in the air & falls like as bit of paper. The stone-chat seems to be scarcer. saw a couple with yet black heads & bright red breasts are much more common in water

23rd.— saw two more shrikes & found near the place 2 bees & beetle impaled

25 remember having seen last year two other fields distant. the same thing. Price1 states he has found a young bird in the same state.—

29 May Without doubt Cocks & Hens feed their young. Caught one of them whilst the other came. in this instance Parus Major

1 June Flycatchers do not seem to be at all plentiful.—

12 June Shot a bird with bright red breast & crown of head. Sennet or Redpole?

16 June Saw several Butcher Birds hawking for bees &c much in the same manner as flycatchers do.—

26 June Shot a cormorant & in it there were several worms. I suppose of course the Ascaris carbonis.— the capacity of the stomach was very great. there being four sole about half a foot long in it. these birds evidently "ducked the flash." —
  Our field was cut.

29 June Found young partridges which had only been born a few days

10-12 July Water Hen makes a sound like a young Hawk. Chicks. Chick being every [where] & then interrupted

12 July One of the redpoles makes a noise like a pewit only of course very piano & much gentler

4 August I saw the Nuthatch bury nuts in a chink then breaking them

1 September 7. & 1/2 brace of partridges & Hare

2 September 6 & 1/2

4 September 2 & 1/2

5 September 4 & Hare
    Lady-cows are also very numerous

6 September Saw as I believe a young Cuckoo ∴ Do the young Cuckoos always remain so late?

7 September Shot the Sternus after a very windy night
    3 & 1/2 & Hare

28 October Observed the larger Titmouse picking the berry from a yew tree & breaking them like a Nuthatch

23 December Saw Grey Wagtail & Water Ouzel under Braid Hills

25 December A remarkably foggy day. So much so that the trees condensed the vapour & caused it to fall like large drops of rain
    Saw a hooded Crow feeding with some rooks. by the sea shore. near Leith.

Forrest[16] gives an account of the species in Shropshire and lists resident[s]... summer migrants...birds of passage...winter migrants...waifs and strays...' stating that: 'Shropshire has been fortunate in regard to the manner in which birds have been observed and recorded from the early part of the century to the present time' and acknowledges a number of ornithologists. His list is presented here. We have a good idea of those species found in the vicinity of Shrewsbury from publications dated 1850[17] and 1878[18] (entries have been marked below) which-gives us some idea of what Darwin is particularly likely to have encountered around his home.

=*Mistle thrush	(Stormcock) Plentiful all the year round
=*+Thrush	(Throstle) Plentiful everywhere
=*Redwing	Common winter visitor
=*Fieldfare (Feltyfare)	Common winter visitor
White's thrush (T. varius)	Specimen..rare...shot at Moreton Corbet...1892
=*+Blackbird	Very common
=*Ring Ouzel	Occurs every summer, chiefly in the hilly parts of the County
=*Wheatear	Visits us in numbers on its Spring and Autumn migrations...
=*Whinchat (U-tick)	Common in summer wherever gorse bushes are found and on meadows along the Severn Valley
=*Stonechat	Common in Summer on moorlands
=*Redstart (Fiery-brand tail)	Common bird in summer 'A few years ago a pair succeeded in rearing a brood in the Quarry, Shrewsbury'
Black redstart	One killed near Wem in 1878
=*+Robin redbreast	Very common
=*Nightingale	Does not seem often to occur North of Shrewsbury, though it is found sparingly every year along the Severn Valley up to that point
=*Whitethroat (Nettle creeper, Jack straw)	Very common
=Lesser whitethroat	Found all over the County
=*+Blackcap	Fairly plentiful summer visitor
=*Garden warbler	Rather common
=*+Golden crested wren	Common where conifers grow Regulus cristatus

=*Fire crested wren* R. ignicapillus	Its has occurred five or six time in Shropshire, no less than three in Shrewsbury
=*+Chiffchaff*	A common and very early Summer visitor
=*+Willow wren* P. trochilus	(Peggy whitethroat, Haybird, Willow warbler) Numerous everywhere
=*Woode wren* (Yellow wren) P. sibilatrix.	Found in many large open woods
=*Reed warbler*	Occurs on most of the larger meres
Great reed warbler	A specimen of this rare large species was shot at Ellesmrere about 1886
=*Sedge warbler*	Common
=*Grasshopper warbler*	A bird rarely seen owing to its shy skulking habits...found all over the County
Hedge sparrow (Hedge warbler)	Common
=*Dipper or Water Ouzel*	Common on most streams
Bearded tit	This rare Tit seems to have been resident in former time at Aqualate Mere, on the borders of Shropshire and Staffordshire
=*+Long tailed Tit* (Canbottlin)	Very common
=*+Great tit*	Very common
=*Coal tit*	Common in large woods
=*Marsh tit*	Not uncommon
=*+Blue tit* (Tom tit)	Commonest of all the Tits
=*+Nuthatch*	Rather local in its distribution, but numerous in certain places (for example in the Quarry, Shrewsbury, where it breeds every year).
+Wren (Jenny wren)	

=*+*Tree creeper* (Creeper)	Not at all uncommon It is abundant in the Quarry, Shrewsbury
=**Pied Wagtail* (Water wagtail)	Common in summer
=**Grey wagtail*	More common in winter than summer; breeds in hilly country, near small streams
=**Yellow wagtail* (Ray's wagtail)	A summer migrant
=*Tree Pipit*	Common in summer
=**Meadow pipit* (Titlark)	Common in summer, especially on high ground
=*Richards Pipit*	Rare. One was killed near Shrewsbury in October 1866
Rock pipit	This is properly a shore bird...specimen killed at Berwick..1877
Golden Oriole	Has occurred several time in Shropshire
=**Great grey shrike* (Ash coloured shrike)	A rare winter visitor
=**Red backed Shrike* (Butcher bird)	It is found sparingly all over the County
**Waxwing* (Chatterer)	A rare winter visitor
=**Spotted flycatcher* (Miller)	Common all over the County in Summer
=**Pied flycatcher*	Rather uncommon Summer visitor
=*+*Swallow*	Very plentiful
=**House martin* (Martin)	Not so numerous as the Swallow
=**Sand martin*	Found all over the County wherever sandbanks occur
*=*Greenfinch* (Green Linnet, Green Grosbeak)	Abundant everywhere
*=*Hawfinch* (Grosbeak)	It used to be reckoned rare, but of late years has multiplied very much

=*Goldfinch (Seven coloured Linnet, Proud tailor, Sheriffs man)	Still fairly numerous in spite of bird catchers
=*Siskin	Abundant in some Winters
=*Sparrow	Far too numerous, owing to the ruthless slaughter of its natural enemy, the Sparrow Hawk
=Tree sparrow	Frequent in stubble fields
=*+Chaffinch (Pyefinch)	Very abundant everywhere
=Brambling (Mountain finch)	Occurs every winter
=*Linnet	Abundant where gorse grows
=Mealy Redpole (Acanthis linaria)	Rare or else generally overlooked
=*Lesser redpole	Common in Winter, and a few spend the summer here, nesting at Shrewsbury
Twite (Mountain Linnet)	Very rare, except on the Welsh border
=*+Bullfinch	Not uncommon in woods, and nests in thick bushes near Shrewsbury etc.
=*Crossbill	Winter visitor of very uncertain occurrence
Parrot crossbill	Rare
*=Corn bunting (Common bunting, Bunting)	Far from common in Shropshire
=*Yellow hammer (Writing-master)	Abundant everywhere
Cirl bunting	Very rare, more probably overlooked from its close resemblance to the yellow hammer
Reed bunting (Reed sparrow, Blackheaded Bunting)	Fairly common by water in summer, and about stack-yards in winter

=*Lapland bunting*	Very rare
Snow bunting	Very rare
=*+Starling*	Exceedingly numerous everywhere
=*Rose-coloured starling* (Pastor)	Twice in the county..1841...1857
Chough	One...killed in...1862
=*+Jay*	Common in thick woods in spite of constant persecution by game-keepers
=*+Magpie*	Common
=*Jackdaw*	Abundant everywhere
=*Raven*	Now very rare
=*+Carrion crow*	Still plentiful in the wilder parts of the County
Hooded crow	Very rare
=*Rook*	One of the most familiar and abundant of our birds
=*+Skylark* (Lark)	Very plentiful
=*Wood lark*	It occurs very sparingly throughout Shropshire
Short toed lark	Very rare
=*+Swift* (Jack Screamer, Squealer)	
=*Nightjar* (Goatsucker, Fern Owl)	Not uncommon in ferny glades in upland woods
Wryneck	Found sparingly in the southern parts of the County
=*+Common or Green Woodpecker* (Yawkle)	Common to all those parts of the County that are well timbered, especially the neighbourhood of Shrewsbury
=*+Great spotted woodpecker* (Pied woodpecker)	Fairly common

=*Lesser woodpecker (Barred woodpecker)	It is often overlooked, but is not really uncommon
=*Kingfisher	Fairly numerous on the Severn and its tributary brooks and on some pools in the County
=*Hoopoe	About a dozen times in the County
=*+Cuckoo	Very abundant
*=Barn or White Owl (Yellow owl)	The most plentiful of the owls in Shropshire, and now that farmers and others recognise its usefulness in destroying mice , and do not shoot it, it is gradulally increasing in numbers
=*Long eared owl	Rather common
=Short eared owl	A winter visitor frequently moors and open ground
=*Brown, Tawny or Wood owl	It is found in thick woods, especially fir plantations
Tengmalms owl	A specimen...shot near Ruyton...1872
Eagle owl	Occasional
Marsh harrier	Now very rare in Shropshire
*Hen harrier (female/juvenile Ringtail)	Almost as rare as the last
Montagues Harrier	Shot at Petton ..1860
=*Common buzzard	Rarely escapes the gun of the gamekeeper It was formerly common
Rough legged buzzard	A rare wanderer
White tailed eagle	At least eight time in the county
=*+Sparrow hawk	In spite of unrelenting persecution this beautiful Hawk is certainly the most numerous of its tribe in Shropshire

Kite	Old Writers speak of the Kite as of quite common occurrence, but it must now be regarded as very rare
=*Honey buzzard*	A rare visitor
=*Peregrine Falcon*	Breeds still in North Wales, especially along the coasts, and every year a few appear in Shropshire
Iceland falcon	
=*Hobby*	Formally Often obtained near Shrewsbury, but now rather rare
Orange legged Hobby	Caught near Shrewsbury 1868
=*Merline* Still	Occurring not infrequently on the Longmynd range and along the Wesh border
=*Kestrel* (Windhover)	Fairly numerous where it is not molested
Osprey	
=*Cormorant*	
Shag or Green Cormorant	
=*Gannet or Solan Goose*	
=*Heron*	Frequently seen on rivers and pools
Squacco Heron	It is rare in Shropshire
=*Night heron*	
Little Bittern	One shot in the Quarry, Shrewsbury
=*Bittern*	It is now very rare
=*Glossy Ibis*	Occurred only once in Shropshire
Grey lag goose	It is very rare in Shropshire
=*White fronted goose*	Winter visitor of uncertain occurrence
Bean goose	More numerous than the other wild geese

Pink footed goose	A smaller bird than the last, and occurs less frequently in Shropshire
Egyptian goose	There is some doubt whether it may be admitted to the list as a wild species
Canada goose	From time to time specimens of this fine bird are seen in an apparently wild state
Barnacle goose	Very rare, but has occurred in the County many years ago
=Brent goose	It is rare in Shropshire
Wild swan or Whooper	Now very rare
Bewicks Swan	Now very rare one killed on the Severn about 1862
Tame or Mute Swan	Common on many ornamental waters in a domesticated condition and numerous on the meres...A pair used to nest under the English Bridge, in Shrewsbury
Sheldrake	Specimens Occur from time to time in the County
*=*Wild duck of Mallard*	Many nest with us regularly
Gadwall	Has occurred only twice in Shropshire
=Shoveler Duck	Mostly an uncertain visitor to the County
=Pintail duck	Has occurred several times in the winter
*=*Teal*	Getting more numerous
Garganey	A very rare duck occurring chiefly on spring and autumn migration; none have been seen in Shropshire lately
*=*Wigeon*	Not uncommon during winter
=Pochard or Red headed Poker	Frequents most of our larger pools during winter, often in numbers

=*Tufted duck*	Another fairly common visitor
=*Scaup duck*	It is decidedly rare in Shropshrie
=*Golden Eye*	Not uncommon during severe winters, especially on the Severn
Long tailed Duck	A rare visitor
Black Scoter	Its visits to Shropshire are very irregular
=*Velvet Scoter*	It has only been obtained once in the County, near Shrewsbury
=*Goosander*	Occurs almost every winter on the Severn and the larger pools.
=*Red breasted Merganser*	Much less common than the Goosander
=*Smew*	Very irregular visitor to Shropshire
=*+Wood pigeon* (Quice, Quist, Ring Dove)	Exceedingly numerous in all our woods
=*Stock dove*	Very common, though not so numerous as the last
+*Rock dove*	It is difficult to say with certainty whether or not those found in the open are escaped tame birds reverting to the wild state
=*Turtle Dove* (Wrekin Dover)	Fairly common in the County, especially round the Wrekin
Sand Grouse	Records in Shropshire
Black grouse (Blackcock and Greyhen)	Numerous in the southern, but rare in the northern parts of the County
Red grouse	Few if any red grouse in Shropshire before 1840...two pairs from Yorkshire turned out on the hills above Chruch Stretton...have spread to other hills in Shropshire
=*+Pheasant*	Common everywhere

Ring necked Pheasant	Far out numbers the old breed
=*Partridge*	Very common and too well known to need any description
=*Red legged partridge*	Rare in Shropshrie
=*Quail*	A regular summer visitor though never numerous
=*Corncrake or Landrail* meadows.	Plentiful, especiallyin lowland
=*Spotted crake*	Occurs in Shropshire from time to time on its spring and autumn migrations
=*Water rail*	Frequenting quiet reaches of the Severn and many pools
=*Moorhen or Water hen* (common gallinule)	Very abundant on our ponds
=*Coot* (Bald-headed coot)	Not quite as abundant as the Water hen.
Crane	A rare and splendid bird
Little bustard	Rare bird...once only in Shropshire
Stone curlew (Thick-knee)	Only once recorded in Shropshire
Dotterel	Very rare in the county
=*Ringed plover*	Only a casual visitor to Shropshire
=*Golden plover*	Occuring almost every winter in Shropshire
=*Peewit or Lapwing* (Plover)	They are found chiefly on lowland meadows, or other open country
=*Turnstone*	Rare in Shropshire
=*Oyster catcher* (Sea-pie)	It is plentiful on the neighbouring coasts of North Wales, and has occurred in the County
Avocet	Sometimes occurred in the Shropshire meres

=*Grey Phalarope*	Visits us frequently on its migrations, generally in autumn
Red necked Phalarop	Much more rare bird
=*Woodcock*	A well known bird come to us in 'flights' in October
=*Snipe* (Full snipe)	Another bird dear to sportsmen, and difficult to hit on account of its peculiar zig zag flight. The extraordinatry drumming noise with it makes while on the wing, during the breeding season, has given rise to much controversy and is alluded to at some length in Darwin's '*Descent of Man*'. The snipe is found on the Longmynd and in most boggy places and a few nest with us in marshy situations
Great snipe (Double snipe)	An autumn visitor which has occurred several times in Shropshire.
=*Jack snipe* (Judcock)	Irregular winter visitor
=*Dunlin*	Rarely visits Shropshire
=*Curlew sandpiper*	One shot on Shrewsbury racecourse.. five at Barrow
Purple sandpiper	Very rare in Shropshire
=*Knot*	It has occurred
Ruff	Only recorded twice in Shropshrie
=*Common sandpiper* (Summer snipe)	Heard in summer on most of our rivers and brooks especially near the Welsh border
=*Green sandpiper*	Occurs pretty often in Shropshire
=*Redshank*	Occurs from time to time, generally on the Severn and Teme
=*Greenshank*	It is rare in the County

Bar tailed Godwit	Has occurred at times in Shropshire on its migrations
Black tailed Godwit	A very rare spring and autumn visitor
=*Curlew	Is numerous on our Shropshire moorlands
Wimbrel	A rare visitor to Shropshire moors
=Black tern	Has occurred several times in different parts of the County, the most recent being at Oxon Pool 1871... Rednal 1873... Gobowen 1883... Walcot Park 1894
Sandwich Tern	Found dead near Shrewsbury...1897
Roseate Tern	Shot, about 1830, at Longden-on-Tern
=Common Tern or Sea Swallow	Often seen on or near the Severn in autumn and spring...In the summer of 1898 one of these pretty birds stayed for more than a week on the Severn below the English Bridge, Shrewsbury.
=Arctic Tern	Occurs in Shropshire, and in May 1842, immense numbers appeared on the Severn, in an exhausted condition...
Little Tern	Occurs less frequently
=Sabine's Gull	Found dead at Nobold...1874 shot at Sandford, near Oswestry..1893
=Little Gull	Obtained at Coalbrookdale...in 1874...at Atcham
=Black-headed Gull	Not infrequent during the winter months
=*Common gull	It occurs in Shropshire from time to time, especially on the Severn near Cressage – generally immature birds in autumn

=*Herring Gull*	Often seen here in winter, especially in tempestuous weather
=*Lesser black-backed gull*	Often seen flying across the country in autum and spring. About forty were counted...1898, and seen by several people about Shresbury and Church Stretton
Great Black-backed Gull	Only a rare wanderer to Shropshire
=*Glaucous Gull* Oswestry	Two young birds...obtained...at Pradoe, 1856...Bomere Pool..1863
=*Kittiwake*	This pretty bird occurs in Shropshire almost every winter...four occurred in Shrewsbury in one week in Feb. 1899
Great Skua	Only recorded twice in the County
=*Pomatorhine Skua*	One killed by flying against the spire of St. Alkmund's Church, Shrewsbury, and there are three in the collection at Hawkstone from Shrewsbury, Shifnal and Baschurch
=*Richardson's Skua*	After a heavy gale in Oct 14th 1881, three were found dead and others seen in the County
Long-tailed or Buffon's Skua	In the Hawkstone collection, shot near Astley...one...found dead near Garmston...1891
=*Razorbill*	Caught at Bromfield in the winter of 1878-9
Guillemot	Very abundant on the neighbouring coasts of North Wales, the Guillemot has occurred several times in the County, in autumn and spring
Black Guillemot	Very rare, but has visited Shropshire in Winter

=Little Auk	A specimen in the Hawkstone collection, was caught near the Welsh Bridge, Shrewsbury; and others have been obtained at Shifnal, Acton Scott, Haughmond, Hodnet, Ludlow and Ellesmere
Puffin	One found on Corndon Hill...Tasley, Bridgnorth...1887...Pontesbury...1894
Great Northern Diver	Adult female ..shot on Ellesmere..in 1863 and several young birds have been obtained from time to time on the Severn
Black-throated Diver	In the Hawkstone collection..obtained in 1862, at Gredington
Red-throated diver	Rare in Shropshire.. Market Drayton ...1890..Baschurch...same year... Shrawardine Pool...1897
=Great crested grebe	It is resident throughout the year, and breeds on several of our larger pools and meres
Red-necked Grebe	Very rare in Shropshire...one killed on the *Severn near Wroxeter*...another close to Shrewsbury...1888
=Slavonian or Horned Grebe	It has occurred in Shropshire several times in winter, the most recent being at Montford Bridge in 1894. One was killed by a boy with a stone in the Quarry, Shrewsbury in Dec. 1890
=*Dabchick or Little Grebe	Common on most of our pools...
=Manx Shearwater	Sept 1859, two were caught, one on the Severn, in Shrewsbury, the other near Shifnal...two..near Oswestry..three...near Ludlow, Ditton Priors, and Cressage...1884... Shrewsbury...Aston on Clun and Halston, near Oswestry

| =*Fork-tailed Petrel* | It has been obtained about ten times in the County |
| =**Storm Petrel* | Occurred at Wellington, Hawkstone, Ellesmere, Ludlow, and other places after storms... |

* marks those birds mentioned around Shrewsbury by Leighton 1850[19] plus Least willow wren (likely to be chiff chaff), Passerine warbler (possibly Garden Warbler, though that is already listed), Pine Grosbeak, Greater redpoll (could be the Linnet with slightly different plumage)

= marks those birds mentioned around Shrewsbury in book by Phillips 1878[20]

N.B. Some new species names confirmed by British Trust for Ornithology[21]

+ Bird species recorded one year at Downe Bank Nature Reserve, Downe[22]

What of birds around Downe? All in all over 60 species of bird have been recorded around Downe in recent years.[23] A taste of the range of birds one can meet can be drawn from a field visit I took a few years ago. One May morning at 5.30am I took a walk with some conservation volunteers along the western edge of Cudham Valley. On that occasion we came across Chiff chaff, crow, pheasant, blue tit, wren, magpie, robin, song thrush, green woodpecker, chaffinch, blackbird, wood pigeon, great tit, long-tailed tit, lesser whitethroat, dunnock, whitethroat, blackcap, jackdaw, song thrush, tree creeper, great spotted woodpecker, starling and jay. A list of bird species recorded one year at Downe Bank Nature Reserve is marked in the main bird list[22].

Darwin's son, Francis, reports Darwin's knack of finding birds around Downe:[24] '...Sometimes when alone, he stood still or walked stealthily to observe birds or beasts...He always found birds' nests even up to the last years of his life, and we, as children, considered that he had a special genius in this direction. In his quiet prowls he came across the less common birds, but I fancy he used to conceal it from me as a little boy because he observed the agony of mind which I endured at not having seen the siskin or goldfinch or whatever it may have been.'

We know that Darwin used to collect eggs as a child. Darwin wrote: [25] 'I was very fond of collecting eggs, but I never took more than a single egg out of a bird's nest, except on one single occasion, when I took all, not for their value, but from a sort of bravado'. There is an account of Darwin meeting a boy,[26] in Downe and explaining to him how to prepare eggs:

'I had been bird's nesting in some woods not far from Down House when suddenly I found myself confronted by a very tall man with a grey beard, wearing a black cloak and a flat, wide-brimmed hat rather like the ones clergymen wore. I was terrified at first, but he spoke very kindly to me and showed me a place where a wren had built her nest. There were three eggs in it and I wanted to take one of them, but he told me I mustn't. In spite of this, he went on to tell me how to blow eggs so as to preserve them, which I thought was very funny. When I returned home to Cudham my father told me who the old man was and said he probably knew more about birds' eggs than any person living.'

Darwin[27] wrote various scientific observations about a range of birds. One of these makes reference to plumage: 'Colour is thought an unimportant character by naturalists; but when we see as it has been fancifully said that "the ptarmigan is lichen in summer & snow in winter, that the red grouse is heather, & black grouse peaty earth"; & when we remember the main check to the increase of our game birds, is owing to birds & beasts of prey, I can see no reason to doubt that in birds varying in colour as does the red grouse, that the finest tints of colour might be selected owing to such individuals suffering less.'

Darwin's fascination in birds changes later in his career; the focus very much becomes that of change in birds through domestication. We know that the Darwins kept pigeons at the Mount. The Shropshire Archaeological & Natural History Society[28] recalls: 'They petted and reared birds and other animals', 'the beauty, variety and tameness of The

Mount pigeons were well known in the town and far beyond'.This is a practice Darwin continued at Down House. In 'The Variation of Animals and Plants Under Domestication'[29] he wrote: 'I have been led to study domestic pigeons with particular care, because the evidence that all the domestic races have descended from one known source is far clearer than with any other anciently domesticated animal. Secondly, because many treatises in several languages, some of them old, have been written on the pigeon, so that we are enabled to trace the history of several breeds. And lastly, because, from causes which we can partly understand, the amount of variation has been extraordinarily great. The details will often be tediously minute; but no one who really wants to understand the progress of change in domestic animals will regret this; and no one who has kept pigeons and has marked the great difference between the breeds and the trueness with which most of them propagate their kind, will, think this care superfluous. Notwithstanding the clear evidence that all the breeds are the descendants of a single species, I could not persuade myself until some years had passed that the whole amount of difference between them had arisen since man first domesticated the wild rock-pigeon.

I have kept alive all the most distinct breeds, which I could procure in England or from the Continent; and have prepared skeletons of all. I have received skins from Persia, and a large number from India and other quarters of the world. Since my admission into two of the London pigeon-clubs, I have received the kindest assistance from many of the most eminent amateurs.'

The Natural History Museum[30] informed me that they: 'hold just over 300 bird specimens directly connected with Darwin's collecting. About 160 of these are skins and skeletons from his research into domestic varieties [including 120 pigeon and 40 chickens and ducks]...during the later 1850s, including the famous fancy pigeons he kept at Down House. The rest are from the Voyage of H.M.S. Beagle...including the famous mockingbird and finch specimens from the Galapagos [also 2 canary skeletons, feral birds from Madeira]. No British wild specimens are presently known from [the] collections – no bird specimens earlier than the Voyage of *The Beagle*...survive anywhere and his later bird collecting activities appear to have been exclusively motivated as part of his research, rather than a general interest in natural history collecting'.

IN THE THICK OF IT

What range of trees would Darwin have witnessed in Shropshire's land-scape? Well, we know that the Mount had woodland on the banks of the Severn from an 1866 map of the estate, though a sketch of the Mount, re-produced in Transactions of the Shropshire Archaeological & Natural His-tory Society[1], shows few canopy-layer trees present. Nowadays this wood-land comprises of ash, sycamore and large-leaved limes with wych elm, English elm, hazel, hawthorn, elder, holly, blackthorn and yew. Exotic tree species, undoubtedly planted by the Darwin's themselves, are also evident, one of which appears to be a type of sweet chestnut. Though the woodland floor is covered in a thick layer of ivy, one surprise for me to see was just how much Cuckoo Pint (*Arum maculatum*) occured in the woodland. This is a species Darwin[2] later studied in more detail.

He wrote: '...in the common *Arum maculatum*, I found in some flow-ers from 30 to 60 midges & minute Diptera of three species, & as many were lying dead at the bottom, & as the filaments on the spadix above the anthers seemed to offer some difficulty to their escape, I concluded that after once entering a flower they probably never left it. To try this I quietly tied gauze over a flower & came back in an hour's time, when I found that several had crawled out of the spathe & were in the gauze: I then gathered a flower & breathed hard into it several times, soon several very minute Flies crawled out...dusted all over, even to their wings, with pollen, & flew away; three of them I distinctly saw fly to another arum about a yard off; they alighted on the spathe & then suddenly flew down into the flower. I opened this flower & found that not a single anther had burst, but at the bottom of the spathe, near to but not on the stigmas, I found a few grains of pollen, which must unquestionably have been brought by the above or other midges from another individual arum. I may mention that in some other arums which had their anthers burst I saw these midges crawling over the stigmas & leave pollen on them.'

It is interesting that Darwin chose to perhaps mimic the woodland of the Mount at Down House years later. The Darwin's planted an area of woodland in the grounds in 1846, through which the 'Thinking Path' was laid. Francis[3] wrote: 'The Sandwalk was planted by my father with a variety of trees such as hazel, alder, lime, hornbeam, birch, privet and dogwood and with a long line of hollies all down the exposed side'. Atkins[4] also highlights the large old Ash and Beech trees already growing in the area and that the woodland had a 'Light Side' and 'Dark Side'. According to Emma[5], it: 'turned out in time a very pleasant addition to the place'. Emma ensured that it was planted up with bluebells, primroses and ground ivy of which she was particularly fond[6]. All these flowers naturally occurred in abundance on the verges and in the surrounding woodlands of the area. One can only presume that Emma was bringing a piece of the countryside into the security of the estate. She paid local boys to weed out dogs mercury and jack-by-the-hedge; Emma did not forgive Darwin for laughing at: 'her dismay and the whole misadventure'[7] when one time a boy pulled out the wrong plants!

The 'General Aspects' show that woodland of Shropshire was then, as now, most abundant to the southern half of the county. Unless Darwin regularly travelled in the south of Shropshire, he therefore would have had little close contact with a wooded landscape. It may well be the reason why his fascination with woodlands and their species swells when he moves to Downe, where ancient woodland is right on his doorstep. However there is one exception; a woodland to the west of the Mount called 'Sheltons Rough'. Its extent hasn't changed much since Darwin's day and it is clearly visible rising up ahead as one walks westwards along the Severn Way. It is apparently not ancient woodland.[8] Darwin wrote in 1842[9]: 'I will give a short journal: on Friday I walked beyond Shelton Rough, towards Ross

Hall;—an immense walk for me.— The day was very boisterous, with great black clouds & gleams of light, & I felt a sensation of delight, which I hardly expected ever to experience again.— There certainly is great pleasure in the country even in Winter.— This walk was rather too much for me' He also corresponded:[10] 'I go out for a turn on the terrace several times a day & mean after Luncheon to attempt Shelton Rough,—but the fine ash-trees there have all been cut down.'

Watts[11] writes of Shropshire's woodlands and hedgerows:

'The tree most characteristic of the county is unquestionably the oak, which is found everywhere and frequently attains great size and beauty. It is especially prevalent in the Forest of Wyre and the Severn Gorge. It is accompanied by ash, elm, poplar, alder, beech, sycamore, maple, mountain ash, horse chestnut, willow, crab, hawthorn, elder, walnut and hazel. Birch and Spanish chestnut grow freely in the coalfields and even on the disused pitmounds. Larch, holly and Scots pine are plentiful on the sandy soils; the last and birch grow on the high lands; yew and beech on the limestone out-crops such as Wenlock Edge. There are extremely fine yews at Acton Burnell and Buildwas, and large oaks at Holt Preen, Kinlet and Willey... In Linley Park, near More, are some of the earliest larches introduced into Britain...The hedges are mostly hawthorn, but holly, hazel, privet and sometime spindlwood and beech are used; mixed with these grows the blackberry and at time the maple; honeysuckle, convolvulus, wild rose, or hop climb over them; and on the hedge banks grow primroses, the blue speedwell, wood sorrel (cuckoo's bread and cheese), cuckoo pint and wild strawberry.'

Leighton's 1841 book[12] lists the following woody species for Shropshire. The asterixed species are those highlighted as growing in and around Shrewsbury in 1878.[13]

+*Acer pseudoplatanus* Greater maple or sycamore woods. Hedges plantations; common but not truly wild

+*Acer campestre* Common maple. Hedges and thickets, not uncommon

+*Alnus glutinosa Alder. Moist meadows, banks of rivers and pools; frequent

+Fraxinus excelsior Ash. List of wood

Berberis vulgaris Barberry. Hedges; not unfrequent

* Betula alba Common birch. Hilly woods and in boggy soils; frequent

Buxus semperivens Box tree. Limestone districts; rare

Cerasus padus Bird cherry. Woods and hedges, rare

+C. avium Wild Cherry. Woods; frequent

Crateagus oxycantha Whitethorn, hawthorn, may. Woods and hedges

Castanea vulgaris Spanish chestnuts. Woods apparently wild

*Carpinus betulus Common hornbeam, Woods and hedges

+Cornus sanguinea Wild cornel or dogwood. Woods, hedges and thickets; common, apparently in this County not confined to any particular soil

+*Corylus avellana Hasel-nut. Hedges and copses, common

+Euonymous europea Spindle. Woods, hedges and thickets; not very common

=+*Fagus sylvatica Beech. Woods doubtful if wild

+Ilex aquilifolium Holly. Hedges, woods and on dry hills

Juniperus communis Juniper. Woods and heaths; rare

+Ligustrum vulgare Privet. Woods and thickets in the Limestone districts; rare

+Prunus spinosa Blackthorn. Hedges; frequent

P. insititia Wild bullace tree. Woods and hedges

+P. domestica Plum. Woods and hedges, scarcely wild

Pyrus communis Wild pear tree. Hedges

P. malus Crab apple. Woods and hedges

P. torminalis Wild service tree. Woods and hedges; rare

+*P. aucuparia* Mountain ash, Rowan, Quicken-tree. Hilly woods; not common

+*P. aria* Whitebeam tree.

Populus alba White poplar Abele. Hilly woods

Poplar canescens Grey poplar. Woods

**P. tremula* Aspen. Woods

**P. nigra* Black poplar. Banks, woods and shady places, very common

*Quercus robur Common british oak. Woods and hedges

Q. intermedia Intermediate oak. Hilly woods

**Q. sessiliflora* Sessile-fruited oak. Hilly woods

+*Rhamnus catharticus* Buckthorn. Woods, hedges and thickets; not common

R. frangula Alder buckthorn. Woods and thickets; Not very common

Ribes grossularia Common gooseberry. Hedges and thickets; scarcely wild, common

R. nigrum Blackcurrant. Woods and swampy places, not common

+*R. rubrum* Redcurrant. Woods and hedges, perhaps scarcely wild

+*Sambucus nigra* Elder. Woods, coppices, hedges, frequent

Sambucus ebulus Dwarf elder. Pastures and waste places; not very common

*Salix fragilis Crack willow. Hedges, banks of rivers etc.

**S. russelliaria* Bedford willow (Salix x fragilis var. russelliana). Banks of rivers, marshy wood

**S. alba* White willow. Riversides, moist woods etc.

**S. undulate* Sharp-leaved triandrous willow (Salix x mollissima var. undulata). Banks of brooks and wet places

**S. triandra* Almond willow or long-leaved triandrous willow. Sides of brooks, edges etc.

**S. viminalis* Osier. Banks of rivers, brooks etc.

S. stipularis Auricled osier (Salix x stipularis). Hedges, woods, wet places etc

S. cinerea Grey willow or sallow. Banks of rivers and moist woods

S. *helix* Rose willow Osier. Holts, hedges and banks of rivers

S. *lambertiana* Boyton willow. Hedges, banks of rivers

S. *forbyana* Fine basket osier. Meadows and wet places

S. *oleifolia* Olive leaved sallow. Marshy places and hedges

S. *aurita* Round leaved sallow. Moist woods and thickets

+S. *caprea* Great round leaved sallow. Woods, hedges etc.

S. *sphacelata* Witherpointed sallow. Banks of streams, wet woods etc.

S. *ferruginea* Ferruginous willow. Banks of streams

S. *holosericea* Soft shaggy-flowered willow. Hedges and marshy places

S. *acuminate* Long leaved willow. Moist woods and hedges

S. *aquatica* Water sallow. Wet hedgerows, swampy places etc.

S. *hoffmanniana* Short leaved triandrous willow. Riverside

S. *amygdalina* Almond leaved willow. Banks of rivers

S. *pentandra* Sweet bay-leaved willow. Banks of river and watery places

S. *decipiens*. Low meadows, moist hedges etc

S. *ritellina* Yellow willow or golden osier. Hedges and banks of rivers etc

S. *fusca* Dwarf silky willow.

S. *smithiana* Silky leaved osier. Meadows and osier grounds

+*Taxus baccata* Yew. Hilly places

Tilia europea Common lime or linden tree. Woods and hedgerows

T. *parvifolia* Small leaved lime. Woods and hedges

Ulmus campestris Common small leaved elm. In hedges

U. suberosa Cork barked elm. In hedges

U. glabra Smooth leaved elm. Woods and hedges

*U. Montana Broad-leaved Wych Elm. In woods and hedges

+*Viburnum opulus* Guelder rose. Woods, hedges and coppices; not unfrequent

= Shown in 'Ecological Flora of the Shropshire Region' 1985 as widespread and 'frequent throughout the region' in parks, old gardens, plantations, shelterbelts and hedges.[14]

* Listed in Phillips 1878 book on Shrewsbury[15] and included *Quercus pedunculata* (as well as *Quercus robur*), *Betula pendula* (Silver birch), *Betula glutinosa* (nonsense, according to the Natural History Museum), *Betula pubescens* (White birch), *Pinus sylvestris* (Scots pine), *Salix purpurea* (Purple willow).

N.B. Some names confirmed by Natural History Museum, London.[16]

+ Species found in Downe hedgerows (2008) also *Crataegus sp.*, *Ulmus sp. Quercus sp.*, *Ligustrum ovalifolium*, *Buddleia*, Norway maple, *Betula pubescens*, Sweet chestnut, Horse chestnut, *Tilia sp.* Hornbeam, Butcher's Broom, *Viburnum lantana*, *Follopia japonica*, *Symp alba*, *Salix sp*, Portuguese laurel, *Quercus ilex*, *Rhododendron sp.*, *Pinus sp. Laburnum*, *Malus domestica*, *Prunus sp.*, *Malus sylvestris*, *Betula pendula*, *Cotoneaster sp*, *Leylandii*, *Pyrus sp*, *Ruscus aculeatus*, *Prunus laurocersus*, *Larix sp*, *Populus sp.*

Nowadays there is nearly 25,000ha of woodland – of broadleaved, mixed and conifer – in Shropshire, which covers around 7% of the county.[17] Around half of this is semi-natural broadleaved woodland, much of it ancient. The Ancient Woodland Inventory for Shropshire shows that just after the Victorian period, there were losses of around 600 ha of irreplaceable ancient woodland from 1901 – 1925. Most losses were due to agriculture or plantation forestry, although some were due to development or mineral extraction. Lack of appropriate management has now become one of the threats to woodland quality.[17]

The landscape familiar to Darwin around Downe is reflected in the 1844 Tithe Maps and the 1868 OS maps, which I was fortunate to study during my review of conservation management plans for the area. They most clearly revealed the extent of woody species, whether this be of woodlands or hedgerows. In comparison to modern maps, it was evident that two key changes had occurred since Darwin's time; a decrease in the size of a place Darwin knew as 'The Big Woods' (Cudham Wood & Cudham Lodge Woods) and an expansion in the extent of 'secondary woodland' – woodland that develops on abandonment of arable and pastoral farmland. It is no coincidence that most of the ancient woodland remaining occurs on the clay-with-flint soils, which historically would have been more difficult to cultivate. Lordfield Shaw and Blackbush Shaw are just two examples of the strips of woodland lying at the edge of the clay-with-flint plateau land. They include woodland banks, some of the twelve kilometres of ancient wood banks in the area.

Most of the woodland around Downe comprises oak and ash as the dominant species, with hazel coppice providing a prominent understorey. However, there is an extra facet that must have been distinctly different to Darwin, compared to Shropshire; the existence of beech. These especially occur on the chalky soil in the Downe countryside and there are plenty of places where one can see the shallow roots of the beech trees running along the tops of banks. One can't help but wonder, with these precarious foundations, how on earth their smooth, grey trunks and weight of shiny leaves manage to keep upright! Darwin mentions beeches growing near to Down House[18]: 'On the south side of Cudham wood a beech hedge has grown to Brobdignagian size, with several of the huge branches crossing each other and firmly grafted together.' Beeches are also referred to by Emma Darwin[19]: 'The terrace was sheltered from the north-east by a rough shaw of beeches and an undergrowth of sloes, travellers joy, service-trees and hawthorn'. Emma[20] also refers to the: '...gnarled old beeches good for children to climb...'

For me, one of the treats to find within a hedge or woodland is the Spindle. It is associated with ancient woodlands, but particularly those on calcareous soil. It is a tree that really stands out from everything else around it because of the colour of its fruit – florescent pink – and seed – orange . The square stem is unusual to see in nature too. During the 1860s Darwin studied spindle around Downe. In Shropshire, in his day, spindle was 'not very common'. His observations of spindle were important in demonstrating that within a species there are naturally occurring variants in reproductive forms, with hermaphrodite and male and female forms in existence. He saw that the amount of fruit and seeds borne by the different trees varied but that some trees consistently produced more fruit than others.

Darwin wrote[21] in 1877 'Thirteen bushes growing near one another in a hedge consisted of eight females quite destitute of pollen and of five hermaphrodites with well-developed anthers. In the autumn the eight females were well covered with fruit, excepting one, which bore only a moderate number. Of the five hermaphrodites, one bore a dozen or two fruits, and the remaining four bushes several dozen; but their number was as nothing compared with those on the female bushes, for a single branch...yielded more than any one of the hermaphrodite bushes.' He also wrote[22] '...We thus see that the female bushes differ somewhat in their degree of fertility, and the polleniferous ones in the most marked manner...This case appears to me very interesting as showing how gradually an hermaphrodite plant may be converted into a dioecious one.'

Woody species are not the only consideration when it comes to the character of a woodland or hedgerow; the ground flora is also a charismatic feature. It is so pleasurable welcoming in the Spring and witnessing the awakening of plants from the woodland floor. Some of these are what are known as 'ancient woodland indicator species'; they hold with them a sense of history as they 'indicate' the existence and stability of woodland cover since at least 1600 AD.

Ancient Woodland Vascular Plant Indicators for Shropshire (*)[23] and the contrasting 'indicator species' for Kent[24] are as follows:

Acer campestre Field maple

Adoxa moschatellina Moschatel

Agrimonia procera Fragrant agrimony

Agropyron caninum Bearded couch

*Allium ursinum Ramsons

Alnus glutinosa Alder

Anagallis minima Chaffweed

*Anemone nemorosa Wood anemone

Aquilegia vulgaris Columbine

*Blechnum spicant Hard fern

*Bromus benekenii Lesser hairy brome

Bromus ramosus Hairy brome

Calamagrostis epigejos Wood small reed

*Campanula trachelium Nettle-leaved bellflower

Cardamine bulbifera Coral root bittercress

Cardamine impatiens Narrow-leaved bittercress

*Carex laevigata Smooth-stalked sedge

Carex ovalis Oval sedge

*Carex pallescens Pale sedge

*Carex pendula Pendulous sedge

*Carex remota Remote sedge

*Carex strigosa Thin-spiked wood sedge

*Carex sylvatica Wood sedge

Carpinus betulus Hornbeam

Centaurium pulchellum Lesser centaury

Cephalanthera longifolia Narrow-leaved Helleborine

*Chrysosplenium alternifolium Alternate-leaved golden saxifrage

*Chrysosplenium oppossitifolium Opposite-leaved golden saxifrage

Circaea lutetiana Enchanters nightshade

Conopodium majus Pignut

Convallaria majalis Lily of the valley

Cordalis claviculata Climbing corydalis

Crataegus laevigata Midland hawthorn

Daphne laureola Spurge laurel

Dipsacus pilosus Small teasel

Dryopteris aemula Hay-scented buckler fern

Dryopteris pseudomas (D. affinis) Scaly male fern

Epipactis helleborine Broad-leaved helleborine

Epipactis leptochila Narrow-lipped helleborine

* *Epipactis phyllanthes* Green-flowered helleborine

Epipactis purpurata Purple helleborine

Equisetum sylvaticum Wood horsetail

Euonymus europaeus Spindle

Euphorbia amygdaloides Wood spurge

Festuca gigantea Giant fescue

Frangula alnus Alder buckthorn

Galium ordratum Woodruff

Gnaphalium sylvaticum Heath cudweed

Helleborus foetidus Stinking hellebore

Helleborus viridis Green hellebore

Holcus mollis Creeping soft grass

Hyacinthoides non-scripta Bluebell

Hypericum androsaemum Tutsan

Hypericum maculatum Imperforate St. John's Wort

Hypericum montanum Pale St. John's Wort

Ilex aquifolium Holly

Iris foetidissima Stinking iris

Lamiastrum galeobdolon Yellow archangel

Lathraea squamaria Toothwort

Lathyrus montanus Wood vetch

Lathyrus sylvestris Narrow-leaved everlasting pea

Luzula forsteri Southern woodrush

Luzula pilosa Hairy woodrush

Luzula sylvatica Great woodrush

Lysimachia nemorum Yellow pimpernel

Malus sylvestris Crab apple

* *Melampyrum pratense* Cow wheat

Melica uniflora Wood melick

Milium effusum Wood millet

Monotropa hypopitys Yellow bird's nest

Naricissus pseudonarcissus Wild daffodil

Neottia nidus-avis Birds nest orchid

Ophrys insectifera Fly orchid

Orchis mascula Early purple orchid

Orchis purpurea Lady orchid

Oxalis acetosella Wood sorrel

Paris quadrifolia Herb paris

Phyllitis scolopendrium Harts tongue fern

Pimpinella major Greater burnet saxifrage

Platanthera bifolia Lesser butterfly orchid

Platanthera chlorantha Greater butterfly orchid

Poa nemoralis Wood meadow grass

Polygonatum multiflorum Common solomon's seal

Polygonum dumetorum Copse bindweed

Polypodium vulgare Common polypody

Polystichum aculeatum Hard shield fern

Polyystichum setiferum Soft shield fern

Populus tremula Aspen

Primula vulgaris Primrose

Prunus avium Cherry

Pyrus communis Wild pear

Quercus petraea Sessile oak

Radiola linoides Allseed

Ranunculus auricomus Goldilocks buttercup

Rhamnus cartharticus Buckthorn

Ribes nigrum Black currant

Rosa arvensis Field rose

Ruscus aculeatus Butcher's broom

Sanicula europea Sanicle

Scirpus sylvaticus Wood club rush

Scrophularia nodosa Common figwort

Scutellaria minor Lesser skullcap

Sedum telephium Orpine

Serratula tinctoria Sawwort

Solidago virgaurea Goldenrod

Sorbus aria Whitebeam

Sorbus aucuparia Rowan

Sorbus torminalis Wild service tree

Stachys officinalis Betony

Stellaria neglecta Greater chickweed

Thelypteris oreopteris (Oreopteris limbosperma) Lemon-scented fern

Tilia cordata Small leaved lime

Ulmus glabra Wych elm

Vaccinium myrttillus Bilberry

Valeriana dioica Marsh valerian

*Veronica montana Wood speedwell

*Viburnum opulus Guelder rose

*Vicia sylvatica Wood vetch

Viola odorata Sweet violet

**Viola reichenbachiana* Early dog violet

Wahlenbergia hederacea Ivy-leaved bellflower

* As well as those asterixed above, Shropshire species include: *Moehringia trinervia* (Three-nerved sandwort), *Dryopteris carthusiana* (Narrow Buckler-fern), *Elymus caninus* (Bearded couch), *Potentilla sterilis* (Barren strawberry), *Prunus avium* (Wild cherry), *Taxus baccata* (Yew), *Tilia platyphyllos* (Large leaved lime), *Fragaria vesca* (Wild Strawberry), *Geum rivale* (Water Avens), *Cornus sanguinea* (Dogwood), *Mercurialis perennis* (Dog's Mercury), *Geranium sylvaticum* (Wood Crane's-bill), *Myosotis sylvatica* (Wood Forget-me-not), *Campanula latifolia* (Great Bellflower), *Arum maculatum* (Lords and Ladies), *Festuca altissima* (Wood Fescue), *Melica nutans* (Mountain Melick), *Bromopsis ramosa* (Wood Brome), *Hordelymus europaeus* (Wood Barley), *Gagea lutea* (Yellow Star-of-Bethlehem), *Listera ovata* (Twayblade).

Sir John Lubbock (of High Elms Estate, Downe, and Darwin's friend)[25] highlighted the species supported through the coppice cycle:

'When the copse is first cut there is a wonderful outburst of wild wood-flowers, anemones, primroses, cowslips, bluebells, stitchwort, bugle, yellow archangel, woodspurge and many others. Attached to this phase are many butterflies, moths and other insects, but there is not yet enough corn for birds, or shelter for their nests. They begin to increase about their third year of the cycle. The flowers become taller, and are less numerous, still the copse is at the height of its interest and beauty. Nightingales,

blackcaps, titmice, willow wrens and other warblers find convenient nesting places. Year by year the beech and hazel and ash shoots grow longer,
the sunlight is more and more excluded and gives place to a soft gloom.
The flowers become fewer, paler and weedier; the small birds draw off to
the edges of the wood...Then come the woodcutters and the cycle begins
again'.

Darwin[26] wrote in 1844: 'The first period of vegetation and the banks are
clothed with pale blue violets to an extent I have never see equalled and
with Primroses. A few days later some of the copses were beautifully en-
livened by *Ranunculus auricomus*, wood anemones and a white *Stellaria*.
Subsequently large areas were brilliantly blue with blue bells. The flowers
here are very beautiful and the number of flowers, together with the darkness of the blue of the common little *Polygala* almost equalled it to an
alpine Gentian'. Indeed: Bluebells are a beautiful rich blue with a delicate
scent; Wood anemone has a flower like a daisy that opens and shuts in the
sunshine; Yellow archangel has a flower just like the statuesque angel in a
church; Moschatel with four faces giving rise to its name the 'Town Hall
Clock'; Wild strawberry with its simple white flowers and yellow centre
transform into strawberries all spring and summer; Dog's mercury provides a bright green covering across the woodland floor; woodruff has
whorls of leaves and a cluster of white flowers, Greater stitchwort comple-
ments the others as *Gypsophila* does in floral bouquets.

The white Wood sorrel, with leaves like clover, caught Darwin's attention [27]: 'It is an interesting fact in relation to our present subject that, as
Prof Batalin informs us in a letter, dated February, 1879, the leaflets of
Oxalis acetosella may be daily exposed to the sun during many weeks, and
they do not suffer if they are allowed to depress themselves; but if this be
prevented, they lose their colour and wither in two or three days. Yet the
duration of a leaf is about two months, when subjected only to diffused
light; and in this case the leaflets never sink downwards during the day.'

He also wrote: 'As the...downward movements of those of *Oxalis*, have
been proved to be highly beneficial...when subjected to bright sunshine,

it seems probable that they have been acquired for the special purpose of avoiding too intense an illumination.'[28]

One of the more curious plants that grows in ancient woodland is the toothwort, *Lathrea squamaria*, and this is plentiful in the woods around Downe. Darwin observed[29]: 'The flower stem...which is destitute of true leaves, breaks through the ground as an arch...the passage...cannot fail to be greatly facilitated by the extraordinary quantity of water secreted at this period of the year by the subterranean scale-like leaves; not that there is any reason to suppose that the secretion is a special adaptation for this purpose; it probably follows from the great quantity of sap absorbed in the early spring by the parasitic roots.' Leighton[30] writes of its distribution in Shropshire: 'Woods and coppices, parasistic on the roots of hazel, ash and other trees; rare.'

The history of the woodland at Downe Scout Activity Centre – a fragment of Darwin's 'Big Woods' – is quite clearly reflected in the trees and other vegetation present on the site today. Much of the woodland appears ancient in character and is listed in the '*London Inventory of Ancient Woodlands in Greater London*'. Though there have been changes on site, such as replanting with conifers and the development of scrub and secondary woodland, 1871 maps of the site show parts of the wood with exactly the same boundaries, such as Bird House Wood. Bird House Wood and adjacent Bromley Croft have a suite of ground flora associated with ancient woodland. I remember coming across a lone early purple orchid when first coming to Bromley. The main canopy consists of ash, and sub-dominant species of rowan, oak and sweet chestnut with an understorey of hazel, elder and holly. Mature oak trees are scattered throughout this woodland. The eastern edge of this woodland contains old pollarded beech trees. The other woody species present on site are Birch, Spindle, Privet, Dogwood, Hawthorn, Field maple, Yew, Whitebeam, Crab apple, Sycamore, Lime, Wild Cherry and Blackthorn, so all in all a very diverse woodland. You can get a sense of the ground flora on this site by visualis-ing the following species that I recorded with others in this wood:

White flowers:

Greater stitchwort (*Stellaria holostea*), Goose grass (*Galium aparine*), Hedge bedstraw (*Galium mollugo*), Woodruff (*Galium odoratum*), Wood anemone (*Anemone nemorosa*), Wood sorrel (*Oxalis acetosella*), Burnet saxifrage (*Pimpinella saxifrage*), Pignut (*Conopodium majus*) Cow parsley (*Anthriscus sylvestris*), Wild strawberry (*Fragaria vesca*), Three veined sandwort (*Moehringia trinervia*). Sanicle (*Sanicula europaea*), Bramble (*Rubus fruticosus*), Garlic mustard (*Alliaria petiolata*).

Yellow flowers:

Lesser celandine (*Ranunculus ficaria*), Goldilocks (*Ranunculus auricomus*), Yellow pimpernel (*Lysimachia nemorum*), Honeysuckle (*Lonicera periclynum*), Slender St John's-wort (*Hypericum pulchrum*), Yellow archangel (*Galeobdolon luteum*) , Herb bennet (*Geum urbanum*), Wall lettuce (*Mycelis muralis*).

Blue and purple flowers:

Common dog violet (*Viola riviniana*), Self heal (*Prunella vulgaris*), Bluebell (*Hyacinthoides non-scripta*), Wood speedwell (*Veronica montana*), Bugle (*Ajuga reptans*), Ground ivy (*Glechoma hederacea*), Sweet violet (*Viola odorata*), Germander speedwell (*Veronica chamaedrys*), Common figwort (*Scrophularia nodosa*).

Pink flowers:

Cuckoo flower (*Cardamine pratensis*), Field rose (*Rosa arvensis*), Foxglove (*Digitalis purpurea*), Hedge woundwort (*Stachys sylvatica*), Early purple orchid (*Orchis_mascula*), Broad leaved willowherb (*Epilobium montanum*), Enchanters nightshade (*Circaea lutetiana*), Cut leaved Cranesbill (*Geranium dissectum*).

Greenish flowers:

Wood spurge (*Euphorbia amygdaloides*), Wood dock (*Rumex sanguineus*), Dogs mercury (*Mercurialis perennis*), Lords and Ladies (*Arum macula-*

tum), Town hall clock (*Adoxa moschatellina*), Black bryony (*Tamus communis*), Ivy (*Hedera helix*).

Grasses & Sedges:
Giant Fescue (*Festuca gigantean*), Wood sedge (*Carex sylvatica*), *Melica uniflora* (Wood melick), Wood False Brome (*Brachypodium sylvaticum*), *Milium effusum* (Wood millet), Rough-stalked meadow grass (*Poa trivialis*), Hairy Brome (*Bromus ramosus*), Wood meadow grass (*Poa nemoralis*), creeping soft grass (*Holcus mollis*), Tufted Hair-grass (*Deschampsia caespitosa*).

Ferns:
Harts tongue (*Phyllitis scolopendrium*), Broad buckler fern (*Dryopteris dilatata*), Male fern (*Dryopteris filix-mas*), Golden male fern (*Dryopteris affinis*).

Some of the most spectacular tree specimens in the landscape around Downe include those within the parkland landscapes. Holwood House, house of First Baron Cranworth (owner from 1853–1868) and then Lord Derby was a place Darwin's family used to visit on many an occasion. During the medieval period the area was used as common land. Here there remain veteran oak trees which host a number of lichen species (some of the ninety found around Downe[31]) and would probably, if surveyed, uncover a wide range of invertebrate species, for which veteran trees are famed. The absence of grazing in recent times has meant the development of other trees in the vicinity of these veterans. It is quite an experience to duck under the branches of the tangled web of hawthorns and come across one of these magnificent oaks.

Another tree abundant at this site is the Horse Chestnut. Darwin puzzled over these trees. He wrote:[32]

'Why should we wonder at thousands of wasted male flowers when we see much waste of flowers of all kinds? I have also somewhere got some notes on the prodigious waste of insect life, by the sticky scales on the buds, the thousands, and all uselessly killed.'

He also wrote :[33]
'I examined flowers from 6 different trees at Holwood & in all it was clear that many male flowers considerably open before females & so lose their pollen uselessly. I conclude I may say a multitude of male pollen produced uselessly, at least the great number of such flowers are produced uselessly – Better say a vast amount of pollen wasted. Hooker says he has looked & confirms my account same in Maple. After careful examination I may say no difference in pollen of Hermaphrodite & Male flowers.'

The trees listed for Shropshire in Darwin's time[34] are similar to those around Downe, however Shropshire had a presence of box and juniper and various poplar trees, and there would appear to be many more species and varieties of elm and willow than I believe have ever been encountered at Downe. The 'Rare Plants of Shropshire' list[34] now shows juniper to be extinct in Shropshire. Junipers are referred to on Downe Bank by Francis [36] 'Another favourite place was "Orchis Bank," above the quiet Cudham valley, where fly- and musk-orchis grew among the junipers, and *Cephalanthera* and *Neottia* under the beech boughs; the little wood "Hangrove," just above this, he was also fond of, and here I remember his collecting grasses, when he took a fancy to make out the names of all the common kinds.' The specimens that occur nowadays on the site are believed to have been planted at some point in the last century. Box has never been known in recent times at Downe. Shropshire still remains one of the country's strongholds for black poplar.[37]

Woodlands, and other habitats, can actually be classed into communities of plants, dependent on the dominant tree and herbaceous species present. These are called National Vegetatation Classification (NVC) communities. It allows someone standing in a woodland in Shropshire or in

Downe to judge whether their woodlands are of similar character. There are 18 main woodland types and seven scrubs or underscrubs, most of which are divided further to give a total of 73 different sub-communities.

Just in 'Downe Bank and High Elms Site of Special Scientific Interest' we can identify: W14, which is Beech-Bramble woodland (none present in Shropshire[38]); *W10a, which is Pedunculate oak-Bracken-Bramble (present in Shropshire[39]); W12, which is Beech-Dogs Mercury woodland, Sanicle sub-community (none present in Shropshire[38]); *W8a/d, which are Ash-Field Maple-Dogs Mercury woodland Primrose-Ground Ivy sub-community and Ash-Field Maple-Dogs Mercury woodland Ivy sub-community (present in Shropshire, for example at Earls Hill and Harton Hollow)[38, 38a]; W13, which is Yew woodland, Whitebeam sub-community (none present in Shropshire[38]). At Downe Scout Activity Centre and West Kent Golf Course, the 'Big Woods' remnants also include community-type W10b/c (also present in Shropshire[38])

According to an old classification system developed by Peterken (1981)[39] in relation to 'stand types', we can find the following types of woodland present in Shropshire these days:[40]

Calcareous ash-wych elm woods – Blodwel Wood

Wet ash-wych elm woods – College Coppice

Calcareious ash-wych elm woods on dry and/or heavy soils – Tick Wood

Western valley ash-wych elm woods – Habberley Valley

Wet ash-maple woods – Incham Coppice

Dry ash-maple woods – Coats Wood, Wenlock Edge

Acid pedunculate oak-hazel-ash woods – Hargrove Wood

Southern calcareous hazel-ash woods – Sallow Coppice, Limekiln Wood

Acid sessile oak-hazel-ash woods – Saplins Wood

Sessile oak-ash-lime woods – Tick Wood

Acid sessile oak-lime woods – Hawthorn Dingle

Upland sessile oak woods – Clunton Coppice

Lowland sessile (and mixed) oak woods – Wyre Forest

Lowland pedunculate oak woods – Wyre Forest

Lowland pedunculate oak woods – Rough Marl

Valley alder woods on mineral soils – Thatchers Wood, Brook Coppice

Wet valley alder woods – White Mere, Sweat Mere

Bird cherry-alder woods – Flat Coppice, Plowden Wood

Invasive elm woods

Let's now turn our attention to hedgerows in Shropshire. There is no up to date estimate of the extent, longevity or richness of hedgerows in Shropshire. It is, however, obvious that they form an important element of the landscape. Initial local surveys undertaken by Church Stretton Community Wildlife Group[41] suggest that some 63% of hedgerows in their survey area are 'species rich'. Hedgerows in the area have been found to contain thirty different woody species, with hazel being the most frequent dominant species. However half the hedges have been found to be 'defunct', containing gaps a person could comfortably walk through, and only 18% contain mature trees. On the plus side, honeysuckle was found to be present in 27% of the hedges surveyed. I have investigated some hedgerows growing west of The Mount, in the bend of the River Severn. Maps reveal that the pattern of hedgerows which surround the grazed fields has not changed since Darwin's time. I found these hedgerows to mainly comprise hawthorn, though elder, holly, blackthorn, rowan, hazel, field maple and ash all make an appearance. The hedgerows had not been managed in recent times and so they had developed into wide thickets or gappy lines of trees.

We know that Darwin observed the abundance of hedgerows and studied some of the associated species around Downe, but he must also have noted the hedgerows in Shropshire because he writes in 'General Aspect' (1843):[42] 'The number of different kinds of bushes in the hedgerows, entwined by Traveller's joy and the two bryonies, is conspicuous, compared with the hedges of the northern counties.' Emma Darwin[43] writes of hedges in Downe: `...At the edge of the table land on which the village and house stand are steep valleys crowned at the top with old hedges & hedgerows very disorderly & picturesque & with enormous clusters of Clematis & blackberries and a great variety of yews, services &c...'

A hedgerow survey was undertaken around Downe in the noughties and I was involved in interpreting the results[44]. Over 200 hedges were recorded in the area and the vast majority were found to have been in existence 150 years before, so demonstrating that hedgerows were and continue to be an important element of Darwin's landscape. Earlier research showed that there had been a tendency for the hedgerows to have been derived from assarting of fields or potentially from the planting of hedgerows with young trees and shrubs obtained from local woods. Darwin noted one method for the colonisation of the hedges by plants:[45] 'Hedgerow planted by self years ago when I hired field...The following now sprung up in hedge – presumably the seeds having been brought by birds...' The additional evidence of longevity is provided by the existence of banks in association with two-thirds of the network.

It was found that there was an overwhelming tendency for hedgerows to be less than 200m in length and to be connected with one or two other hedgerows, so giving an indication of the density of fields with wooded boundaries. Almost the whole resource was found to provide cross-sectional areas of at least 3m² per hedgerow, illustrating appropriate (not too severe or frequent) cutting and therefore better provision of shelter for fauna, especially birds.

A greater proportion of hedgerows were found to be 'shrubby' and almost all the resource had gaps fewer than 10%. The hedgerow network was found to be composed of a wide range of tree and shrub species, with over fifty represented, the majority being native. Between five and six species of tree or shrub could be expected within a 30m length of hedgerow.

An average of three isolated standard trees per one hundred metre length of hedgerow was found to occur. A quarter of hedgerows were found to have ancient tree representatives of oak and ash in particular and these would have formed important 'isolated trees' in existence in the landscape in Darwin's time. The majority of hedgerows were found to have more than one metre of perennial herbaceous vegetation at their base. The ground flora associated with the hedgerows included more than 150 species. Grasses, especially Agrostis species, tended to dominate alongside ivy, bramble, nettle and dogs mercury. In addition, there was representation of a wide range of climbing plants across the hedgerow resource, some making only occasional appearance, such as hops and honeysuckle.

What was the abundance of climbing species in Darwin's Shropshire? Leighton[46] presented the following:

Rosa spinosissima Burnet leaved rose. Heaths etc rare

Rosa villosa Villous rose. Hedges etc; not uncommon

Rosa tomentosa Downy leaved rose. Hedges and thickets; not unfrequent

*Rosa rubiginosa True sweet briar. Hedges etc. rare

*Rosa canina Common dog rose. Thickets, hedges etc; very common

Rubus schleicheri Schleicher's bramble. Hedges etc

R. dumetorum. Hedges etc. common

R. caesius Dewberry. Ditches, borders of fields, hedges etc frequent

R. saxatilis Stone bramble. Stony, mountainous places, rare

R. idaeus Raspberry. Moist margins of woods and moist heaths, frequent

R. suberectus Upright bramble. Somewhat boggy heaths, sides of streams etc rare

R. plicatus Plaited leaved bramble. Moist boggy places, rare

R. fissus Cleft bramble. Moist boggy places; rare

R. affinus. Waste places and hedges; not uncommon

R. rhamnifolius Buckthorn leaved bramble. Hedges, thickets etc; common

R. discolour Discoloured bramble. Hedges, thickets etc, frequent

R. fruiticosus Shrubby bramble. Hedges and thickets, frequent

R. carpinifolius Hornbeam-leaved bramble. Hedges, thickets etc

R. leucostachys White spiked bramble. Hedge, thickets etc. frequent

R. vulgaris Common bramble. Wastes, thickets etc.

R. villicaulis Hairy stemmed bramble. Hedges, woods etc, not very common

R. echinatus Echinate bramble. Thickets etc, not common

R. fusco-ater Brownish-black bramble. Woods etc.

R. pallidus Pale bramble. Woods, thickets etc. frequent

R. radula Hairy bramble. Hedges, thickets etc. frequent

R. leightoni Leighton's bramble. Hedge in Shrewsbury

R. kohleri Kohler's bramble. Wastes, thickets etc; not common

Rosa arvensis Trailing dog rose. Woods, hedges, thickets etc. common

*Clematis vitalba Travellers Joy. Hedges, rare

*Bryonia dioica Red berried bryony. Thickets and hedges, frequent

*Humulus lupulus Hop. Hedges; frequent; apparently wild

*Tamus communis Black bryony. Hedges and thickets; frequent

*Solanum dulcamara. Woody nightshade. Moist hedges and thickets; common

*Honeysuckle. Woods, hedges and thickets; frequent

*Hedera helix. An evergreen of excessive elegance and an universal favourite, ever enfolding our hedges, rocks, ruins and trunks of trees, in a rich entangled mantle of verdure and beauty

* Climbing species found in Downe hedgerows (2008) Also present were *Convolvulus arvensis, Clematis montana, Calystegia sepium,* cleavers, *Rose sp, Rosa arvensis.*

Darwin observed many of the climbing species around Downe and undertook more intensive studies on them at his home. For black bryony he noted[47] 'Tamus communis (Dioscoreaceæ). A young shoot from a potted tuber placed in the greenhouse; follows the sun;[48] A plant placed in a room; a semicircle was performed in travelling from the light in 1 h. 33 m., in travelling to the light in 1 h. 13 m.: difference of rate 20 m.';[49] 'After a tendril has once firmly coiled itself round a stick, it is difficult to imagine of what use the adhesive cellular layer can be. Owing to the spiral contraction which soon ensues, the tendrils were never able to remain, excepting in one instance, in contact with a thick post or a nearly flat surface; if they had quickly become attached by means of the adhesive layer, this would evidently have been of service to the plant.

For white bryony Darwin noted:[50] 'The tendrils of *Bryonia dioica*...are sensitive and revolve.' And again: 'Though the tendril is highly flexible, and though the extremity travels, under favourable circumstances, at about the rate of an inch in two minutes and a quarter, yet its sensitiveness to contact is so great that it hardly ever fails to seize a thin stick placed in its path.' He wrote:[51] 'I have more than once gone on purpose during a gale to watch a Bryony growing in an exposed hedge...the Bryony safely rode out the gale, like a ship with two anchors down...'

For wild clematis he wrote[52] '*Clematis vitalba* – I saw many proofs that the petioles of plants growing naturally are excited to movement by very slight pressure. For instance, I found petioles which had clasped thin withered blades of grass, the soft young leaves of a maple, and the lateral flower-peduncles of the quaking-grass or *Briza*: the latter are only about as thick as a hair from a man's beard, but they were completely surrounded and clasped. The petioles of a leaf, so young that none of the leaflets had expanded, had partially seized on a twig. The petioles of almost every old leaf, even when unattached to any object, are much convoluted; but this is owing to their having come, whilst young, into contact during several hours with some object subsequently removed...When winter comes on, the blades of the leaves of *C.vitalba* drop off; but the petioles...remain, sometimes during two seasons, attached to the branches; and, being con-voluted, they curiously resemble true tendrils,...'

For the woody nightshade (Bittersweet) Darwin wrote[53]: 'The *Solanum dulcamara*, as we shall presently see, can twine only round such stems as are both thin and flexible. Most twining plants apparently are adapted to ascend supports of different thicknesses. Our English twiners, as far as I have seen, never twine round trees, excepting the Honeysuckle (*Lonicera periclymenum*), which I have observed twining up a young beech-tree nearly 4 1/2 inches in diameter.' He also wrote:[54] 'Solanum dulcamara one of the feeblest and poorest of twiners: it may often be seen growing as an upright bush, and when growing in the midst of a thicket merely scrambles up between the branches without twining'.

Darwin writes of ivy:[55] 'Root-climbers, as far as I have seen, namely, the Ivy (*Hedera helix*), *Ficus repens*, and *F. barbatus*, have no power of movement, not even from the light to the dark.'

Darwin comments on bramble in his investigations too. He wrote:[56] 'Linne described the fruticose bramble as a species, under name of Rubus fruticosus; but various modern botanists make out 50 to 100 supposed species of Bramble which others call varieties of *R. fruticosus*, & others again group into a small number of species, say half a dozen. To the naturalist who looks at species as not essentially differing from varieties, being only more permanent, with the connecting links extinct, the occasional blending by intermedial forms of two or more apparently distinct species, will not be wonderful; indeed the wonder is to us, with our restricted notions of the lapse of time, that many more cases are not on record.'

You truly get an appreciation of what is growing in hedgerows when you get down to ground level. One of the traditional ways of managing hedgerows is by hedgelaying, where you have to work close to the ground and work intimately with the plants they contain. This is a process whereby a tree or 'pleacher' is cut two-thirds of the way through its base and then bent over and woven between wooden stakes gleaned from woodland management. A number of the hedgerows around Downe provide evidence of this ancient craft, with pleachers whose side branches have long since grown to tree-size in their own right being present. This craft, which I taught others at Downe, has been reinstated in the area in recent decades. It was good to see this practice being undertaken in the Shropshire countryside too.

A BIT OF BOTANISING

We know that Darwin appreciated the flowers growing in and around his garden at The Mount. Darwin recollects[1] broom in the garden at The Mount, following receipt of a letter from Hooker in 1845. Hooker stated: 'The reappearance of plants in certain situations is a curious phenomena of which instances are multiplying daily in this neighbourhood: there are doubtless series of seeds in some grounds lying dormant but not dead: what a curious principle life must be & what an uncomfortable abode it must often have. Cutting open rail-ways causes a change of vegetation in two ways, by turning up buried live seeds, & by affording space & protection for the growth of transported seeds: so that it is often very difficult to determine to which cause the appearance or superabundance of a plant is attributable...The Kings Park was dug up in about 1650...wherever the cuts were made for encampments, the broom appeared, but in a year or two disappeared. In rebellion of 1745, it was again encamped upon & again Broom came up & disappeared: it was afterwards ploughed & immediately became covered with Broom, which has all for the 3d time vanished.' Darwin responded:

'Very curious the case of the broom; I can tell you something analogous on a small scale: my Father when he built his house sowed many broom-seed, on a wild bank which did not come up, owing, as it was thought, to much earth having been thrown over them: about 35 years afterwards, in cutting a terrace, all this earth was thrown up, & now the bank is one mass of broom.'

So what of Darwin's other 'botanising', as his sister put it? There are no records of the species of plants with which Darwin dabbled as a youngster in Shropshire. However, regarding the sorts of plants Darwin would have come across within a five mile radius of Shrewsbury[2], we are lucky enough to have an account:

Clematis vitalba Traveller's Joy

Thalictrum flavum Yellow Meadow Rue

Anemone nemorosa Wood anemone

Ranunculus aquatilis Common water crowfoot

R. hederaceous Ivy leaved water crowfoot

R. ficaria Lesser celandine

R. flammula Lesser spearwort

R. lingua Greater spearwort

R. auticomus A horticultural buttercup

R. acris Meadow buttercup

R. repens Creeping buttercup

R. bulbous Bulbous buttercup

R. hirsutus Hairy crowfoot

R. parviflorus Small flower buttercup

R. arvensis Corn buttercup

Caltha palustris Marsh marigold

Aquila vulgaris Columbine

Berberis vulgaris Barberry

Nymphaea alba White water lily

Nuphar lutea Yellow water lily

Papaver argemone Long prickly-head poppy

P. dubium Long headed poppy

P. rhoeas Field poppy

Chlelidonium majus Greater celandine

Corydalis clariculata Climbing corydalis

Fumaris capreolata A fumatory

F. officinalis Common fumatory

Coronopus ruellii Common wart-cress

Thlaspi arvense Field penny cress

Capsella bursa-pastoris Shepherd's purse

Tiesdalis nudicaulis

Lepidium smithii Purple-anther field pepperweed

L. campestre Field pepperweed

Cochlearia polymorhpha A brassica

C. danica Danish scurvygrass

Armoracia rusticana Horseradish

Subularia aquatica Water awlwort

Draba verna Whitlow grass or Shadflower

Cardamine amara Large bittercress

C. pratensis Cuckoo flower

C. hirsute Hairy bittercress

Arabis thaliana Mouse ear cress

Turritis glabra Tower mustard

Barbarea vulgaris Bittercress

Nasturtium officinale Watercress

N. terrestre Marsh yellow cress

N. sylvestre Creeping yellow cress

Sisymbrium officinale Hedge mustard

S. sophia Flixweed

Erysimum alliaria Garlic mustard

Cheiranthus cheiri Wallflower

Brassica polymorpha Turnip

Sinapsis nigra Black mustard

S. arvensis Field mustard

S. alba White mustard

S. tenuifolia A brassica

Reseda luteola Dyer's weed

Helianthemum vulgare Rockrose

Viola palustris Marsh violet

V. odorata Sweet violet

V. hirta Hairy violet

V. canina Heath dog violet

V. tricolour Heartease

V. arvensis Field pansy

Drosera rotundifolia Round leaved sundew

D. intermedia Oblong leaved sundew

Polygala vulgaris Common milkwort

Elatine hexandra Six stamened waterwort

Dianthus plumarins Wild pink

D. deltoids Maiden pink

Saponaria officinalis Soapwort

Silene inflate Bladder campion

Lychnis flos-cuculi Ragged robin

L. diurnal Pink campion

L. vespertina Sticky cockle

L. githago Common corncockle

Moenchia erecta Upright chickweed

Sagina apetala Annual pearlwort

S. procumbens Birdeye pearlwort

Spergula arvensis Corn spurrey

Arenaria serpyllifolia Thyme-leaved sandwort

A. tennifolia

Stellaria media Chickweed

S. holostea Greater stitchwort

S. glauca Marsh stitchwort

S. uliginosa Bog stitchwort

Cerastium aquaticum Water chickweed

C. glomeratum Sticky mouse ear chickweed

C. trivale (modern equivalent *Cerastium fontanum ssp. triviale*) Mouse-ear chickweed

C. semidecandrum Little Mouse-ear

C. arvense Field chickweed

Linum usitatissimum Common flax

L. catharticum Fairy flax

Malva moschata Musk mallow

M. sylvestris Common mallow

M. rotundifolia Round leaved mallow

Hypericum perforatum Perforate St. John's wort

H. quadrangulum A St. John's wort

H. humifusum Trailing St. John's wort

H. pulchrum Slender St. John's wort

H. hirsutum Hairy St. John's wort

H. elodes Marsh St. John's wort

Acer campestris Field maple

A. pseudo-platanus Sycamore

Erodium cicutarium Common storksbill

Geranium pratense Meadow cranesbill

G. pyrenaicum Hedgerow geranium

G. pusillum Small flowered cranesbill

G. molle Dovesfoot cranesbill

G. dissectum Cut-leaved cranesbill

G. lumbinum (modern equivalent *Geranium columbinum*) Long-stalked Crane's-bill

G. lucidum Shining cranesbill

G. robertianum Herb robert

Oxalis acetosella Wood sorrel

Euonymus europaeus Spindle

Rhamus frangula Alder buckthorn

Sarothamnus scoparius Broom

Ulex europaeus Gorse

U. nanus Dwarf gorse

Genista tinctoria Dyer's broom

G. anglica Petty whin

Ononsis arvensis

O. spinosa Spiny restharrow

Anthyllis vulneraria Kidney vetch

Medicago sativa Lucerne

M. lupulina Black medick

Trifolium repens White clover

T. pratense Red clover

T. medium Zigzag clover

T. arvense Haresfoot clover

T. striatum Knotted clover

T. procumbens Hop clover

T. filiforme Slender trefoil

Lotus corniculatus Birds foot trefoil

L. major (modern equivalent *Lotus pedunculatus*) Greater Bird's-foot Trefoil or Marsh Bird's-foot Trefoil

Ornithopus perpusillus Birds foot

Vicia sylvatica Wood vetch

V. cracca Tufted vetch

V. sativa Common vetch

V. sepium Bush vetch

V. hirsute Hairy tare

V. tetrasperme (modern equivalent *Vicia tetrasperma*) Smooth Tare

Lathyrus pratensis Meadow vetchling

L. sylvestris Narrow leaved everlasting pea

Orobus tuberosus Bitter vetch

Prunus spinosa Blackthorn

P. cerasus Wild cherry

Spiraea ulmaria Meadow sweet

Geum urbanum Herb bennet

G. rivale Water avens

Potentilla anserine Silverweed

P. argentea Hoary cinquefoil

P. reptans Creeping cinquefoil

P. tormentilla Common tormentil

P. fragariastrum Barren strawberry

Comarum palustre Marsh cinquefoil

Fragaris vesca Wild strawberry

Rubus fruticosus Bramble

R. idaeus Raspberry

Rosa villosa Apple rose

R. canina Dog rose

R. arvensis Field rose

Agrimonia eupatoria Agrimony

Alchemilla vulgaris Common lady's mantle

A. arvensis Field lady's mantle

Crataegus oxycanthus Hawthorn

Pyrus malus Crab apple

P. aucuparia Rowan

Epilobium hirsutum Great willowherb

E. parviflorum Small flowered hairy willowherb

E. montanum Broad leaved willowherb

E. palustre Marsh willowherb

E. tetragonum Square stalked willowherb

Myriophyllum spicatum Eurasian water milfoil

M. alterniflorum Alternate flowered milfoil

Callitriche verna Common water starwort

C. platycarpa Various leaved water starwort

C. hamulata Intermediate water starwort

Ceratophyllum aquaticum Rigid hornwort

Lythrum salicaria Purple loosestrife

Peplis portula Water purslane

Bryonia dioica White bryony

Montia fontana Water blinks

Herniaria vulgaris (modern equivalent *Herniaria glabra*) Smooth rupturewort

Scleranthus annus Annual knawel

Ribes nigrum Blackcurrant

Sedum telephium Orpine

S. acre Goldmoss stonecrop

S. reflexum Reflexed stonecrop

S. forsterianum

Sempervivum tectorum Common houseleek

Cotyledon umbilicus Wall pennywort

Saxifraga granulate Meadow saxifrage

S. tridactylites Rue-leaved saxifrage

Chrysosplenium oppositifolium Opposite leaved golden saxifrage

C. alternifolium Alternate leaved golden saxifrage

Adoxa moschatellina Moschatel

Hedera helix Ivy

Cornus sanguinea Dogwood

Hydrocotyle vulgaris Marsh pennywort

Sanicula europaea Sanicle

Conium maculatum Hemlock

Smyrnium olusatrum Alexander

Cicuta virosa Cowbane

Helosciadium nodiflorum Fool's watercress

H. innundatum (modern equivalent *Apium inundatum*) Lesser Marshwort

Aegopodium podagraria Ground elder

Bunium flexuosum Pignut

Pimpinella saxifrage Burnet saxifrage

Sium angustifolium Lesser water parsnip

Oenanthe fistulosa Tubular water dropwort

O. crocata Hemlock water dropwort

O. phellandrium Water fennel

Aethusa cynapium Fools parsley

Silaurs pratensis (modern equivalent unidentifable)

Angelica sylvestris Wild angelica

Heracleum sphondylium Hogweed

Daucus carota Wild carrot

Torilis anthriscus Upright hedge parsley

T. infesta Spreading hedge parsley

T. nodosa Knotted hedge parsley

Scandix pectin-veneris Shepherd's needle

Anthriscus vulgaris Chervil

A. sylvestris Cow parsley

Chaerophyllum temulum Rough chervil

Viscum album Mistletoe

Sambucus nigra Elder

S. ebulus Dwarf elder

Viburnum opulus Guelder rose

Lonicera periclymenum Honeysuckle

Galium verum Lady's bedstraw

G. cruciatum (modern equivalent *Cruciata laevipes*) Crosswort

G. palustre Marsh bedstraw

G. saxatile Heath bedstraw

G. erectum (modern equivalent *Galium album*) White bedstraw

G. aparine Goosegrass

Cherardia arvensis (modern equivalent *Sherardia arvensis*) Field Madder

Asperula odorata Sweet woodruff

Valeriana dioica Common valerian

V. officinalis Valerian

Valerianella olitoria Common corn salad

V. dentate Narrow fruited corn salad

Dipsacus sylvestris Teasal

D. pilosus Small teasal

Scabiosa succisa Devil's bit scabious

S. columbaria Small scabious

Knautia arvensis Field scabious

Tragopogon pratensis Goatsbeard

Picris hieracioides Hawkweed oxtongue

Leontodon hirtus (modern equivalent *Leontodon hispidus*) Rough Hawkbit

L. hispidus Rough hawkbit

L. autumnalis Autumn hawkbit

Hypochoeris glabra Smooth cats ear

H. radicata Wall lettuce

Lactuca muralis Wall lettuce

Sonchus arvensis Field sow thistle

S. asper Prickly sow thistle

S.. oleraceus Common sow thistle

Crepis virens Hawksbeard

Hieracium pilosella Mouse ear hawkweed

H. murorum Wll hawkweed

H. sylvaticum Wood hawkweed

H. boreale (a *Hieracium* species)

Taraxacum officinale Dandelion

Lapsana communis Nipplewort

Cichonium intybus Chicory

Artium lappa Greater burdock

Carduus nutans Musk thistle

C. crispus Welted thistle

C. lanceolatus Spear thistle

C. palustris Marsh thistle

C. arvensis Perennial thistle

Onopordum acanthium Cotton thistle

Carlina vulgaris Dwarf carline thistle

Centauria nigra Common knapweed

C. cyanus Cornflower

C. scabiosa Greater knapweed

Bidens cernua Nodding bur marigold

B. tripartite Trifid bur marigold

Eupatorium cannabinum Hemp agrimony

Artemesia absinthium Wormwood

A. vulgaris Mugwort

Gnaphalium uliginosum Marsh cudweed

Filago minima Small cudweed

F. germanica Common cudweed

Petasites vulgaris Common butterbur

Solidago virgaurea European goldenrod

Senecio vulgaris Common groundsel

S. sylvaticus Woodland ragwort

S. erucifolius Hoary ragwort

S. jacobaea Common ragwort

S. aquaticus Marsh ragwort

Inula conyza Ploughman's spikenard

I. dysenterica Common fleabane

Bellis perennis Common daisy

Chrysanthemum leucanthemum Oxeye Daisy

C. parthenium Feverfew

C. tanacetum Feverfew (modern equivalent *Tanacetum parthenium*)

C. inodorum (modern equivalent *Tripleurospermum inodorum*) Scentless mayweed

C. chamomilla Chamomile

Anthemis nobilis Perennial chamomile

A. arvensis Corn chamomile

A. cotula Stinking chamomile

Achillea ptarmica Sneezewort

A. millefolium Yarrow

Campanula rotundifolia Harebell

C. patula Spreading bellflower

C. trachelium Nettle-leved bellflower

Jasione montana Sheep's bit scabious

Lobelia dortmanna Water lobelia

Erica tetralix Cross leaved heath

E. cineria Bell heather

Calluna vulgaris Heather

Vaccinium oxycoccus Cranberry

Ilex aquifolium Holly

Fraxinus excelsior Ash

Vinca major Greater periwinkle

V. minor Lesser periwinkle

Erythraea centaurium Centaury

Chlora perfoliata Perfoliate yellow wort

Convolvulus arvensis Field bindweed

C. sepium Bindweed

Hyoscyamus nigra Black henbane

Solanum nigrum Black nightshade

S. dulcamara Woody nightshade

Verbascum thapsus Great mullein

Veronica arvensis Wall speedwell

V. serpyllifolia Thyme leaved speedwell

V. scutellata Marsh speedwell

V. anagallis Water speedwell

V. beccabunga Brooklime

V. officinalis Heath speedwell

V. montana Wood speedwell

V. chamaedrys Germander speedwell

V. hederifolia Ivy leaved speedwell

V. agrestis Green field speedwell

V. polita Grey field speedwell

V. buxbaumii Common field speedwell

Euphrasia officinalis An eyebright

E. odontites An eyebright

Rhinanthus crist-galli Yellow rattle

Melamphyrum pratense Common cow wheat

M. sylvaticum Small cow wheat

Pedicularis palustris Marsh lousewort

P. sylvatica Lousewort

Scrophularia nodosa Green figwort

S. aquatica Water figwort

Digitalis perpurea Foxglove

Antirrhinum majus Snapdragon

Linaria cymbalaria Ivy leaved toadflax

L. elatine (modern equivalent *Kickxia elatine*) Sharp-leaved fluellin

L. vulgaris Common toadflax

Limosella aquatica Mudwort

Orobanche rapum Greater broomrape

Lathraea squamaria Toothwort

Verbena officinalis Common vervain

Salvia verbenaca Wild clary

Lycopus europaeus Gypsywort

Mentha rotundifolia Round leaved mint

M. piperita Peppermint

M. aquatica Water mint

M. sativa Sandalwood peppermint

M. arvensis Wild mint

Thymus serpyllum Wild thyme

Calamintha nepeta Lesser calamint

C. officinalis Calamint

C. clinopodium Wild basil

Teucrium scorodonia Wood sage

Ajuga reptans Bugle

Ballota nigra Black horehound

Lamium galeobdolon Yellow archangel

L. album White deadnettle

L. amplexicaule Henbit deadnettle

L. purpureum Red deadnettle

Galeopsis ladanum Broadleaved hempnettle

G. tetrahit Common hempnettle

G. versicolor (modern equivalent *Galeopsis speciosa*) Large-flowered Hemp-nettle

Stachys betonica Betony

S. palustris Marsh woundwort

S. sylvatica Hedge woundwort

S. arvensis Field woundwort

Nepeta glechoma Ground ivy

Prunella vulgaris Self heal

Scutellaria galericulata Common skullcap

S. minor Lesser skullcap

Myosotis palustris Water forget-me-not

M. caespitose

M. sylvatica Wood forget-me-not

M. arvensis Field forget-me-not

M. collina (modern equivalent *Myosotis ramosissima*) Early Forget-me-not

M. versicolor Changing forget-me-not

Lithospermum officinale Common gromwell

L. arvense Field gromwell

Symphytum officinale Comfrey

Borago officinalis Borage

Lycopsis arvensis Wild bugloss

Cynoglossum officinale Hound's tongue

Echium vulgare Vipers bugloss

Pinguicula vulgaris Common butterwort

Untricularia vulgaris Common bladderwort

U. minor Lesser bladderwort

Primula vulgaris Primrose

P. veris Cowslip

Hottonia palustris Water violet

Lysimachia vulgaris Yellow loosestrife

L. nemorum Yellow pimpernel

Anagallis arvensis Scarlet pimpernel

A. tenella Bog pimpernel

Plantago major Greater plantain

P. lanceolata Ribwort plantain

P. coronopus Buckshorn plantain

Litorella lacustris Shoreweed

Chenopodium polyspermum Many seeded goosefoot

C. murale Green fat hen

C. hybridum Maple-leaf goosefoot

C. album White goosefoot

C. bonus-henricus Good King Henry

Atriplex patula Common orache

A. hastate (modern equivalent *Atriplex prostrata*) Spear-leaved Orache

Polygonum bistorta Greater bistort

P. amphibium Water knotweed

P. persicaria Spotted ladysthumb

P. lapathifolium (modern equivalent *Persicaria lapathifolia*) Pale-flowered persicaria or Pale smartweed

P. hydropiper Water pepper

P. aviculare

P. convolvulus (modern equivalent *Fallopia convolulus*) Black-bindweed or Wild buckwheat

Rumex hydrolapthum

R. crispus Curled dock

R. aquaticus Scottish dock

R. pratensis (modern equivalent *Rumex x pratensis*) A Hybrid Dock

R. obtusifolius Broadleaved dock

R. sanguineus Bloody dock

R. conglomerates Green dock

R. maritimus Seashore dock

R. palustris Marsh dock

R. acetosa Common sorrel

R. acetosella Sheeps sorrel

Empetrum nigrum Crowberry

Euphorbia helioscopia Sun spurge

E. exigua Dwarf spurge

E. peplus Petty spurge

E. amygdaloides Wood spurge

Mercurialis perennis Dogs mercury

M. annua Annual mercury

Urtica urens Annual nettle

U. dioica Stinging nettle

Parientaria officinalis Pellitory of the wall

Humulus lupulus Hop

Iris foetidissima Stinking iris

I. pseudacoms Yellow flag iris

Crocus vernus Spring crocus

Narcissus pseudo-narcissus Wild daffodil

Alium vineale Wild garlic

A. ursinum Ramsons garlic

Hyacinthus non-scriptus Bluebell

Narthecium ossifragum Bog asphodel

Ruscus aculeatus Butcher's broom

Tamus communis Black bryony

Colchinum autumnale Autumn crocus

Hydrocharis morsus-ranae Frogbit

Alisma plantago Water plantain

A. ranunculoides (modern equivalent *Baldellia ranuculoides*) Lesser Water-plantain

A. nutans (modern equivalent *Luronium natans*) Floating Water-plantain

Sagittaria sagittifolia Arrowhead

Butomus umbelletus Flowering rush

Triglochin palustris Marsh arrowgrass

Potomogeton pectinatum Fennel pondweed

P. pusillus Lesser pondweed

P. crispus Curly-leaved pondweed

P. perfoliatus Perfoliate pondweed

P. proteus (modern equivalent *Potomogeton lucens*) Shining Pondweed

P. heterophyllus (modern equivalent *Potomogeton gramineus*) Various leaved pond weed

P. rufescens (modern equivalent *Potomogeton alpinus*) Reddish pond weed

P. natans Broadleaved pondweed

P. oblongus Bog pondweed

Zannichellia palustris Horned pondweed

Lemna minor Lesser duckweed

L. polyrhiza Greater duckweed

L. trisulca Ivy leaved duckweed

Arum maculatum Cuckoo pint

Sparganium natans Small burreed

S. simplex Burreed (modern equivalent *Sparganium emersum*)

S. ramosum

Thypha latifolia Reedmace

T. angustifolia Lesser reedmace

Juncus communis (modern equivalent unidentifable)

J. conglomerates Compact rush

J. effuses Soft rush

J. glaucus Blue rush

J. acutiflorus Sharp flowered rush

J. lamprocarpus Jointed rush

J. bufonius Toad rush

Luzula sylvatica Greater wood rush

L. pilosa Hairy wood rush

L. campestris Field woodrush

L. multiflora Heath woodrush

Rhyncospora alba White beak sedge

R. frusca (equivalent *Rhynchospora fusca*) Brown Beak Sedge

Scirpus lacustris Common clubrush

S. sylvaticus Wood clubrush

S. palustris (equivalent *Eleocharis palustris*) Common Spike-rush

S. apuciflorus (modern equivalent unidentifable)

S. fluitans Floating clubrush

Eriophorum vaginatum Harestail cottongrass

E. polystachyon Tall cottongrass

E. latifolium Broadleaved bog cotton

Carex pulicaris Flea sedge

C. stellulata Star sedge

C. curta White sedge

C. remota Remote sedge

C. intermedia (modern equivalent unidentifable)

C. muricata

C. divulsa Grey sedge

C. vulpine True fox sedge

C. teretiuscula

C. vulgaris Black sedge

C. stricta Upright sedge

C. acuta Acute sedge

C. flava Yellow sedge

C. pallescens Pale sedge

C. fulva (equivalent to *Carex x fulva*)

C. binervis Green ribbed sedge

C. panacea Carnation sedge

C. limosa Mud or Shore sedge

C. sylvatica Wood sedge

C. psydo-dyperus Hop sedge

C. glauca Blue sedge

C. praecox Russick star sedge

C. pilulifera Pill sedge

C. filiformis Downy fruited sedge

C. hirta Hairy sedge

C. ampullaceal (modern equivalent *Carex rostrata*) Bottle Sedge

C. vesicaria Bladder sedge

C. paludosa Lesser pond sedge

Phalaris arundinacea Reed canary grass

P. canaeriensis Annual canarygrass

Chara aspera A stonewort

Note All plants are 'within five to six miles' of Shrewsbury. Grasses, trees and orchids of Victorian Shrewsbury are listed elsewhere in this book.

N.B Some modern names were confirmed by the Natural History Museum, London[3]; an up-to-date 'A Flora of Shrewsbury' was published in 2011.[4]

A full 'A Flora of Shropshire'[5] was published in 1841 by Darwin's fellow Shropshire school mate and Cambridge student, Leighton. The list is too long to replicate here but Leighton wrote: 'The result has been that 876 species of flowering plants have been ascertained and described as natives of Shropshire'. Leighton dedicated the book to Reverend Henslow, Professor of Botany at Cambridge – also a mentor of Darwin's. Darwin appears to have had a copy of the book in his collection as he later refers to an extract of it in his 'The Variation of Animals and Plants Under Domestication'[6]: '...a weeping and almost prostrate yew (*Taxus baccata*) was found in a hedge in Shropshire; it was a male, but one branch bore female flowers, and produced berries; these, being sown, produced seventeen trees, all of which had exactly the same peculiar habit with the parent-tree.'

Darwin also writes to Leighton in 1841[7]:

My dear Sir

A few days since I was struck by the difference in aspect of a *Cynoglossum* from the common species. Being no Botanist I did not even know there were two species, till on consulting your work. I have no doubt it was the *C. sylvaticum*, as it was of a much paler green, with narrower leaves & of a more upright growth. Observing that you do not appear to have seen a Shropshire specimen it has occurred to me that you would like to know where I saw my plant, for the chance of a non-botanist having observed correctly.— the following diagram will best show position...Should you think it worth while to visit this spot, will you be so kind as to take the trouble at any time to inform me whether it is the *C. sylvaticum*...

Believe me | My dear Sir | Yours very faithfully | Charles Darwin.

The Shropshire Botanical Society[8] wrote a piece on this letter in their news-letter in 2004 stating that the plant is unlikely to have been *C.sylvaticum* but rather *C. officinale*, Hound's tongue.

Kohn[9] has indicated that 'In the early 1840's...Darwin did a fair amount of botanical rambling between Shrewsbury and Maer...during summer visits to his & his wife's family. He made many observations and kept extensive notes on floral structure – mostly of garden flowers, but there are also quite a few field observations. In general he is pretty vague about locations...'

Lowland heath and moorland is a key feature of Shropshire's coun-tryside and for Darwin, would have been 'unavoidable'. To give some idea of the variety of plantlife growing within these special habitats, I've come across the following species whilst visiting Prees Heath, Cramer Gutter and Stiperstones:

Calluna vulgaris Heather

Erica cinerea Bell heather

Deschampsia flexuosa Wavy hair grass

Agrostis capillaris Common bent

Festuca ovina agg. Sheeps fescue

Potentilla erecta Tormentil

Galium saxatile Heath bedstraw

Ulex gallii Western gorse

Danthonia decumbens Heath grass

Luzula campestris Field wood rush

Hypnum jutlandicum Hypnum moss

Pseudoscleropodium purum Neat feather moss

Polytrichum juniperinum Juniper haircap moss

Achillea millefolium Yarrow

Carex pilulifera Pill sedge

Viola canina Heath dog violet

Dicranum scoparium Broom moss

Anthoxanthum odoratum Sweet vernal grass

Hypericum pulchrum Slender St. John's wort

Rumex acetosella Sheeps sorrel

Hypochaeris radicata Cat's ear

Cerastium fontanum Common mouse ear

Holcus lanatus Yorkshire fog

Senecio jacobaea Common ragwort

Rhytidiadelphus squarrosus Springy turf moss

Chamerion angustifolium Rosebay willowherb

Juncus effusus Soft rush

Trifolium repens White clover

Tortula ruralis Twisted or star moss

Reseda luteola Weld

Viola arvensis Field pansy

Hypericum perforatum Perforate St. Johns wort

Narthecium ossifragum Bog asphodel

Eriophorum angustifolium Common cotton grass

Molinia caerulea Purple moor grass

Erica tetralix Cross leaved heath

Trichophorum caespitosum Deer grass

Vaccinium oxycoccos Cranberry

Carex echinata Star sedge

Drosera rotundifolia Round leaved sundew

Sphagnum papillosum Papillose bog moss

Sphagnum capillifolium Acute leaved or Small red peat moss

Sphagnum tenellum Soft bog moss

Carex binervis Green ribbed sedge

Luzula multiflora Heath woodrush

Lotus pedunculatus Large birds foot trefoil

Carex ovalis Oval sedge

Agrostis canina Velvet bent

Ranunculus flammula Lesser spearwort

Juncus acutiflorus Sharp flowered rush

Nardus stricta Mat grass

Carex flava Large yellow sedge

Potentilla anserina Silverweed

Prunella vulgaris Self heal

Vaccinium myrtillus Bilberry or Whortleberry

Pteridium aquilinum Bracken

Vaccinium vitis-idaea Cowberry

Pleurozium schreberi Big red stem moss

Sorbus aucuparia Rowan

Dicranum spp. A brown moss

Empetrum nigrum Crowberry

Sphagnum recurvum Recurvum bog moss

Galium palustre Marsh bedstraw

Sphagnum palustre Blunt-leaved bogmoss

Festuca rubra agg. Red fescue

Juncus squarrosus Heath rush

Juncus bulbosus Bulbous rush

Potamogeton polygonifolius Bog pondweed

Anagallis tenella Bog pimpernel

Epilobium palustre Marsh willowherb

Succisa pratensis Devil's Bit Scabious

Cirsium palustre Marsh thistle

I can find no specific reference by Darwin to Shropshire's heathland but in an account he made of that present at Maer and in Surrey, we discover something more of the ecology of this important habitat . 'Many cases are on record showing how complex and unexpected are the checks and relations between organic beings, which have to struggle together in the same country. I will give only a single instance, which, though a simple one, has interested me. In Staffordshire, on the estate of a relation where I had ample means of investigation, there was a large and extremely barren heath, which had never been touched by the hand of man; but several hundred acres of exactly the same nature had been enclosed twenty-five years previously and planted with Scotch fir. The change in the native vegetation of the planted part of the heath was most remarkable, more than is generally seen in passing from one quite different soil to another: not only the proportional numbers of the heath-plants were wholly changed, but twelve species of plants (not counting grasses and carices) flourished in the plantations, which could not be found on the heath. The effect on the insects must have been still greater, for six insectivorous birds were very common in the plantations, which were not to be seen on the heath; and the heath was frequented by two or three distinct insectivorous birds. Here we see how potent has been the effect of the introduction of a single tree, nothing whatever else having been done, with the exception that the land had been enclosed, so that cattle could not enter.[10]

I was interested by one particular [bird]: young oaks were springing up of all ages by hundreds, in parts at the distance of a mile from any oak tree, here & there actually appearing as if they had been sown broadcast; but I was assured that this never had been the case; & the woodmen told me that there was not the least doubt how they came there; that they had repeatedly seen rooks dropping acorns in their flight across the woods: there was no rookery near, & the line of flight would take the birds across the heath where there were no oaks, so that this <curious> most efficient means of dispersal must have been wasted for centuries, until the decay of the leaves of the fir trees & the growth of other plants had made a bed on which the acorns soon after being dropped could germinate. I have given instances to show what an effect the introduction of a single quadruped can indirectly produce on the vegetation of a country; & here we see that the introduction of a tree, with no other change whatever, can produce as great an influence on other plants, birds & insects.[11]

But how important an element enclosure is, I plainly saw near Farnham, in Surrey. Here there are extensive heaths, with a few clumps of old Scotch firs on the distant hill-tops: within the last ten years large spaces have been enclosed, and self-sown firs are now springing up in multitudes, so close together that all cannot live.

When I ascertained that these young trees had not been sown or planted, I was so much surprised at their numbers that I went to several points of view, whence I could examine hundreds of acres of the unenclosed heath, and literally I could not see a single Scotch fir, except the old planted clumps. But on looking closely between the stems of the heath, I found a multitude of seedlings and little trees, which had been perpetually browsed down by the cattle. In one square yard, at a point some hundred yards distant from one of the old clumps, I counted thirty-two little trees; and one of them, judging from the rings of growth, had during twenty-six years tried to raise its head above the stems of the heath, and had failed. No wonder that, as soon as the land was enclosed, it became thickly clothed with vigorously growing young firs. Yet the heath was so extremely barren and so extensive that no one would ever have imagined that cattle would have so closely and effectually searched it for food.'[12]

Darwin is likely to have explored grassland in Shropshire. The Shropshire Biodiversity Action Plan states that species-rich grasslands are one of the most threatened and rapidly disappearing habitats in Shropshire. 'They occur on both neutral and calcareous soils...They encompass traditionally managed hay meadows, old pastures and other undisturbed areas of grasslands such as churchyards and roadside verges.' The 'Lowland Species Rich Grassland' Habitat Action Plan for Shropshire[13] states that there is approximately 335ha of Lowland Meadows and 43ha of Lowland Calcareous Grassland in the county. 'Unimproved neutral grasslands are scattered throughout the county but with some concentrations in areas around the Clee Hills, the Wyre Forest and along Wenlock Edge. Calcareous grasslands are particularly associated with the limestone areas around Oswestry and Wenlock Edge, and on former clay workings in the Telford area.' It's amazing to think that these grasslands are 'survivors', having avoided ploughing, fertilising, reseeding or treatment with chemicals. Their management essentially involves the prevention of their invasion by trees, through hay cutting or grazing.

The Habitat Action Plan[13] states that 'Neutral and calcareous grasslands can be distinguished by their characteristic assemblage of species. Unimproved neutral grassland typically contains a range of grasses such as Crested Dog's Tail, Sweet Vernal Grass and Meadow Foxtail, often with a colourful array of wildflowers such as Yellow Rattle, Oxeye Daisy, Betony, Devil's-bit Scabious and Black Knapweed. Calcareous grassland occurs over limestone or other base-rich rocks and the soils are typically thin and nutrient poor. Many plants have adapted to these conditions and calcareous grasslands can be extremely rich in species. The sward is composed of a wide range of grasses including Quaking Grass, Glaucous Sedge, orchids species, Fairy Flax, Yellow-wort, Small Scabious and Rock-rose.' The National Vegetation Classification grassland communities present[13] are:

MG4: *Alopecurus pratensis – Sanguisorba officinalis* (rare in Shropshire)

MG5: *Cynosurus cristatus – Centauria nigra*

MG8: *Cynosurus cristatus – Caltha palustris* (rare in Shropshire)

MG1e: *Arrhenatherum elatius* grassland, *Centauria nigra* sub-community

CG1: *Festuca ovina – Carlina vulgaris*

CG2: *Festuca ovina – Avenula pratensis* [*Helictotrichon pratense*] (as *H. pratense* is not found in Shropshire this is an unusual form of this grassland)

CG3: *Bromus erectus*

CG6: *Avenula pubescens* [*Helictrotrichon pubescens*]

CG7: *Festuca ovina - Hieracium pilosella - Thymus polytrichus*

I have visited a number of meadows in Shropshire. The Shropshire Wildlife Trust site at Melverley Farm is a very interesting one. Here one gets a sense of the diversity meadows offer. Here I enjoyed the carpet of little Eyebrights, alongside buttercups, common spotted orchids, betony, devil' bit scabious and yellow rattle. Veins of plants of damper areas also embellished the site including rushes, ragged robin and marsh marigold. Llanymynech Nature Reserve, with chalk grassland, is well worth a visit, to get some impression of the habitat Darwin came to love around Downe – we know that Darwin visited the area as part of his geology studies. Though not an owner of large meadows at The Mount in Shropshire, Darwin did have his own meadows at Down House, on clay-with-flint soils. Great House Meadow was cut for hay and in a bad year earned the family £30. [14] Francis,[15] recalled it as: 'a great sea of tall grasses, pink with sorrel and white with dog daisies'. Darwin recorded 142 plant species (not including mosses or fungi) in Great Pucklands meadow throughout 1855; 119 plants were found in a modern survey undertaken by scientists and three generations of Charles Darwin's descendants in 2009[16].

Unimproved grasslands of calcareous soils have that 'extra something special' and are renowned as one of the most floristically diverse habitats in Britain. They occur in a number of locations around Downe. Darwin wrote:[17] 'After several fruitless searches in Surrey and elsewhere, we found [Down] house and purchased it. I was pleased with the diversified appearance of vegetation proper to a chalk district, and so unlike what I had been accustomed to in the Midland counties; and still more pleased with the extreme quietness and rusticity of the place.'

Some of the areas that support chalk grassland these days appear to have been under arable land use in Darwin's time, but even where this was the case, chalk grassland flowers would have been growing in the margins of the land and throughout the crops due to the cultural agricultural practices of the time.

I personally adore all flowers of the chalk grasslands, for their diverse companionship of species and their spectacular variation in colour and structure. But somehow, fairy flax and squinancywort always bring a smile to my face as it's a miracle they are ever in a position to grow, so delicately, at all in the dry soil of chalk grassland. The Grass vetchling (*Lathyrus nissolia*), is also a delight to see. A particularly special bonus about chalk grassland is the smell it exudes as leaves are crushed underfoot; this activates one's senses. The culprits range from the aromatic herbs of thyme, marjoram and basil to the pungent smell of wild parsnip (on the rare list in Shropshire[18]).

We have an overview of a piece of chalk grassland Darwin knew from an account made by his daugther,[19] Henrietta Darwin: 'It was a sure sign of my father's feeling pretty well that he ventured from his safe 'Sand-walk', down a pleasant field at the end of the kitchen garden, over a stile, and then along a grassy terrace, looking across the quiet green valley on to the woods beyond. The terrace was sheltered from the north-east by a rough shaw of beeches and an undergrowth of sloes, traveller's joy, service-trees and hawthorn, and this bank was particularly gay with the flowers that love a chalk soil – little yellow rock-rose, milkwort, orchises, ladies' fingers, hare-bells, coronilla, scabious and gentian. My father would pace to and fro, and my mother would sometimes sit on the dry chalky bank waiting for him, and be pulled by him up the little steep pitch on the way home.'

Darwin commented on the competitive nature of plants in chalk grassland[20]: 'One set of plants will allow another to live only on some bare chalk banks, though not perfectly suited to them; but the relation of different plants to each other growing on the same plot of ground must be equally important. Cut a piece of turf and look at the inextricable mass of roots, each growing rapidly in the line where it can find food: it is like a battle between voracious animals devouring the same prey.'

The following is a list of species (excluding orchids) I commonly encountered on chalk grasslands I helped survey and manage around Downe.

Ophioglossum vulgatum Adder's-tongue Fern

Lithospermum officinale Common Cromwell

Acinos alpinus Basil Thyme.

Agrimonia eupatoria Agrimony

Gentianella amarelle Autumn gentian

Lotus corniculatus Birdsfoot trefoil

Centaurea nigra Black knapweed

Medicago lupulina Black medick

Silene vulgaris Bladder campion

Pimpinella saxifrage Burnet saxifrage

Carlina vulgaris Carline thistle

Centaurium erythraea Common centaury

Polygala vulgaris Common milkwort

Cerastium holostoides Common mouseear

Helianthemum chamaecistus Common rock rose

Primula veris Cowslip

Potentilla reptans Creeping cinquefoil

Cruciata laevipes Crosswort

Cirsium acaule Dwarf thistle

Linum catharticum Fairy flax

Knautia arvensis Field scabious

Tragopogon pratensis Goatsbeard

Centauria scabiosa Greater knapweed

Hypericum hisutum Hairy St. John's Wort

Viola hirta Hairy violet

Galium mollugo Hedge bedstraw

Plantago media Hoary plantain

Heracleium sphondylium Hogweed

Anthyllis vulneraria Kidney vetch

Galium verum Ladies bedstraw

Origanum vulgare Marjoram

Lathyrus pratensis Meadow vetchling

Pilosella officinarum Mouse-ear hawkweed

Hypericum perforatum Perforate St. John's wort

Inula conyza Ploughman's spikenard

Senecio jacobaea Ragwort

Trifolium pratense Red clover

Plantago lanceolata Ribwort plantain

Ononis repens Rest harrow

Sanguisorba minor Salad burnet

Onobrychis viciifolia Sainfoin

Prunella vulgaris Self heal

Scabiosa columbaria Small scabious

Vicia cracca Tufted vetch

Clinpodium vulgare Wild basil

Daucus carota Wild carrot

Achillea millefolium Yarrow

Rhinanthus minor Yellow rattle

Blackstonia perfoliata Yellow wort

Euphrasia agg. Eyebright

Aster sp. Aster

Cirsium vulgare Spear thistle

Dipsacus fullonum Wild teasal

Euphorbia amygdaloides Wood spurge

Pastinaca sativa Wild parsnip

Polygala vulgaris Common milkwort

Potentilla sterilis Barren strawberry

Potentilla reptans Creeping cinquefoil

Primula vulgaris Primrose

Prunella vulgaris Self heal

Senecio erucifolius Hoary ragwort

Torilis japonica Upright hedge parsley

Veronica filiformis Slender speedwell

Vicia sativa Common vetch

Viola riviniana Common dog violet

Primula veris Cowslip

Centaurea nigra Common knapweed

Cerastium fontanum Common Mouse-ear

Convolvulus arvensis Field Bindweed

Crepis capillaris Smooth Hawk's-beard

Euphrasia nemorosa Eyebright

Galium mollugo Hedge Bedstraw

Galium verum Lady's Bedstraw

Hypericum perforatum Perforate St John's-wort

Knautia arvensis Field Scabious

Leontodon hispidus Rough Hawkbit

Leucanthemum vulgare Oxeye Daisy

Odontites vernus Red Bartsia

Torilis japonica Upright Hedge-parsley

Tragopogon pratensis Goat's-beard

Veronica chamaedrys Germander Speedwell

Asperula cynanchica Squinancywort

About a mile away from Down House, I was involved in creating a new meadow to link existing areas of chalk grassland which Darwin knew well. Seeds were collected by hand, captured in a seed harvesting machine and spread from bales of meadow hay by conservation volunteers. It was amazing to see how the initially boring sward of vegetation that developed came bit by bit to support the full range of chalk grassland species one expected for the area. Majoram provided the most obvious flush of flowers in the early years and within eight years we had our first common spotted orchid growing in the field. The 'link' provided an effective corridor for insects. Butterfly transect surveys showed how the grassland provided an essential piece of foraging habitat for butterflies of the area.[21] A brief investigation[22] of invertebrates one late summer (a suboptimum time for surveying), over some six hours of collecting by a consultant, revealed that the chain of chalk grasslands at this site – Musk Orchid Bank & Hangrove Fields – supported 185 species, 63 of which were beetles. Nationally scarce species found included the Wasp Spider (*Argiope bruennichi*), the mining bee, *Lasioglossum xanthopus*, Roesel's Bush Cricket (*Metrioptera roeselii*), a ground beetle, *Platyderus ruficollis*, and a pyralid moth, *Sitochroa palealis*. A further fourteen Nationally Local species were also found.

The following observations of meadows were made by Darwin and brings home to me what an achievement grassland creation is:

[23] '...on the struggle for existence...of sixteen kinds of seed sown in my meadow, fifteen have germinated, but now they are perishing at such a rate that I doubt whether more than one will flower' 1857.

[24] 'Seedlings, also, are destroyed in vast numbers by various enemies;...I marked all the seedlings of our native weeds as they came up, and out of 357 no less than 295 were destroyed, chiefly by slugs and insects.'

[25] '...the greatest amount of life can be supported by great diversification of structure...I found that a piece of turf...which had been exposed for many years to exactly the same conditions supported twenty species of plants.' 1859.

Spring at Downe is particularly marked on the chalk grassland by the abundance of primroses and cowslips. They always attracted much interest from residents whenever I organised a guided walk on their folklore and management. I was interested to find in 'Ecological Flora of the Shropshire Region' (1985)[26] that cowslips are more widespread than primroses in Shropshire's countryside. Leighton, however, describes cowslip in 'meadows and pastures; abundant' and primroses in 'Woods, hedgebanks and pastures; abundant'.[27]

Darwin was the first to have discovered the variation in flower structure of primroses, the fact that there are thrum-eyed and pin-eyed versions of the species[28]. He wrote: 'Whether or not the dimorphic condition of the Primulæ has any bearing on other points in natural history, it is valuable as showing how nature strives, if I may so express myself, to favour the sexual union of distinct individuals of the same species. The resources of nature are inimitable; and we know not why the species of *Primula* should have acquired this novel and curious aid for checking continued self-fertilization through the division of the individuals into two bodies of hermaphrodites with different sexual powers, instead of by the more common method of the separation of the sexes, or by the maturity of the male and female elements at different periods, or by other such contrivances.'

He also wrote: 'The claim of the three forms...namely the common cowslip, primrose and Bardfield Oxlip...to be ranked as distinct species has been discussed at greater length than that of almost any other plants. Linnaeus considered them varieties, as do some of the most ditinguished botanists of the present day; whilst others who have carefully studied these plants do not doubt that they deserve to be ranked as distinct species...I think, that the latter view is correct;...that the common Oxlip, which is found in most parts of England, is a hybrid between *P. veris* and *vulgaris*.

The cowslip differs so conspicuously in general appearance from the Primrose, that nothing need here be said with respect to their external characters. But some less-obvious differences deserve notice. As both species are heterostyled, their complete fertilisations depends on insects. The cowslip is habitually visited during the day by the larger humble-bees (viz. *Bombus muscorum* and *hortorum*), and at night by moths...The primrose is never visited (and I speak after many years' observation) by the larger humble-bees, and only rarely by the smaller kinds; hence its fertilisation must depend almost exclusively on moths. There is nothing in the structure of the flowers of the two plants which can determine the visits of such widely different insects. But they emit a different odour, and perhaps their nectar may have a different taste.' [29]

Of late spring and summer it was the orchids that attracted Darwin's eye. Darwin commented[30] in 'Various Contrivances by which Orchids are Fertilised by Insects' (1877): 'Kent appears to be the most favourable country in England for the order [of Orchids], and within a mile of my house nine genera, including thirteen species, grow; but of these one alone, Orchis morio, is sufficiently abundant to make a conspicuous feature in the vegetation; as is Orchis maculate in a lesser degree in open woodlands. Most of the other species, although deserving to be called rare, are sparingly distributed.' A few years ago the first sighting of a Violet Helleborine was encountered at High Elms Country Park – a treat to all who knew where it grew.

There are many accounts of Darwin and his family observing the pollination of various orchids, such as Bee and Early Purple orchids, in the Downe countryside. Just to take one example, the Pyramidal Orchid, Darwin wrote[31]:

'I have been examining Orchis pyramidalis, and it almost equals, perhaps even beats, your Listera case; the sticky glands are congenitally united into a saddle-shaped organ, which has great power of movement, and seizes hold of a bristle (or proboscis) in an admirable manner, and then another movement takes place in the pollen masses, by which they are beautifully adapted to leave pollen on the two lateral stigmatic surfaces. I never saw anything so beautiful.' Elsewhere, he wrote[32]: 'In no other plant, or indeed in hardly any animal, can adaptations of one part to another, and of the whole to other organised beings widely remote in the scale of nature, be named more perfect than those presented by...Orchis [pyramidalis]'. He added: 'With respect to Orchis pyramidalis, which possesses, as we have

seen, an elongated nectary...I selected twenty-three species, enumer-
ated in the following list, with the pollina of this Orchid, which can
easily be recognized, attached to their proboscides'[33]. The following
species were listed: Common blue, small copper, marbled white,
large skipper, small skipper, grizzled skipper, six-spot burnet, five-
spot burnet, scarce footman, The Clay, The Rustic, The Uncertain,
Northern Rustic, Shaded broad-bar, The Shears, Clouded Border,
Reddish Light Arches, Burnet Companion, The Blackneck, Wood
Carpet, The Four-Spotted, *Sitochroa palealis* (moth) and *Sitochroa
verticalis* (moth).[31] Kent Wildlife Trust has stated that: 'Darwin recognized this orchid [as] one of the supreme examples of evolutionary co-adaptation between plant and animal in the natural world.'[34]

Darwin wrote an article called 'Fertilisation of British Orchids by Insect
Agency' to explain to people the various roles of pollinators[35] '...different
insects haunt different Orchids, and are necessary for their fertilisation.
From the wide difference in shape of the flower of *Orchis* and *Ophrys*, I
should have anticipated that they would be visited and fertilised by different insects. In *Listera*, for instance, it is chiefly Ichneumonidæ, and sometimes flies, which by day perform the marriage ceremony. In the case of
most Orchids it is nocturnal moths. *Orchis pyramidalis*, however, is visited by Zygæna, and I have examined one of these day-sphinxes with three
pair of pollen-masses firmly attached to its proboscis. There can hardly be
a doubt that the Butterfly Orchis is visited by different moths from most
of the smaller Orchids; and I have recognised its peculiar pollen-masses
attached to the sides of the face of certain moths. It is probable that the
same kind of moths would visit all the species of true Orchis, which closely resemble each other in structure...the *Epipactis latifolia*, growing in my
garden and flowering well, had not its pollen-masses removed; though in
its own home, several miles distant, the flowers are regularly visited and
thus fertilised. We thus see that the seeds of an Orchid might be carried
by the wind to some distant place, and there germinate, but that the species would not be perpetuated unless the proper insects inhabited the site.'

Darwin's admiration for the group gives rise to the publication of '*the Various Contrivances by which Orchids are Fertlised by Insects*'. In part he aims to dispel the belief that their beauty, perfume and medicinal properties were purely for the benefit of humanity but that their form was designed to accommodate insects. He wrote in a covering letter[36] 'The subject of propagation is interesting to most people, and is treated in my paper so that any woman could read it', by which he was not being disparaging to female intelligence but rather excusing the fact that the book was examining reproduction!

Though apparently not an object of affection for Darwin in Shropshire, Leighton[37] lists the following orchids in Shropshire:

=*Orchis morio* Green winged meadow orchid. Meadows and pastures; not unfrequent

=*Orchis mascula Early purple orchis. Woods and pastures; not unfrequent

O. ustulata Dwarf dark-winged orchis. Pastures in the limestone districts, rare

O. maculata Spotted palmate orchis. Pastures; not unfrequent

=*O. latifolia* Marsh orchis. Marshes and moist meadows; not unfrequent

**O. pyramidalis* Pyramidal orchis. Pastures and waste ground in the limestone districts; not unfrequent

Gymnadenia conopsea Fragrant gymnadenia. Dry hilly pasture, chiefly in the limestone districts

Gymnadenia galbida Small white gymnadenia. Mountain pasture; very rare

=*Habenaria viridis* Green habenaria (Frog orchid). Dry hilly pastures, non unfrequent

Habenaria chlorantha Yellow butterfly habenaria. Pastures in the limestone districts; not unfrequent

=*Habenaria bifolia* Smaller butterfly orchis (Lesser butterfly orchid). Pastures in the limestone districts; no unfrequent

*Ophrys apifera Bee Ophrys. Limestone districts; not unfrequent

O. aranifera Spider Ophrys. Limestone districts; very rare

*O. muscifera Fly Ophrys. Limestone districts; very rare

Neottia spiralis. Limestone districts; not common

=**Listera ovata* Twayblade. Woods and moist pastures; frequent

L. cordata Heart leaved twayblade. Sides of mountains in heathy spots; very rare

=**Neottidium avis avis (Neottia nidus-avis)* Common birds nest orchid. Shady woods, not common

=**Epipactis latifolia* Broad leaved helleborine. Woods; not unfrequent

E. palustris Marsh helleborine. Marshy places in the limestone districts; not common

Cephalanthera ensifolia Narrow-leaved White helleborine. Hilly woods; rare

* Those asterixed and Man Orchid, White helleborine, Common spotted orchid, Musk orchid, Fragrant orchid, Lady orchid, Greater Butterfly orchid, Autumn Lady's-Tresses were found around Downe in Victorian times.[38]

= Listed in Phillips 1878 book of Shrewsbury[39]

The 'Rare Plants of Shropshire'[40] lists many hybrids and the following orchids as now being rare or extinct in Shropshire:

Cephalanthera longifolia Narrow-leaved Helleborine (Extinct 1891)

Coeloglossum viride Frog Orchid 'scarce'

Dactylorhiza purpurella (Northern Marsh Orchid) as rare

Epipactis leptochila (Narrow lipped Helleborine) as extinct 1993

Epipactis palustris (Marsh Helleborine) as rare

Epipactis phyllanthes (Green flowered Helleborine) as rare

Epipogium aphyllum (Ghost Orchid) as extinct 1892.

Listera cordata (Lesser Twayblade) as extinct 1920

Ophrys insectifera (Fly Orchid) Extinct 1944

Orchis ustulata (Burnt Orchid) Extinct 1904

In summer, *Verbascum* occurs on the disturbed ground on the chalky soils around Downe. Great Mullein *Verbascum thapsus*, soars over the other vegetation with it's bunny-ear leaves, whilst White Mullein *V. lychnitis* grows as a knee-high dainty white spike of a flower. In recent times these have been most prevalent in the location of old bonfire sites and scrub-cleared areas on the chalk slopes around Downe. The '*Ecological Flora of the Shropshire Region*' describes Great Mullein as: 'frequent throughout region' and 'unpalatable'[41] (Leighton describes it on 'hedgebanks and waste ground; not uncommon)[42] and White Mullein as only occurring in historic records including: 'Near Snow Pool, Dryton, Wroxeter' by Serjeantson (1861–1916) [41]. (Leighton describes it as on 'roadsides, pastures and waste places; rare').

Darwin's studies of *Verbascum* looked at the hybridisation of plants under both controlled investigations and in the wild. The 'inefficiency' of producing sterile forms and the variation in 'potency' of pollen, the occurrence of self-fertility and self-sterility were investigated by him. In two letters, for example, Darwin writes[43]: 'Have you any white and yellow varieties of *Verbascum* which you could give me or propagate for me or lend me for a year? I have resolved to try Gaertner's wonderful and repeated statement, that pollen of white and yellow varieties, whether used on the varieties or on distinct species, has different potency. I do not think any experiment can be more important on Origin of Species; for if he is correct, we certainly have what Huxley calls new species arising. I should require several species of *Verbascum* besides the white & yellow varieties of the same species. – It will be tiresome work, but if I can anyhow get the plants it shall be tried.' Darwin writes on another occasion: 'Here is a fact which may possibly interest you. In a field here I find many *Verbascum thapsus & lycnitis*; & lots of varieties making an almost perfect series between those two distinct forms. I am sure many species have been run together on less perfect evidence. But lo and behold every one of these intermediate forms are absolutely sterile! And no doubt are natural hybrids. I found 33 of these hybrids in one field!!!'[44]

Autumn gentian and Field scabious mark the autumn on chalk grassland around Downe, two of the few plants that leave their flowering til the end of summer. The scabious is a fantastic plant; its blue-lilac disc attracting many butterflies to sip from them as the flowers dance in the autumn breeze. I could never quite bring myself to cut the small colony at Musk Orchid Bank in Downe as it had never quite seeded when we came to do the September 'cut and rake'. The chalk slope west of 'The Terrace' at Downe is probably where Darwin observed, Autumn gentian, *Gentianella amarelle* and examples of it occur on the site in present times. The 'Ecological Flora of the Shropshire Region' (1985) shows it to occur in few locations in Oswestry upland and Wenlock Edge to Benthall Edge areas.[45] (Leighton describes it as 'In high limestone pastures; not very common).[46]

The studies undertaken by Darwin of Gentian indicated that variation in species, such as naturally-occurring single- and double-flowering, may be induced by something other than nutrients in soil, which was normally the assumption. He wrote: 'The plants of the Gentiana in both states grow mingled together on a very hard, dry, bare chalk bank; but those with the abortive flowers grow on rather the barest spots, where it was surprising that anything could grow. You state in your "*Theory of Horticulture*," that the origin of double flowers is not well understood. Some have attributed it to excess of food; but the dry chalk bank surely was not too rich a soil; and I may mention that late last autumn, I found on an adjoining field of wretchedly sterile clay, great numbers of the Ranunculus repens, producing semi-double flowers, some having three, some additional rows of petals. The partial or entire sterility of double flowers is generally attributed to their doubleness; but is not this putting the effect before the cause? It is well known that plants...when placed out of their natural conditions, become, often from apparently slight and unintelligible causes, sterile.'[47]

'...The plants of the Gentiana bearing the little tufts are generally, but not always, dwarfer than the perfect plants; their leaves are less pointed, and the entire plant is much less symmetrical. The much greater number of the imperfect flowers on one plant than are ever produced of the perfect, shows, I presume, that the metamorphic change must be determined early in the plant's life. Except in their small size, less beauty, and in the occasional presence on the same stem of flowers in different stages of monstrosity, these purple tufts seem to be essentially similar in their nature to the double flowers of Horticulturists.'[48]

The beauty of the wildflowers of grasslands often leads one to overlook the grasses - 'the elephants in the room'. Grasses are an obviously important component of chalk grassland, but can be a nightmare to identify especially when they are half-chewed! It is heartening to read that Darwin found difficulty in their identification too. He wrote:[49] 'I have just made out my first grass, hurrah! hurrah! I must confess that fortune favours the bold, for, as good luck would have it, it was the easy Anthoxanthum odoratum – nevertheless it is a great discovery; I never expected to make out a grass in my life.' Francis wrote[50]: 'I remember his collecting grasses there when he took a fancy to make out the names of all the common grasses. (I think it was here that Lenny as a little boy found one that my father had not seen before and had it by him all dinner remarking "I are an extraordinary grass finder". It is amazing how many grasses can be found within a small area of grassland. I had to gather some once to show girl guides the range they could use to make an 'Extraordinary Grassfinder' bookmark as part of a Darwin Challenge badge – they were quite beautiful bunched up together.

Darwin wrote of grasses[51]: 'When the fertilisation is not aided by the voluntary flight of insects, these could seed well only when growing in masses: I believe many Grasses are in this predicament, namely depending to a great extent on other individuals for their fertilisation; are not visited by insects; grasses are commonly social'. He also wrote[52]: 'We know that it has been experimentally shown that a plot of land will yield a greater weight if cropped with several species of grasses than with 2 or 3 species. Now every single organic being, by propagating so rapidly, may be said to be striving its utmost to increase in numbers.'

What grasses would Darwin have come across in Shropshire? Leighton lists the following in 1841[53]:

Lolium perenne Perennial darnel or rye grass. Waysides, pastures and waste places; frequent

Lolium temulentum bearded rye. Grass cornfields

Lolium arvense. Cornfields

L. festucaceum spiked darnel. Moist pastures and meadows; not unfrequent

Nardus stricta mat. Grass moors and heaths, not uncommon

Agropyron repens (Triticum repens) Creeping couch. Grass fields and waste places; too frequent

A. caninum (Triticum caninum) fibrous rooted couch. Grass woods and hedges; not common

Brachypodium sylvaticum. Dry copses, thickets and Slender False oat grass hedges; frequent

Hordeum pratense Meadow barley. Moist meadows and pastures; not common

H. murinum Wall barley. Waste grounds and by waysides; not common

Phalaris canariensis Canary grass. Cultivated and waste ground; doubtless naturalised

* *Phleum pratense* Cats Tail Grass (Timothy grass). Meadows and pastures

* *Phleum nodosum* (Common timothy). In barren, dry ground; common

Seslaria caerulea Blue moor grass. Limestone districts; rare

Anthoxanthum odoratum. Sweet scented vernal grass. Meadows and pastures. Very common

Alopecurus pratensis Meadow fox tail grass. Meadows and pastures. Common

* *Alopecurus geniculatus* Floating fox tail grass. In pools and wet grassy places, sometimes on dry ground. Not unfrequent

Alopercurus agrestis. Slender fox tail grass. Fields and waysides. Not common

Briza media common quaking grass. Meadows and pastures. Frequent

Melica nutans Mountain melic grass. Woods. Not common

M. uniflora wood melic grass. Shady woods. Not unfrequent

Glyceria fluitans floating sweet grass. In stagnant waters and slow streams. Frequent

G. spectabilis Reed sweet grass. Sides of rivers, ponds and ditches. Not very common

Catabrosa aquatica Water whorl grass. Banks of rivers and pools of water

Poa annua Annual meadow grass. Meadows, pastures, roadsides, waste and cultivated ground. Everywhere variety villosa equally common

P. compressa Flat stemmed meadow grass. On walls and in dry barren ground. Not common

P. nemoralis Wood meadow grass. Woods and thickets. Not very common

P. trivialis Roughish meadow grass. Meadows and pastures. Common

P. pratensis smooth stalked meadow grass. Meadows and pastures. Common

Sclerochloa rigida Rigid Hard grass. Dry barren soils chiefly in the limestone districts

* *Milium effusum* Spreading Millet grass (Wood millet). Moist, shady places. Not common

Molinia caerulea Purple molinia. On the turfy boggy margins of pools and wet moors. Not common

Baldingera arundanacea Reed band grass. Sides of rivers, ponds and pools. Common

Arundo phragmites common reed grass. Margins of pools. Not unfrequent

Dactylis glomerata Rough cock's foot grass. Waysides, meadows and hedgerows. Abundant

Festuca ovina sheeps fescue grass. Pastures and waste grounds. Not common

* *F. duriuscula* Hard fescue grass. Pastures and waste grounds. Not common

F. pratensis Meadow fescue grass. Moist meadows and pastures. Not common

F. arundinacea Tall fescue grass. Moist meadows, banks of river. Rare

F. gigantea Tall fescue grass. Shady woods. Not common

Vulpia myurus Wall vulpia walls. Waste and barren places. Not common

V. bromoides Barren vulpia. Dry hilly pastures and wastes. Not common

Danthonia decumbens. Dry hilly pastures

Bromus secalinus Smooth rye brome grass. Cornfields. Not common

B. racemosus Smooth brome grass. Meadows and pastures. Not common

Bromus mollins Soft brome grass. Meadows, pastures, banks, roadsides. Everywhere

B. asper Hairy wood brome grass (Upright brome). Moist woods. Not unfrequent

B. sterilis Barren brome grass. Waste grounds, fields, hedges. Common

B. erectus Upright brome grass. Roadsides in the limestone districts. Rare

Holcus lanatus Meadow soft grass. Meadows and pastures. Common

H. mollis Creeping soft grass. Pastures and hedges. Common

* *Agrostis vulgaris* Fine bent grass. Meadows, pastures and dry borders of fields. Common

Agrostis alba Marsh bent grass (creeping bent). Pastures, roadsides moist places. Common

A. spica Silky bent grass. Sandy fields occasionally flooded. Rare

Calamagrostis epigejos Wood small reed. Shady moist places. Rare

lanceolata purple flowered small reed. Moist margins of pools. Rare

Avena fatua Wild oat. Cornfields. Not frequent

A. pubescens Downy oat grass. Dry hilly places in limestone districts. Not common

A. flavescens Yellow oat grass. Dry meadows and pastures. Frequent

Aira caespitosa Turfy hair grass. Moist shady places. Plentiful

 A. flexuosa Waved hair grass. Heaths and hilly places. Not uncommon

A. caryophyllea Silvery hair grass. Gravelly hills and pastures. Not unfrequent

A. praecox Early hair grass. Hedgebanks and hilly pastures. Not uncommon

Arrhenatherum avenaceum Common oat like grass (Meadow Oat Grass). Hedges and pastures. Frequent

Note * are those included in Phillips 1878 book of Shrewsbury[54] also included were, *Arundo calamagrostis* (a type of reed), *Triodia decumbens*, *Glyceria aquatica* (Water meadow grass), *Cynosurus cristatus* (Crested dogs tail), *Festuca elatior* (a meadow fescue), *Bromus commutatus* (Meadow brome).

WATERY INVESTIGATIONS

What were Darwin's early encounters with watery habitats?

Darwin used to fish on the River Severn at the bottom of his garden. Darwin wrote:[1] 'I had a strong taste for angling, and would sit for any number of hours on the bank of a river or pond watching the float... When at Maer I was told that I could kill the worms with salt and water, and from that day I never spitted a living worm, though at the expense probably of some loss of success'. I wonder what he would have caught? Though I admit to not understanding the thrill of hooking a fish, I have always envied fisherman's opportunity to see a fish close up and distinguish its features so as to identify it. Seeing fry and trout in the river, accidentally catching numerous bullheads in a river sample and hearing the plops of jumping fish was as far as my experiences went in Shropshire.

One of the clearest nineteenth century accounts of fish in Shropshire is from Forrest 1899[2]; he describes the following:

Perch...common in pools and quiet parts of rivers that are more or less sluggish...The Severn is fairly well stocked with Perch; the more so in the Shrewsbury district, since bush-netting has been greatly restricted in this part of the river. Most of the large sheets of water in Shropshire contain plenty of these excellent 'coarse fish'...

Pope. Local name 'Jack Ruffe'...common in the Severn and is to be found on the muddy bottoms, where the stream is fairly deep and slow...

Bullhead or Miller's Thumb...found in most of our smaller streams, lurking under stones...

Stickleback. Local name Tittlebat...plentiful in our smaller streams...

Ten-spined stickleback..found...in ditches on the Weald Moors...

Flounder...years ago, before the time of Severn navigations weirs..Flounders used to be taken in Shropshire; and one or two older Shresbury residents still relate that in their youthful days they occasionally capture specimens when bottom fishing...

Eel Common...in most pools, canals, and rivers...

Allis Shad...

Twaite Shad...

Carp...they are prolific and long lived...

Gudgeon...occurs in many parts of the Severn, Vyrnwy, Rea and most of the tributaries...

Roach...found in most streams and pools; often in abundance...

Rudd...is caught in Bomere and Shomere Pools, near Shrewsbury, and in Fennymere, near Baschurch...

Chub...is perhaps the most common fish in the Severn and tributaries...

Dace...sporting in large numbers in the Severn, Rea, Tern, Teme and other rivers in the County...

Minnow...found abundantly in the Severn and in most tributary streams...

Tench...found in many ponds, especially such as have muddy bottoms...

Bream...found in Berrington, Fennymere, Hawkstone and other pools as well as in the Severn...

Bleak...not uncommon in the Severn, near Shrewsbury, and in certain brooks running into it...

Loach Local name, Stone Loach...like the Bullhead...found in similar situations...

Salmon...formerly caught in numbers in the Severn, close to Shrewsbury, but the pollution of the river and the excessive netting of the lower reaches, combined with other changes in the channel, has completely altered the state of affairs and now comparatively few fish pass up...

Sea trout or Salmon Trout...were at one time frequently taken both in the-Servern and in the Vyrnwy...

The Common brown trout...is the only one natural to the Severn and other local streams...once pretty plentiful in the Severn...it is becoming much scarcer, in consequence of over fishing and the depredations of Pike...

Grayling...fairly numerous in the Severn notably at The Isle, Atcham, Cronkhill and other places where the bed of the river is gravelly, and there is a gliding current. The Teme and several rivers in Ludlow district are among the best...

Pike or Jack...have greatly increased in the Severn and Vyrnwy of late years...

Sturgeon...1802...a fine specimen was caught in the Severn below Shrewsbury Castle...

Sea Lamprey...the Severn in particular has long been celebrated for its Lampreys. This species does not often now occur as high up as Shrewsbury, though it was not uncommon in former year..One was caught below the Welsh Bridge a year or so ago...

Lampern or River Lamprey Local name Seven Eyes...common in our Shropshire streams..

Mud Lamprey or Sand Pride...closely resembles the last in habits and appearance, and is common in our brooks.

A later account of Shropshire fish-life states:[3] 'Crayfish occur in some of the streams. Salmon though once frequent are now comparatively rare in the Severn; the brown trout, grayling, and chub are common, but the barbell is seldom seen. Pike and eels are everywhere, and the river lamprey occurs. Perch, carp and tench are caught in the ponds, and the rudd lives in Bomere and Shomerer Pools.'

The River Severn obviously made an impression on Darwin. Darwin later made many references to the Severn on his voyage of *The Beagle*, using it as a standard of measurement: 'Its width here is about 60 yards generally it must be once half as wide as the Severn at Shrewsbury. The tortuous course of the river is marked by numerous willow trees beds of reeds'[4]; 'The river is rapid tortuous; it is about twice as large as the Severn (when half banks full) at Shrewsbury'[5]; 'four times as wide as the Severn at Shrewsbury.'[6] Darwin does not appear to have made any specific accounts of rivers in Shropshire other than the Severn.

Nowadays one can find wetland plants such as meadowsweet, marsh woundwort and purple loosestrife growing along the Severn river, close to the boundary of the former Mount grounds. There grows another modern addition too; the Himalayan Balsam (*Impatiens glandulifera*). It is a plant that was introduced to Britain in 1839 from Northern India and was first recorded in the wild in 1855.[7] Darwin is unlikely to have known it, but would he have been impressed at how this introduced plant could come to dominate many of Britain's riverbanks in the summer? Would he have gathered that its success was based on the fact that Britain had not evolved herbivorous insects and plant pathogens to control it whilst in their native range the plant would be kept in equilibrium with the surrounding plant community? You get a hint that he might from something he wrote about St. Helena on 13 July 1836 'numbers of indigenous plants being 52, to 424 imported species, of which latter so many come from England...Many English plants appear to flourish here better than in their native country...These numerous species, which have been so recently introduced, can hardly have failed to have destroyed some of the native kinds.'[8]

Darwin didn't have a pond in his garden at the Mount. We know, however, that Darwin did his share of pond-dipping. He recollects in 1817 [9.] 'At 8 1/2 years old I went to Mr. Case's School....I was very timid by nature. I remember I took great delight at school in fishing for newts in the quarry pool.' The Quarry was Darwin's local 'park'. Between 1324 and 1588 it was known as the Wet or Water Quarry because it was liable to flood.[10] The park was created in 1719. It is desribed by Leighton[11] as a 'fine public promenade' occupying 'a rich sloping meadow of about twenty acres...which supplied a considerable part of the red sandstone visible in the older portions of the walls and churches of the town.' It was a site that had 'long been designated 'The Dingle' and...planted with a bold clump of most magnificent horse chestnut and lime trees...' It was said that 'The still retirement and pleasing gloom of this delightful grove from which the noise of the busy town, and even a prospect of its buildings, are almost entirely excluded'. The park still contains a large pond.

We know from Forrest[12] that amphibians were abundant in Victorian Shropshire. He wrote the following: 'Common frog...No description is necessary of such a well-known animal, found generally in all localities suited to its habits...Common toad. Plentiful all over Shropshire...the Toad is quite...useful to the gardener as the Frog, in keeping down slugs and insect pests. The fact is recognized by many intelligent gardeners, who encourage Toads to stay amongst the beds, and even fetch them to place in greenhouses and frames...Natterjack. This is a rather better-looking Toad than the common species, the colours being brighter...in Shropshire it has only been recorded at Lutwyche...and at Broseley...There is little doubt that it often passes unnoticed, as few persons take any interest in such humble creatures as Toads...Great Warty Newt Provincial name, Askel.. fairly common in Shropshire...Common or Smooth Newt Provincial name Askel. Considerably smaller than the last and easily distinguished by the smooth skin, devoid of warts or pimples...Palmate or Webbed Newt...It appears that in districts where it occurs, it often exists in such numbers as to replace the Common Newt, which may be present in small numbers, or absent altogether. Mr J. Steele Elliot reports that the Palmate Newt is extremely numerous in the Wyre Forest, and the authors has received it from the neighbourhood of Shifnal. He has not found it near Shresbury, but there is little doubt that further search would reveal other Shropshire localities for the species'.

Watts (1939)[13] wrote: 'Three species of newts ('askels') occur, and the natterjack toad sparingly, while of course both frogs and ordinary toads are abundant.' Nowadays, residents of Darwin's Gardens (residential street) report the common toad, common frog and 'newts' in their gardens.[13] The smooth newt and great crested newt have formally been recorded in recent times in the tetrad[14]

Darwin later wrote on embryonic development, using newts as an example:[16] 'The student of Nature wonders the more and is astonished the less, the more conversant he becomes with her operations; but of all the perennial miracles she offers to his inspection, perhaps the most worthy of admiration is the development of a plant or of an animal from its embryo. Examine the recently laid egg of some common animal, such as a salamander or newt. It is a minute spheroid in which the best microscope will reveal nothing but a structureless sac, enclosing a glairy fluid, holding granules in suspension. But strange possibilities lie dormant in that semi-fluid globule. Let a moderate supply of warmth reach its watery cradle, and the plastic matter undergoes changes so rapid, yet so steady and purpose-like in their succession, that one can only compare them to those operated by a skilled modeller upon a formless lump of clay. As with an invisible trowel, the mass is divided and subdivided into smaller and smaller portions, until it is reduced to an aggregation of granules not too large to build withal the finest fabrics of the nascent organism. And, then, it is as if a delicate finger traced out the line to be occupied by the spinal column, and moulded the contour of the body; pinching up the head at one end, the tail at the other, and fashioning flank and limb into due salamandrine proportions, in so artistic a way, that, after watching the process hour by hour, one is almost involuntarily possessed by the notion, that some more subtle aid to vision than an achromatic, would show the hidden artist, with his plan before him, striving with skilful manipulation to perfect his work.

As life advances, and the young amphibian ranges the waters, the terror of his insect contemporaries, not only are the nutritious particles supplied by its prey, by the addition of which to its frame, growth takes place, laid down, each in its proper spot, and in such due proportion to the rest, as to reproduce the form, the colour, and the size, characteristic of the parental stock; but even the wonderful powers of reproducing lost parts possessed by these animals are controlled by the same governing tendency. Cut off the legs, the tail, the jaws, separately or all together, and, as Spallanzani showed long ago, these parts not only grow again, but the redintegrated limb is formed on the same type as those which were lost. The new jaw, or leg, is a newt's, and never by any accident more like that of a frog. What is true of the newt is true of every animal and of every plant; the acorn tends to build itself up again into a woodland giant such as that from whose twig it fell; the spore of the humblest lichen reproduces the green or brown incrustation which gave it birth; and at the other end of the scale of life, the child that resembled neither the paternal nor the maternal side of the house would be regarded as a kind of monster.'

Darwin also wrote about the physical appearance of newts[16]: 'The sexes of salamanders or newts often differ much both in colour and structure. In some species prehensile claws are developed on the fore-legs of the males during the breeding-season; and at this season in the male *Triton palmipes* the hind-feet are provided with a swimming web, which is almost completely absorbed during the winter; so that their feet then resemble those of the female. This structure no doubt aids the male in his eager search and pursuit of the female. With our common newts (*Triton punctatus* and *cristatus*) a deep, much-indented crest is developed along the back and tail of the male during the breeding-season, being absorbed during the winter. It is not furnished, as Mr St. George Mivart informs me, with muscles, and therefore cannot be used for locomotion. As during the season of courtship it becomes edged with bright colours, it serves, there can hardly be a doubt, as a masculine ornament. In many species the body presents strongly contrasted, though lurid tints; and these become more vivid during the breeding-season. The male, for instance, of our common little newt (*Triton punctatus*) is "brownish-grey "above, passing into yellow beneath, which in the "spring becomes a rich bright orange, marked every-where with round dark spots." The edge of the crest also is then tipped with bright red or violet. The female is usually of a yellowish-brown colour with scattered brown dots; and the lower surface is often quite plain. The young are obscurely tinted. The ova are fertilised during the act of deposition and are not subsequently tended by either parent. We may therefore conclude that the males acquired their strongly-marked colours and ornamental appendages through sexual selection; these being transmitted either to the male offspring alone or to both sexes.'

Darwin was brought up right on top of the Shropshire-Cheshire plain where meres and smaller pools of glacial origin are scattered. The Shropshire Biodiversity Partnership[17] wrote: 'The low rolling landscapes of north Shropshire are made of surface clay, sands and gravels, resulting from ice sheets hundreds of metres thick effectively bulldozing the landscape. The landscape is predominantly flat with many water-filled hollows or meres, some of which filled with accumulated vegetation and have developed into mosses. The mosses and meres are of international importance for biodiversity and characteristic features of the north Shropshire Plain' Strangely, Darwin does not appear to have made direct reference to the very watery landscape in the north of the county, despite must having been very aware of them.

One pond, located just two miles from The Mount is Oxon Pool, a small kettlehole mere – now belonging to Shropshire Council. It was well known to botanists in Victorian times[18] as a locality for some rare species, such as *Cicuta virosa* and *Hypericum elodes*. It has been studied within each of the 19 (noted with*) 20 and 21 Centuries (noted with =). The plants that can be found there are as follows[18].

Calliergon cordifolium Heart-shaped Spear-moss

=Kindbergia praelonga* Common Feather-moss

Nymphaea alba White Water-lily

Nuphar lutea Yellow Water-lily

Chelidonium majus Greater Celandine

R. sceleratus Celery-leaved Buttercup

R. flammula Lesser Spearwort

Lotus pedunculatus Large Bird's-foot-trefoil

Comarum palustre Marsh Cinquefoil

U. dioica ssp. *galeopsifolia* Fen Nettle

Alnus glutinosa Alder

Salix fragilis Crack Willow

=*S.* ×*rubens* Hybrid Crack-willow

S. cinerea Grey Willow

*Hypericum elodes Marsh St John's-wort

Epilobium hirsutum Great Willowherb

E. parviflorum Hoary Willowherb

*E. palustre Marsh Willowherb

=*Rorippa sylvestris* Creeping Yellow-cress

Nasturtium officinale Water-cress

=*Cardamine pratensis* Cuckoo-flower

C. flexuosa Wavy Bitter-cress

=*C. hirsuta* Hairy Bitter-cress

Persicaria maculosa Redshank

=*P. lapathifolia* Pale Persicaria

P. hydropiper Water-pepper

Polygonum aviculare agg. Knotgrass

=*Rumex conglomeratus* Clustered Dock

Stellaria. alsine Bog Stitchwort

Cerastium fontanum Common Mouse-ear

C. glomeratum Sticky Mouse-ear

S. flos-cuculi Ragged Robin

Hottonia palustris Water-violet

Galium palustre Common Marsh-bedstraw

Pentaglottis sempervirens Green

Myosotis scorpioides Water Forget-me-not

*M. laxa Tufted Forget-me-not

Callitriche sp. Water-starwort

=*C. stagnalis* Common Water-starwort

Scrophularia nodosa Common Figwort

Galeopsis bifida Bifid Hemp-nettle

Scutellaria galericulata Skullcap

*S. minor Lesser Skullcap

Lycopus europaeus Gipsywort

*Mentha ×verticillata Whorled Mint

*Pedicularis palustris Marsh Lousewort

Arctium minus Lesser Burdock

Cirsium vulgare Spear Thistle

C. palustre Marsh Thistle

Gnaphalium uliginosum Marsh Cudweed

Tanacetum parthenium Feverfew

S. sylvaticus Heath Groundsel

=*Bidens cernua* Nodding Bur-marigold

Hydrocotyle vulgaris Marsh Pennywort

*Oenanthe fistulosa Tubular Water-dropwort

O. aquatica Fine-leaved Water-dropwort

*Cicuta virosa Cowbane

Angelica sylvestris Wild Angelica

=*Lemna minor* Common Duckweed

L. minuta Least Duckweed

=*L. trisulca* Ivy-leaved Duckweed

Alisma plantago-aquatica Water-plantain

=*Potamogeton berchtoldii* Small Pondweed

Iris pseudacorus Yellow Iris

Sparganium erectum Branched Bur-reed

Typha latifolia Great Reedmace

=*Juncus articulatus* Jointed Rush

J. bufonius Toad Rush

J. effusus Soft Rush

Schoenoplectus lacustris Common Club-rush

Carex pseudocyperus Cyperus Sedge

*C. rostrata Bottle Sedge

=*C. elata* Tufted Sedge

Phalaris arundinacea Reed Canary-grass

When Darwin picked out his newt from the pond in Shrewsbury, there can surely be no doubt that he would have noticed the other wildlife – namely invertebrates – occupying the pond too. With children, there is no greater temptation in the natural world than to chase around and be mesmorised by the strange creatures that lie beneath a water's surface. What invertebrates can be found at Oxon Pool these days?[19]:

Dugesia polychroa A flatworm

Dugesia tigrina A flatworm

Polycelis nigra A flatworm

Helobdella stagnalis A leech

Glossiphonia complanata leech

Theromyzon tessulatum leech

Bithynia tentaculata Snail

Lymnaea peregra Wandering snail

Lymnaea stagnalis Great pond snail

Sphaerium corneium Freshwater clam

Asellus aquaticus Waterlouse

Crangonyx pseudogracilis Freshwater shrimp

Ceriodaphnia megalops Water flea

Simocephalus vetulus Water flea

Cloeon dipterum Mayfly

Enallagma cyathigerium Common blue damselfly

Pyrrhosoma nymphula Large red damselfly

Nepa cinerea Water scorpion

Notonecta glauca Backswimmer

Acilius canaliculatus Beetle

Gyrinus marinus Whirligig beetle

Haliplus flavicollis Beetle

Anacaena limbata Beetle

Chironomidae Non-biting midge

Additional records for the site from Shropshire Ecological Records Network:

Rana temporaria Common frog

Bufo bufo Common toad

Triturus cristatus Great crested newt

Triturus vulgaris Smooth newt

Ischnura elegans Blue-tailed damselfly

Aeshna grandis Brown hawker

Aeshna mixta Migrant hawker

Aeshna cyanea Southern hawker

Additional species of dragonfly recorded at Bomere and Shomere pools (3 miles from the Mount)[20]

Anax imperator Emperor Dragonfly

Calopteryx splendens Banded Demoiselle

Calopteryx virgo Beautiful Demoiselle

Coenagrion puella Azure Damselfly

Coenagrion pulchellum Variable Damselfly

Cordulia aenea Downy Emerald

Erythromma najas Red-eyed Damselfly

Gomphus vulgatissimus Club-tailed Dragonfly

Lestes sponsa Emerald Damselfly

Libellula depressa Broad-bodied Chaser

Libellula quadrimaculata Four-spotted Chaser

Sympetrum sanguineum Ruddy Darter

Sympetrum striolatum Common Darter

The Banded demoiselle, Club tailed dragonfly and White-legged damselfly have been recorded in recent times in the tetrad The Mount occurs.[21]

In a query raised by Darwin about dragonflies, R. McLachlan responded [22]: 'I do not think that Dragon-flies will give any important results as to protective sexual peculiarities. I think I may say that they are of all insects the least liable to the attacks of birds &c. In themselves they are the tyrants of the insect world, & have few enemies. Universal aggressors yet seldom aggrieved. Very many species, European & exotic, vary in colour in the sexes. In the true Libellulidæ, when this obtains, the male is usually blue & the female yellow, yet I see not how the latter & more conspicuous colour can protect. It is to be remarked also that these insects take a considerable time to attain their full coloration & that at first both sexes are like coloured. Thus the males of Libellula depressa does not acquire its blue tint of body until nearly a fortnight after its first appearance as an imago; & it is probable that until its period of puberty, so to speak, has arrived, it is unfit for reproduction. I look upon the colours of Dragon flies more in the light of sexual attractions than protections...In some Dragon flies the rule of Dimorphism in the female is known to obtain. You have no doubt observed among a host of blue Agrions hovering over a pond, several individuals of an orange-colour— these are always female. This is not confined to one species but is found in many; yet I know not the reason of this difference in the colour of certain individuals. So far as I know they are equally fertile with their blue sisters. It may be owing to the existence of a family tendency. In the true Libellulas where differences of coloration exist, the female is always yellow or orange, & so in the Agrions a tendency to assume the same tint may be more or less latent.'

So what of the wetlands around Downe? Henrietta, Darwin's daughter, wrote:[23] '...across the valley, the shingled spire of Cudham church shewing above its old yews. The view was strongly characteristic of the country, and had the somewhat melancholy charm of our chalk landscape – the waterless, uninhabited valley, the rolling contour of the country, yews in the hedges, and here and there a white chalk-pit.' It's true that the valleys are devoid of rivers, however maps of Darwin's time show that there were a handful of ponds in the landscape. One example was a pond in Downe village itself. I was lucky enough to view a colour print of an etching circa 1890 by W. H. Boot showing the pond being sampled by local cattle. A few miles north of where Down House stands are also the ponds at Keston Common, now owned by the London Borough of Bromley, and the River Ravensbourne.

Darwin wrote:[24] '...this power in fresh-water productions of ranging widely, though so unexpected, can I think, in most cases be explained by their having become fitted, in a manner highly useful to them, for short and frequent migrations from pond to pond, or from stream to stream; and liability to wide dispersal would follow from this capacity as an almost necessary consequence.' Darwin's Landscape Laboratory Partnership[25] explains: 'Darwin had taken a special interest in the distribution of fresh water species ever since noticing, while he was collecting specimens during H.M.S. Beagle voyage, how uniform they were in comparison with land species, while they might have been expected to be varied from their isolation in separate bodies of water between land barriers. He suggested a possible evolutionary answer in On The Origin of Species that only organisms adapted for transport from one body of water to another would survive the frequent drying out of many ponds. When he found surface-water ponds in the countryside around Downe and Cudham, he took the opportunity to test his idea in a number of them'.

Darwin studied the dispersal, survival and germination of plant seeds from waterbodies. He visited Cudham pond and collected samples of mud to then germinate the seeds within them. He wrote: 'April 6th. Got some... mud from two spots, under decaying leaves & roots of water plants, 4 or 5 inches from margin & 3 or 4 inches under water; & a little red clayey mud from margin chiefly in another spot; Little Pond by Cudham School. This mud with fibrous Matter was divided into 2 portions; in one weighing when damp about 2 ¼ oz. 27 Monocot & Dicot. came up making 29 plants. In the other lot, weighing when damp 1 ½ oz. 14 Monocot. came up & 10 Dicot. = Making 24. plants. So that in under 1/4 lb of damp mud 51 plants came up. (May 10th)'[26] Darwin also wrote: 'I do not believe that botanists are aware how charged the mud of ponds is with seeds...I took in February three table-spoonfuls of mud...I kept it covered up in my study for six months, pulling up and counting each plant as it grew; the plants were of many kinds, and were altogether 537 in number.[27]

Darwin tested seed tolerance to sea-water too. Darwin wrote[28]: 'I have begun making some few experiments on the effects of immersion in sea water on the germinating powers of seeds, in the hope of being able to throw a very little light on the distribution of plants, more especially in regard to the same species being found in many cases in far outlying islands and on the mainland.'

Darwin tested how duckweed and water snails could be transported by ducks[29] He wrote: 'When ducks suddenly emerge from a pond covered with duck-weed, I have twice seen these little plants adhering to their backs; and it has happened to me, in removing a little duck-weed from one aquarium to another, that I have unintentionally stocked the one with shells from the other. But another agency is perhaps more effectual: I suspended the feet of a duck in an aquarium, where many ova of fresh-water shells were hatching; and I found that numbers of the extremely minute and just-hatched shells crawled on the feet and clung to them so firmly that they could not be jarred off...These molluscs, though aquatic in nature, survived on the duck's feet, in damp air, from twelve to twenty hours; and in this time a duck might fly at least six hundred miles...'

Darwin wrote further on the role of birds in explaining the distribution of species across islands and geographical areas: 'Some plants might under favourable conditions be transported over...the sea 300 or even more miles...and if cast on the shore of an island not well stocked with species, might become naturalised'.[30]

We are lucky to have a more detailed account of the little pond in Cudham (near Downe) which Darwin studied[31]:

Cudham Pond. — Aug'. 10– 1864. — Now almost dry with much mud after wonderfully dry summer. — Not near Road— No infall or outfall— visited by Water-hens— Cattle & sheep may have been driven into field from distant pasturage— Dry Chalk Platform. no other pool near— Long-made.—

Sparganium simplex

Potamogeton natans?

Veronica scutellata

Ranunculus flammula

Alisma plantago

Lemna

Rush [Juncus sp.]

Glyceria fluitans

Another grass

Newt

Cyclas

Lymnea

Water Coleoptera & Hemiptera (winged)

I was involved in doing an amphibian survey on the very same pond. One year in Spring I counted thousands of tadpoles, six toads, two frogs and three small newts. (Small newt is a legitimate description as young palmate and smooth newts are indistinguishable). One autumn, I led a group of volunteers in de-leafing the pond using chromes and it was interesting to feel that the base of the pond was solid with flints; a practice that was typical in many ponds to prevent cattle puncturing the clay lining.

It was interesting to read of the plant species Darwin found in this pond. I undertook a plant survey of ponds in the Borough and those he found are still present in many of them. Of those present in the downland landscape I found:

Juncus inflexus Hard rush

Butomus ubellatus Flowering rush

Juncus articulatus Jointed rush

Juncus bufonius Toad rush

Schoenoplecus lacueris Bulrush

Carex pendula Pendulus sedge

Lemna minor Common duckweed

Lemna auricular Ivy-leaved duckweed

Certophyllum demersum Rigid hornwort

Potomogetan natans Broadleaved pondweed

Lagarosiphon major Curly leaved elodea

Iris pseudacorus Yellow flag iris

Nymphaea alba White water lily

Alisma plantago-aquatica Common water plantain

Typha latifolia Greater reedmace

Sparganium erectum Branched burreed

Elodea nutalli Soft elodea

Lythrum salicaria Purple loosestrife

Caltha palustris Marsh marigold

Glyceria declinata Glaucous sweetgrass

Glyceria fluitans Floating sweetgrass

Veronica beccabunga Brooklime

Ranunculus lingua Greater spearwort

What snails and other invertebrates can now be found in ponds around Downe? The Borough commissioned a brief survey of invertebrates in Keston Ponds some years ago and found the following species.[32] As for Darwin in Cudham Pond, Hemiptera, Coleoptera, and Lymnea were found here too.

Mollusca *Ferrisia wauteri* Freshwater limpet alien

Mollusca *Gyraulus albus* White ramshorn

Mollusca *Gyraulus laevis* Smooth ramshorn local

Mollusca *Hippeutis complanatus* Flat ramshorn

Mollusca *Radix auricularia* Ear Snail

Mollusca *Radix balthica* Wandering snail

Mollusca *Lymnaea stagnalis* Great pond snail

Mollusca *Physa fontinalis* Bladder snail

Mollusca *Pisidium sp.* Pea mussel

Mollusca *Planorbarius corneus* Great ramshorn

Mollusca *Planorbis carinatus* Keeled ramshorn

Mollusca *Planorbis planorbis* Ramshorn

Mollusca *Potamopyrgus antipodarum* Jenkins spire snail

Mollusca *Sphaerium corneum* Horny orb mussel

Flatworms *Dendrocoelium lacteum* Flatworm

Flatworms *Dugesia lugubris* Flatworm

Flatworms *Dugesia tigrina* Flatworm alien

Flatworms *Polycelis nigra* Flatworm

Flatworms *Polycelis tenuis* Flatworm

Leeches *Erpobdella octoculata* Leech

Leeches *Glossiphonia heteroclita* Leech local

Leeches *Haemopis sanguisuga* Horse leech

Leeches *Helobdella stagnalis* Leech

Leeches *Hemiclepsis marginata* Leech

Leeches *Piscicola geometra* Fish leech

Leeches *Theromyzon tessulatum* Duck leech

Crustacea *Asellus aquaticus* Water slater

Crustacea *Crangonyx pseudogracilis* Freshwater shrimp

Crustacea *Gammarus pulex* Freshwater shrimp inflow

Megaloptera *Sialis lutaria* Alderfly

Ephemeroptera *Cloeon dipterum* Pond Olive

Ephemeroptera *Caenis horaria* Angler's curse

Ephemeroptera *Caenis luctuosa* Angler's curse

Odonata *Aeshna cyanea* Southern Hawker

Odonata *Anax imperator* Emperor dragonfly

Odonata *Coenagrion puella* Azure damselfly

Odonata *Enallagma cyathigerum* Common Blue damselfly

Odonata *Erythromma najas* Red-eyed damselfly

Odonata *Ischnura elegans* Blue-tailed damselfly

Odonata *Pyrrhosoma nymphula* Large red damselfly

Odonata *Sympetrum sanguineum* Ruddy darter

Odonata *Sympetrum striolatum* Common darter

Hemiptera *Cymatia coleoptrata* Lesser water boatman

Hemiptera *Gerris gibbifer* Water skater

Hemiptera *Gerris lacustris* Water skater

Hemiptera *Gerris sp* Water skater nymphs

Hemiptera *Hesperocorixa moesta* Lesser water boatman

Hemiptera *Hesperocorixa sahlbergi* Lesser water boatman

Hemiptera *Hydrometra stagnorum* Water measurer

Hemiptera *Ilyocoris cimicoides* Saucer bug

Hemiptera *Micronecta scholtzi* Water singer local

Hemiptera *Microvelia pygmaea* Micro-water cricket nationally scarce

Hemiptera *Microvelia reticulata* Micro-water cricket

Hemiptera *Nepa cinerea* Water scorpion

Hemiptera *Notonecta glauca* Water boatman

Hemiptera *Plea minutissima* Least water boatman

Hemiptera *Sigara dorsalis* Lesser water boatman

Hemiptera *Sigara falleni* Lesser water boatman

Hemiptera *Velia caprai* Water cricket inflow

Coleoptera *Agabus bipustulatus* Diving beetle

Coleoptera *Anacaena limbata* Scavenger beetle

Coleoptera *Galerucella nymphaeae* Leaf beetle

Coleoptera *Helochares punctatus* Scavenger beetle nationally scarce

Coleoptera *Helodidae* Marsh beetle larvae

Coleoptera *Hydrobius fuscipes* Scavenger

Coleoptera *Hydroporus angustatus* Diving beetle

Coleoptera *Hydroporus gyllenhalii* Diving beetle

Coleoptera *Hydroporus incognitus* Diving beetle

Coleoptera *Hydroporus memnonius* Diving beetle

Coleoptera *Hydroporus obscurus* Diving beetle

Coleoptera *Hydroporus palustris* Diving beetle

Coleoptera *Hydroporus planus* Diving beetle

Coleoptera *Haliplus flavicollis* Crawling water beetle

Coleoptera *Haliplus ruficollis* Crawling water beetle

Trichoptera *Agraylea multipunctata* Micro-caddis

Trichoptera *Agraylea sp.* Micro-caddis

Trichoptera *Oxyethira sp* Micro-caddis

Trichoptera *Agrypnia varia* Cased caddis

Trichoptera *Glyphotaelius pellucidus* Cased caddis

Trichoptera *Micropterna lateralis* Cased caddis inflow

Trichoptera *Mystacides longicornis* Cased caddis

Trichoptera *Holocentropus dubius* Caseless caddis

Trichoptera *Holocentropus picicornis* Caseless caddis

Trichoptera *Hydropsyche angustipennis* Caseless caddis inflow

Diptera *Ceratopogonidae* Biting midge larvae

Diptera *Chironomidae* Non-biting midge larvae

Diptera *Culicidae* Mosquito larvae

Diptera *Dixidae* Meniscus midge larvae

Diptera *Ephyhridae* Shore flies larvae

Diptera *Muscidae* Stable flies pupae

Diptera *Psychodidae* Moth flies larvae

Diptera *Ptychopteridae* Lesser crane-flies larvae

Diptera *Sciomyzidae* Snail-eating flies larvae

Diptera *Simuliidae* Black flies larvae inflow

Diptera *Tipulidae* Crane flies larvae

Others *Hydracarina* Water mites

Others *Oligochaeta* True worms

Others *Spongillidae* Sponge outflow

MAMMALIAN AND REPTILIAN ENCOUNTERS

In the 1930's, Watts[1] summarised the status of mammals in Shropshire in this way: 'About the mammals there is little to say...There are no wild deer, though red deer and roe-deer lived here in early historic times, but fallow deer are preserved in numerous parks. Dormice, squirrels and otters are plentiful, and the badger not scarce. Though the polecat and the wild cat are extinct, the weasel and stoat are abundant. There are six species of bat of which two, Daubenton's bat and the whiskered bat, have only recently been recorded.'

Times have changed. I on at least two occasions, saw herds of deer in the vicinity of Ludlow including crossing a road at Mortimer Forest. Dormice have been the subject of a Species Action Plan in Shropshire. They are known to occur in around 50 tetrads, mainly in the southern half of the county and especially along Wenlock Edge. Red squirrels no longer occur in the county; grey squirrels have taken their place. Otters have been joined by minks on the riverside (they have been spotted by The Mount [3]). The polecat is widespread in the county. Shropshire supports at least twelve of the eighteen British species of bat[4].'

Earlier reports on mammals, collated in 1899 by Forrest[5], state: '...the number of species of Mammals is very limited, and cannot be added to from outside unless by human agency, and any species once extinct, cannot occur again...the Black Rat and the Pine Martin disappeared this century; while the Polecat is on the verge of extinction...A noticeable characteristic of our Mammals is that they are, almost without exception, nocturnal in their habits, possibly from fear of man; they conceal themselves by day in holes or amongst herbage, even those which do come abroad by day fly at his approach. This makes the study of their habits in a state of nature one of peculiar difficulty, for there are few naturalist who will spend their nights out of doors for the sake of learning some new fact concerning them. A great deal, however, may be learnt by going to some secluded wood on a fine summer evening and sitting perfectly still. Rabbits, Stoats, various Mice, Squirrels etc will soon appear and disport themselves within a few feets of the observer apparently unconscious of his presence, but – if he stir ever so lightly – they instantly vanish into obscurity.'

A number of different bat species have been recorded on the Down House estate in recent times and include the Common pipistrelle, Soprano pipistrelle, Serotine and Long-eared bat.[6] A resident of Darwin's Gardens (residential street) has reported seeing bats in the wood and along the riverbank near The Mount and no doubt these habitats would have attracted bats in Darwin's day.[7] Common pipistrelle, Daubenton's bat, Noctule bat and Whiskered bat have been formally recorded near the Mount in recent times.[8] The other bat species that definitely occur nowadays in Shropshire are Soprano pipistrelle, Brown-long-eared bat (alongside the Pipistrelles', the commonest), Natterer's bat, Lesser Horseshoe bat, Brandt's bat, Barbastelle, Leisler's bat and Serotine. It is thought that Alcathoe's bat, Bechsteins bat, Nathusius's pipistrelle and Greater Horseshoe bat may be 'possibly present'.[9] For Victorian Shropshire, the following bat species were recognized[10]:

'Of the eleven species of Bat recognized as British, only six are known to occur in Shropshire, and, of these, the Long-eared bat is the most numerous...Noctule or Great Bat...seems to be pretty generally distributed through Shropshire, especially in the neighbourhood of water, but is not so numerous as the Long-eared...Pipistrelle or Common Bat.. Although this Bat is common all over the County, it is not so numerous in Shropshire as the Long-eared...It is, however, more often seen than any other species because it comes abroad at times when all the other Bats are hibernating...Daubenton's Bat is best known by its extreme fondness for water... Mr J. Steele Elliott reports that this Bat is common...along the river Severn generally throughout the County...Natterer's or Reddish-Grey Bat...Eyton states that he had a specimen of this Bat taken at Eyton, near Wellington, Salop. This was in 1840 and is still the only record for the County, though as the species is not a rare one it almost certainly occurs here, but passes unrecognized...Whiskered Bat...Mr Chas. Oldham...writes in the Zoologist 1890...one...was knocked down with a stick in a garden at Hanwood, near Shrewsbury...this is the only record for Shropshire'

Darwin wrote about the morphology of bats: 'In bats which have the wing-membrane extended from the top of the shoulder to the tail, including the hind-legs, we perhaps see traces of an apparatus originally constructed for gliding through the air rather than for flight.'[11] Darwin wrote: 'The framework of bones being the same in the hand of a man, wing of a bat, fin of the porpoise, and leg of the horse,—the same number of vertebræ forming the neck of the giraffe and of the elephant,—and innumerable other such facts, at once explain themselves on the theory of descent with slow and slight successive modifications. The similarity of pattern in the wing and leg of a bat, though used for such different purpose...is likewise intelligible on the view of the gradual modification of parts or organs...' [12] He wrote: 'Morphology...What can be more curious than that the hand of a man, formed for grasping, that of a mole for digging, the leg of the horse, the paddle of the porpoise, and the wing of the bat, should all be constructed on the same pattern, and should include the same bones, in the same relative positions?...the parts may change to almost any extent in form and size, and yet they always remain connected together in the same order. We never find, for instance, the bones of the arm and forearm, or of the thigh and leg, transposed. Hence the same names can be given to the homologous bones in widely different animals...'[13]

Forrest[14] says of 'Hedgehog or Urchin...It is certain that it does not eat fruit, or indeed vegetable matter of any kind...food...worms, slugs, beetles, and young birds...bird's eggs.. They sometimes eat poultry, attacking them at night when asleep on the nest, and putting them to a horrible lingering death by eating into the soft parts of their bodies...they will kill and eat snakes and vipers...In captivity the Hedgehog is useful in destroying cock-roaches in kitchens.. The Hedgehog is common all over the County, and there is a popular superstition that it sucks cows, robbing the calves of their milk...A white Hedgehog was taken near Oswestry a few years ago.' Reading this reminded me of the various myths I had come across when learning about hedgehogs in my youth. It therefore surprised me to read about an-other tale about hedgehogs actually being promoted by Darwin, following his receipt of a letter which had included the statement of a witness to the hedgehog's use of its spines as a foraging tool.[15] '.. you have published an account of hedgehogs apparently carrying away pears and crabs sticking on their spines, you may think the following statement worth insertion as a further corroboration. I have received this account in a letter dated August 5, 1867, from Mr. Swinhoe at Amoy:— "Mr. Gisbert, the Spanish Consul at Amoy, informs me that when he was an engineer on the roads in Spain some years ago, he was fond of shooting and roaming about the country. He states that in the Sierra Morena, a strawberry-tree...was very abundant, and bore large quantities of red, fruit-like, fine, large, red strawberries...Under these trees hedgehogs occurred innumerable, and fed on the fruit...Mr Gis-bert has often seen...hedgehog[s]...trotting along with at least a dozen of these strawberries sticking on its spines. He supposes that the hedgehogs were carrying the fruit to their holes to eat in quiet and security, and that to procure them they must have rolled themselves on the fruit which was scattered in great abundance all over the ground beneath the trees."

Hedgehogs certainly appear to be numerous in south Shropshire, judg-ing from their remains on the road, but I was never to see a live one strolling along in the gloom of the night. A colleague, who lived in Shrewsbury, had had a hedgehog in her garden for a number of years.[16] She said that it must have lived in an unkempt garden a few doors down from her and that it was easy to hear it coming as it shuffled through the undergrowth. Shropshire Mammal Group records[17] show that hedgehogs are very much present in Shrewsbury, so it would not be surprising if Darwin encountered them there in his day. In fact, Milner says that as a young man, Darwin 'sought out the homes of foxes and hedgehogs.'[18]

Forrest[19] presents the following dubious information on moles: '... provincial name, Oont...The presence of the Mole is shown all over the County by the abundance of molehills which are to be seen in pastures, fields, and gardens, everywhere...It has been known to take to the water, and swim well, and will often make a tunnel to a brook or pond for it is a thirsty animal, and goes regularly at noon to the water to drink.' He does not mention their unfortunate position in being considered a pest. I have since coming to Shropshire seen evidence of mole control, witnessing on fences the decaying and mummified bodies of moles caught by farmers. I had never seen a live mole until the day a boy brought one in a bucket to a WATCH group I was helping with. His cat had brought it into the house and had let it go in the hallway. We all admired its smoky grey pelt, its broad front feet and shoulders and its brush of a tail. Darwin wrote on moles[20]: 'How many moles may a person casually examine without perceiving the slightest difference, yet being a thoroughly well known, animal, we hear from Mr. Bell, in his excellent history of British Quadrupeds...that there are several remarkable varieties...' Elsewhere, Darwin wrote:[21] 'The eyes of moles and of some burrowing rodents are rudimentary in size, and in some cases are quite covered up by skin and fur. This state of the eyes is probably due to gradual reduction from disuse, but aided perhaps by natural selection.'

Foxes have been seen by a resident of Darwin's Gardens (residential street) in modern times.[22] Forrest[23] says about Shropshire's foxes: '...In England the Fox is surrounded by a kind of romantic halo owing to its association with the national sport of the country. From time immemorial it has been adopted in literature as the type of cunning and sagacity, and is represented in fable as invariably getting the best of other animals by its cleverness. The wiles it adopts to escape from the pursuing hounds have been so often recorded that there is no need to describe them here, and so dear are these stories to the heart of the Foxhunter that he would be a bold man who would venture to throw discredit upon them. It may be well, however, to point out that the existence of the Fox in England is very artificial, and there is little doubt that, but for the protection afforded by the unwritten lawn which makes it a crime to shoot a Fox, the animal would be nearly or quite as rare as the Wild Cat...In Shropshire the fox is fairly plentiful wherever there is suitable cover, and most landowners preserve it carefully.' Unfortunately I discovered the Shrewsbury Journal[24] make the claim that 'We believe that Darwin...was a keen foxhunter in his youth, and that it was in this field that his great habits of observation were first awakened.' I later was more comforted by Francis Darwin's[25] report of Darwin's more affectionate encounters with foxes at Downe: 'He used to tell us how, when he was creeping along in the 'Big Woods', he came upon a fox asleep in the daytime, which was so much astonished that it took a good stare at him before it ran off. A Spitz dog which accompanied him showed no sign of excitement at the fox, and he used to end the story by wondering how the dog could have been so faint-hearted.' Francis also wrote:[26] 'He used to delight me as a boy by telling me how, in still earlier walks, on dark winter mornings, he had once or twice met foxes trotting home at the dawning'. I have been priviledged as a Londoner to have foxes and their playful cubs in the gardens of two properties in which I lived. One adult female, Foxy as we called her, had learnt to sit outside the kitchen door and peer through the glass in the hope of a morsel of food. Her fiery coat, bushy tail, sharp muzzle and hazel eyes were beautiful to see at close quarters. In Shropshire, I never saw a live fox so supporting the case that nowadays foxes are perhaps at their most dense in urban situations.

Forrest[27] reports on stoats and weasals:

Stoat...This graceful, active, and courageous little animal is plentiful in Shropshire, and more numerous than any of its tribe in spite of the numbers shot every year by gamekeepers...the writer once watched a group of five on the towing-path of the Canal, near Shrewsbury'. Weasel 'It...destroys large numbers of mice and voles...For this reason the Weasel should be encouraged and protected instead of being shot by keepers as it so often is...In Shropshire the Weasel is common everywhere, but not so numerous as the Stoat.' I have not been able to find any information as to whether either of these two mustelids have been encountered near the Mount in modern times. When I'd previously seen a 'stoat-weasel' I had always been so excited at glimpsing it for those few seconds, that I constantly missed my opportunity to note the colour of the tip of their tail – distinctive between the two species. It was therefore a pleasing moment when I saw one aim to cross the road in the middle of the afternoon on Clee Hill. Whilst concentrating on not running it over, I noted a black tail tip – a stoat! The stoat has been recorded in modern times around the locality of The Mount.

Throughout Downe are badger setts, with badger activity being evident from the frequent runs and dung pits. In Shropshire, was the first time I 'counted' seeing a badger. My badger-watching exploits in the past had not come to much; the most I had previously seen was the backside of one in Downe village one night. But in Shropshire I saw the full length of one ahead of me, waddling across the road and sniffing out its regular path as it searched for its 'pedestrian crossing'. Darwin felt that the visual appearance of a species might remain over a long period of time. In a letter to H. Falconer dated 26 December 1863, he wrote:[28] 'has not Owen stated that the Pliocene badger is identical with the recent? Such a case does indeed well show the stupendous duration of the same form.' It was interesting to find on a tour of Darwin's[29] wooded garden in the old grounds of the Mount, that badgers had created spoil on one of the key paths through the site. I wonder whether Darwin went badger-watching as a child or adult? Forrest[30] says of the badger: 'It used to be called the 'Brock' and the word is found in many Shropshire place-names...it is rarely seen in the districts where it resides, and thus it is generally regarded as a rare animal and decreasing in numbers. So far as Shropshire is concerned, this is certainly not the case, and it is found in most parts of the County where there are extensive woodland remote from the dwellings of man...The cruel sport of Badger-baiting is now supposed to be obsolete in England...Opinions differ as to whether the Badger is worthy of protection or not...'

I thought that I'd never see a polecat. My colleague at work said he had had some in his Shropshire garden[30a] and this really surprised me. I didn't even know they occurred in the County at that stage. Amazingly, a couple of days later, on the borders with Herefordshire, I saw one – but not in good circumstances. The car in front of me had just managed to injure it and it was hobbling back and forth across the road in obvious discomfort. Then it suddenly expired. Though on a sharp bend in the road, I took the opportunity to get out of the car to examine its beauty. I knew this would probably be the only one I would ever see at such close quarters again. It's demise has been something I've been desperately keen for forget. Of the Pole cat Forrest[31] says: '...Provincial name, Fitchet...Few animals of its size are so destructive of game, poultry etc. as the Polecat, and the result of the bad character it bears is that it is shot and trapped at every opportunity. Early in the...century it was quite common in Shropshire, and it could not be called rare in 1850, but from that time forward the number has diminished so rapidly that the time cannot now be far distant when it will be as extinct locally as the Marten...recent occurrences.. Craven Arms...1895... Leighton...1897...' Polecats have been recorded in recent times within two miles of the Mount.

Within three weeks of starting work in Shropshire, out of the corner of my eye along the River Clun, near Clunton, I saw something sodden and slippery. It stared at me for a few seconds and then it was gone. I had seen my first otter. And what a thrill it was. It is very likely Darwin would have seen otters along the Severn; the species has been seen in modern times by Darwin's Gardens (residential street)[32]. Forrest[33] reported that..In Shropshire the Otter is found on the Severn and most of the larger streams, and in some parts is numerous...Rev J.B. Meredith, of Kinnerley writes – '... for two years there has been a regular holt on the Morda brook...I had the pleasure of seeing one fishing in the Tanat, and as I continued perfectly still he seemed to have no fear, and at times cames within a dozen yards...' Darwin makes references to otters in some of his writings[34]...'To return to the objection which has actually been made that a land-carnivorous animal could not be changed into an Otter, for it could not live during the transitional state. The genus *Mustela* is closely allied to Lutra or the otter, & indeed was made into one by Linnaeus. Some species of Mustela occasionally haunt the water, & the common Polecat has been known to lay up stores of half-killed frogs; the N. American Vison-Weasel (*Mustela vison* allied to the *M. lutreola* of N. Europe) has webbed feet, a flattened head, short ears, close fur & a tail all like an otter: it can dive well, & preys on fish: but during the winter when the water is frozen, it hunts mice on the land: here then we have an animal allied to the otter, wholly aquatic during part of the year & partly terrestrial during another part. Can it, then, be said that there would be any great difficulty, as far as transitional habits are concerned, in converting a polecat into an otter. The possibility will rest on there being a place open in the polity of nature, which would allow of a polecat living & increasing in numbers, if rendered more & more aquatic in habits & structure. On the same principles an otter could be converted into a seal-like animal; not, perhaps, now when seals actually exist & well fill their place in nature, but before a seal had been formed. It might well happen through natural selection, that an aquatic animal should be converted into a terrestrial animal, retaining perhaps a trace of its former webbed feet; & subsequently have some of its descendants refitted to inhabit the waters.'

In Darwin's day, the squirrel referred to by Forrest would have been the now uncommon Red Squirrel. Forrest[35] explains: '...its sprightly habitat, make it a general favourite. It is all over the County wherever there are woods, especially those that contain beech and hazel trees, on the mast and nuts of which it feeds...When alarmed it scampers away with marvellous agility...It can also run rapidly on the ground by a succession of leaps... It is rare indeed to see a Squirrel miss its footing...'. We know Darwin was familiar with squirrels at least from a reference by Francis at Downe. 'He did not always walk round with swinging step & the click of the ironshod walking stick which is so strongly associated with the place, for sometimes when alone he stood still or walked quietly to see birds & beasts. It was on one of these occasions that some young squirrels mistook him for a part of a tree and ran up his back and legs while their mother barked at them in an agony from the tree.'[36] Darwin wrote of their feeding behaviour: 'I may mention that I once saw some squirrels eagerly splitting those little semi-transparent spherical galls on the back of oak-leaves, for the maggot within; so that they are insectivorous.'[37] These days Downe, The Mount, and other places in Shropshire, only support the introduced grey squirrel.

Forrest[38] says of the Common Dormouse: 'This pretty little creature resembles the Squirrel in general appearance and shape, though in reality is is much more nearly related to the Mice. It is very gental and retiring in its habits, and , as it rarely comes abroad by day, it is generally thought to be rather scarce, This, however, is not really the case, and it is to be found in most copses by those who know how and where to look for it' It is unlikely that Darwin encountered the species in Shropshire, as he didn't live near extensive areas of ancient woodland where it normally resides. Around Downe lives the only population of dormice within Greater London; he could well have encountered them there. It is nowadays a species which has been subject to much conservation work. It is famous for spending half of its year sleeping. Darwin wrote[39]: 'Amongst the rodents two very curious contrasts in the matter of tail are presented by the guinea-pig and the squirrel. The former is gregarious, and any one who has kept a hutch of guinea-pigs must have seen how they protect themselves from loss of heat by packing themselves in rows arranged heads and tails; whilst the squirrel is solitary, and in his nest, during his winter sleep, coils himself up and covers his face with his tail. The same is seen in...the dormouse during hibernation.'

In relation to the Harvest Mouse, Forrest[40] says: 'The tiniest of British Mammals is rather rare in Shropshire, and even where it occurs is very local, being perhaps found in one field and not in the next...Eyton had in his collection a pair with their nest which he found on the Weald Moors' Darwin was familiar with harvest mice; he wrote[41]: 'Professor Henslow kept in confinement some harvest mice (*Mus messorius*) which do not possess a structurally prehensile tail; but he frequently observed that they curled their tails round the branches of a bush placed in the cage, and thus aided themselves in climbing. I have received an analogous account from Dr. Günther, who has seen a mouse thus suspend itself. If the harvest mouse had been more strictly arboreal, it would perhaps have had its tail rendered structurally prehensile, as is the case with some members of the same order.' They have not been reported close to Shrewsbury in modern times. I used to come across harvest mouse nests, which are tennis-ball in size, around Downe, including at Hang Grove and Den Barn Farm. They were very easy to overlook and would most commonly be spotted after an autumn harvest of hay.

What of other rodents around the Mount? Nowadays, a resident of Darwin's Gardens (residential street) has reported 'mice' and 'voles' in the former Mount grounds.[42]

Forrest[43] says of the Wood mouse or long-tailed Field Mouse:' This little animal is abundant all over the County...It occurs in hedgebanks, woods, fields, of grain or grass, stackyards and sometimes even in houses... The write has noticed a curious habit it has of biting off the 'hips' or berries of the Wild Rose and storing them up in old nests of the thrush and blackbird...' We know that Darwin observed field mice in Downe because he makes reference to them as regards their role in a 'food chain' relating to red clover.[44] He wrote: ' I have found that the visits of bees are necessary for the fertilisation of some kinds of clover...100 heads of red clover produced 2700 seeds but the same number of protected heads produced not a single seed...if the whole genus of humble-bees became extinct or very rare in England, the...red clover would become very rare, or wholly disappear...it is quite credible that the presence of a feline animal in large numbers in a district might determine, through the intervention first of mice and then of bees, the frequency of certain flowers in the district!'

It is an exciting task to undertake live small mammal-trapping as a means of identifying the range of species occurring in a special habitat. One of the most unusual to catch is the Yellow-necked mouse, which has a 'yellow bib' on its chest. Forrest[45] reports this as being 'taken by Mr. Dumville Lees, near Oswestry'. He says of the Field Vole of Short-tailed field mouse...'it is usually more numerous, and at times has been known to appear in enormous numbers, causing complete devastation over entire districts. Fortunately this has never happened in Shropshire, but as a warning to those who persist in destroying such natural enemies of the mice as Weasels, Owls, Buzzards and Kestrels...In Shropshire the Field Vole is found in most parts that are under cultivations, and, being noticed chiefly when the grass or wheat is cut, is sometimes called the Harvest Mouse – a name which belongs properly to a very different and much rarer animal...and the Field vole has been taken in the centre of Shrewsbury'. Of the Bank vole he wrote '...the distribution of the Bank vole is very partial, for, while there are large areas in which it is quite unknown, there are other districts in which it is very abundant and the common Field vole comparatively scarce...it has not yet been found near Shrewsbury.' All three species have been recorded in the hectad around The Mount. I would often come across voles, which had been disturbed, whilst cutting and raking chalk grasslands around Downe. I remember once gapping-up a hedgerow with bare-rooted trees along the banks of an old track called Bogey Lane when some voles, disturbed by the vibration of the spades in the ground, crossed one by one over the path to hide in the base of a hedge opposite.

Forrest[45] writes of Shrews or Shrew-mice in Shropshire: 'Common in Shropshire, this little animal is not often seen alive on account of its seeking food only by night. In autumn, large numbers of them are found lying dead in roads and lanes; there are no marks upon them, or we might suppose they got killed in a fight, for Shrews are very pugnacious. This annual mortality is a puzzle'. Shrews in fact are known to forage at all times of the day, taking 'cat naps' of a few seconds along their journeys in the undergrowth. I have often come across dead shrews in the middle of paths and roads myself. Darwin wrote on Shrews 'With Shrew-mice... both sexes possess abdominal scent-glands, and there can be little doubt, from the manner in which their bodies are rejected by birds and beasts of prey, that their odour is protective 46'. The Common shrew, as well as the Pygmy shrew, have been recorded in modern times in tetrad SJ41 around The Mount.

Two small mammals that are most commonly associated with wetlands are the Water Shrew and the Water Vole. Forrest[45] writes about them in the following way: 'Water shrews...As its name implies, it is found in the neighbourhood of water, in which it swims and dives readily....On account of its timidity it is very rarely seen, but there is no doubt it is fairly common in Shropshire, as specimens have been taken in several widely-separated localities, as well as close to Shrewsbury... Eyton had an albino taken near Shrewsbury... Water vole or Water Rat... although it is numerous on all our ponds, pools, canals and streams, this is one of the most harmless and inoffensive of animals'. Water voles have been recorded in recent times in the tetrad in which The Mount occurs, and so may well have been seen by Darwin there too. I saw neither species whilst working in Shropshire.

Two mammal species most associated with humans is the rat and the house-mouse; I was well acquainted with these when living in London. In the latter case, their appearance in the house often coincided with the onset of winter and they would waste no time in swelling their population! Forrest 45 stated: 'Common or Brown rat...was introduced...about the middle of the 18th Century...It very quickly over-ran the Country and exterminated the other wherever it appeared...It is now only too common everywhere, so that a description of its habits is unnecessary... Although it is generally found in or near to houses, the Rat often takes up its quarters in fields and gardens, or on the banks of brooks, and lives there through the summer...'. For the 'Common (House) mouse' Forrest wrote of them in Shropshire: 'The appearance and habits of this animal are so familiar, and it is so plentiful everywhere that description is superfluous...although it usually inhabits houses it often visits gardens and fields adjoin them and hundreds are frequently found at the bottom of corn stacks...' I did not see rats whilst working in Shropshire, despite walking many miles of riverbank, however both House mice and rats have been recorded around The Mount in modern times.

Rabbits proved to be a fascination for Darwin. Darwin would correspond with others about breeding and how particular characteristics could be transferred from generation to generation. He wrote[53]:

'These rabbits have run wild for a considerable time in Sandon Park, and in other places in Staffordshire and Shropshire. They originated, as I have been informed by the gamekeeper, from variously-coloured domestic rabbits which had been turned out. They vary in colour; but many are symmetrically coloured, being white with a streak along the spine, and with the ears and certain marks about the head of a blackish-grey tint. They have rather longer bodies than common rabbits.

Finally, let us sum up the more important modifications which domestic rabbits have undergone, together with their causes as far as we can obscurely see them. By the supply of abundant and nutritious food, together with little exercise, and by the continued selection of the heaviest individuals, the weight of the larger breeds has been more than doubled. The bones of the limbs have increased in weight (but the hind legs less than the front legs), in due proportion with the increased weight of body; but in length they have not increased in due proportion, and this may have been caused by the want of proper exercise. With the increased size of the body the third cervical vertebra has assumed characters proper to the fourth cervical; and the eighth and ninth dorsal vertebræ have similarly assumed characters proper to the tenth and posterior vertebræ. The skull in the larger breeds has increased in length, but not in due proportion with the increased length of body; the brain has not duly increased in dimensions, or has even actually decreased, and consequently the bony case for the brain has remained narrow, and by correlation has affected the bones of the face and the entire length of the skull. The skull has thus acquired its characteristic narrowness. From unknown causes the supra-orbital processes of the frontal bones and the free end of the malar bones have increased in breadth; and in the larger breeds naturalists, with, as far as I know, a single exception, believe that the several domestic breeds of the rabbit are descended from the common wild species; I shall therefore describe them more carefully than in the previous cases. Professor Gervais states: "that the true wild rabbit is smaller than the domestic; its proportions are not absolutely the same; its tail is smaller; its ears are shorter and more thickly clothed with hair; and these characters, without speaking of colour, are so many indications opposed to the opinion which unites these animals under the same specific denomination." Few naturalists will agree with this author that such slight differences are sufficient to separate as distinct species the wild and domestic rabbit. How extraordinary it would be, if close confinement, perfect tameness, unnatural food, and careful breeding, all prolonged during many generations, had not produced at least some effect! The tame rabbit has been domesticated from an ancient period.'[54]

The Natural History Museum in London 'has exotic species [of mammals] collected in South America during *H.M.S. Beagle* Voyage...and included [are]...two feral black rabbits from the Falkland Islands.' The Museum also has 'about twenty specimens of wild or feral rabbits and a dozen of domestic breeds of rabbit obtained by...Darwin at a later date about 1860. They are disarticulated skeletons or just skulls and many lack any locality data. There are some which were obtained from the Island of Maderia, other individuals are from mainland Spain, Northern Ireland and the Shetland Islands. There are two skeletons of wild rabbits annotated 'Kent' and 'Down'...There is also the skull of a domestic lop-eared rabbit which is marked 'Down'. These all relate to Darwin's work on island forms and domestic breeds.'[55]

What might Darwin's experience have been of reptiles in Shropshire? Forrest[56] states the following: 'Common lizard, provincial name Harriman...this pretty and agile little creature...is fairly common on heathy uplands in Shropshire...common in the Wyre Forest, and Mr. Martin J. Harding says he has seen it frequently along the old Potteries Railway line, near Shrewsbury...Sand lizard, less common than the preceding, this species is found more frequently on low-lying ground and on sandy heaths. In Shropshire it has been found on the Weald Moors...near Admaston... and at Bromfield...Blind-worm or Slow-Worm...the creature lives mostly in crevices in the ground, and along hedge-banks, and , like other reptiles, emerges from its retreat when the weather is warm, to bask in the sun. It is then so supremely happy that it becomes oblivious of all else but the pleasant warmth, and can be caught easily by anyone who approaches it quietly...The Blind-worm is plentiful throughout Shropshire, in such situations as are suited to its habits, and this too in spite of the numbers killed every year by the mis-directed zeal of ignorant persons...Common or Ringed Snake. This is the most abundant of the Reptiles in Shropshire, and is found pretty generally throughout the County. It is also the largest British Reptile, occasionally reaching a length of five feet...Viper or Adder. Provincial name Etther. This, our only poisonous reptile, is easily distinguished...In Shropshire the Viper is not nearly so numerous as the Snake. It is entirely absent from the immediate neighbourhood of Shrewsbury, the nearest places where it occurs being Nesscliff and Pim Hills. It is fairly numerous in the neighbourhood of Oswestry and Ellesmere, on Rudge Heath and Whixall Moss in the North; and on Titterstone Clee Hill, and in the Forest of Wyre in the South'

Later, Watts states:[57] Lizards and the blindworm are well known, the ringed snake is fairly common and the viper, our only venomous snake, is found usually in dry, warm, and stony places but is also abundant on the peat of Whixall Moss'. The common lizard has been recorded near the Mount in recent times [58]. Darwin does appear to take an interest in reptiles in various locations. He wrote: '1819. July (ten and a half years). Went to the sea at Plas Edwards. I remember a certain shady green road (where I saw a snake) and a waterfall, with a degree of pleasure'[59] and '3 July 1826 – Caught the *Lacerta agilis*1 with several eggs in its body'.[60]

Common lizards and slow-worms may be regularly seen around Downe, especially on the chalk grasslands. On warm days, the lizards meander between the grass stems with unbelievable ease at high speed. The slow-worms can be most readily seen under artificial 'refugia' of corrugated iron or roofing felt, where they gather to warm-up. Grass snake have been sighted near Berry's Hill and at Holwood Estate, for example. The adder occurs not too far away from Keston Common.

UNDER OUR FEET

Does geology really affect our day-to-day lives? A Geodiversity Action Plan[1] formerly written for Shropshire rightly pointed out 'Our lives and environment are very much influenced by geodiversity, from the distribution of mineral resources and water supplies to the pattern of settlements, farming and wildlife. Geodiversity can add to our understanding of the natural and historic environment and can tell us fascinating stories about the history of the Earth, its ancient plant and animal inhabitants, climates and environments. Geodiversity also underpins biodiversity...with the soil forming the link between them.' You get a real connection with what's under your feet when experiencing a landscape's terrain whilst walking, when your nostrils detect the unmistakable and glorious smell of damp soil after it has rained and when physically moving soil through digging. I have done a lot of digging in Downe and in Shropshire, whilst planting trees and improving rights of way. I confess that once, when I worked with volunteers in the grounds of Down House to replace a kissing gate, I came across a huge round flint. It sits in my garden as a 'Darwin memento'; a flint (one of millions of course) that would have been around when Darwin was walking his grounds!

When I first came to Shropshire, I was very aware that it is one of the richest counties in England for geology. I braved the bitter cold of February to go on a guided walk at the Stiperstones which sought to explain the complexities of the eras that had shaped the landmarks around. But I found it difficult to process. I came away with a folk story of how the Stiperstones had been formed from stones carried in the apron of the Devil and how the new academia of geology must have been revolutionary in Darwin's time. I later found out that there are over 300 Regionally Important Geological Sites in Shropshire and that the county is famous for its fossils, 'including the Condover Mammoth, the Grinshill Rhynchosaurus (a lizard-like reptile pre-dating the dinosaurs) and the Ludlow Bone Bed (a rock layer full of fossil fish bones) and that it has yielded the earliest known evidence of a wildfire'.[2]

So when did Darwin's fascination with geology start? Darwin wrote:[3] '1817 At eight and a half years I went to Mr. Case's school...I was very timid by nature...I had thus young formed a strong taste for collecting...pebbles and minerals...I believe shortly after this or before, I had smattered in botany, and certainly when at Mr. Case's school I was very fond of gardening, and invented some great falsehoods about being able to colour crocuses as I liked...It was soon after I began collecting stones, i.e., when nine or ten, that I distinctly recollect the desire I had of being able to know something about every pebble in front of the hall door: it was my earliest and only geological aspiration at that time.'

This interest continues to grow when Darwin gets older. On 14 March 1822 Erasmus writes:[4] 'I have bought a book which will be very useful, there are directions for finding out the names of minerals...the rules are not very difficult – I dare say I shall be able to obtain some specimens of rocks for you, for Professor Sedgewick said that at the Gog Magog hills (about 4 miles distant) there were a vast number of specimens'. His brother, Erasmus, writes on 25 October 1822 from Christs College, Cambridge[5]: 'I have also found another very nice man...I have bought 2 or 3 little stones from him; 2 specimens of uranite which is a very scarce stone and some leaf copper and a very odd looking thing like a petrefaction called a brain stone...He sells things very cheap and so if you will mention any stones I can probably get them.'

In his youth, Darwin was told that the Bell-stone, which now marks the start of the Shrewsbury Darwin tour[6] was special. 'Mr Cotton...pointed out.. the 'bellstone'; he told me that there was no rock of the same kind nearer than Cumberland or Scotland, and he solemnly assured me that the world would come to an end before anyone would be able to explain how this stone came where it now lay. This produced a deep impression on me, and I meditated over this wonderful stone. So that I felt the keenest delight when I first read of the action of icebergs in transporting boulders, and I glorified in the progress of Geology.'[7]

When he started on his University career, Darwin didn't make the effort to develop his geological knowledge further. Darwin wrote:[8] 'I was so sickened with lectures at Edinburgh that I did not even attend Sedgwick's eloquent and interesting lectures. Had I done so I should probably have become a geologist earlier than I did.'

A few years later, at Cambridge, Professor Henslow encouraged Darwin to study geology after taking his degree. Darwin wrote to Henslow:[9]

'I suspect the first expedition I take clinometer and hammer in hand, will send me back very little wiser and a good deal more puzzled than when I started.' Plans started to be made regarding a trip to Tenerife to study geology and natural history. To his sister Caroline on 28 April 1831 Darwin wrote[10] '...All the while I am writing now my head is running about the Tropics...my enthusiasm is so great that I cannot hardly sit still on my chair. Henslow and other Dons give us great credit for our plan: Henslow promises to cram me in geology – I never will be easy till I see the peak of Tenerife and the great Dragon tree; sandy, dazzling plains, and gloomy silent forest are alternately uppermost in my mind – I am working regularly at Spanish; Erasmus advised me decidedly to give up Italian. I have written myself into a Tropical glow.'

Darwin makes reference to specific geological studies in the area around his home in the summer of 1831: '...on my return to Shropshire I examined sections and coloured a map of parts round Shrewsbury.'[11] In June 1831 Darwin writes to W. D. Fox:[12] 'The Canary scheme goes on very prosperously. I am working like a tiger for it, at present Spanish and Geology, the former I find intensely stupid, as the latter most interesting. I am trying to make a map of Shrops[shire] but don't find it so easy as I expected.'

Some surviving maps in the Cambridge University Library show how Darwin drew copies of Baugh's 1808 map of Shropshire at 1 inch to 1 mile to use as base maps. The towns and villages he drew fall within the following perimenter : Ellesmere, Wem, Newport, Wellington, Bridgnorth, Ludlow, Church Stretton, Bishops Castle, Pontesbury, Pool Quay. 'He coloured areas orange to indicate New Red Sandstone.'[11] The sandstone is coloured as a block from Meole Brace, across Shrewsbury, to Kinnerley.[13]

In July 1831 Darwin visited Llanymynech Hill near Oswestry[14]. Why did this interest Darwin? Kynaston writes: 'Llanymynech Hill forms the southern end of a limestone belt which extends as far as the Great Orme at Llandudno, North Wales...'[15] Originally, this limestone was 'crystallised out of sea water during the carboniferous period, around 360 million years ago. At that time, this area was lying on the equator, slowly journeying north. This was a hot, tropical environment, with rapid evaporation slowly laying down the limestone...full of sea shells or fossilised crinoids.'[16] Darwin recorded his findings on two and a half sheets of notes and made 'extensive use of his compass and clinometer.' His 'immaturity' in the use of geological terms and nomenclature of rocks is evident.[17]

It appears that Shropshire was the perfect place for Darwin to learn about geology. Toghill[18] writes that Shropshire has: '...rocks representative of eleven of the thirteen recognised periods of geological time, ranging in age from about 700 million years old to those formed in the last Ice Age... Shropshire saw many of the great pioneers of British geology in Victorian times...Shropshire is an excellent area to learn about some of the general principles of geology, as well as learning the details of the county's own unique rock sequence and its development through 700 million years of geological time...We can...use the county to explain a large number of aspects of geology: earthquakes, volcanoes, folds, faults, fossils, sedimentary and volcanic environments, which apply not just to Shropshire but to anywhere in Britain...it is always a teaching ground for new generations of geologists...the Cambrian period in Shropshire [contains] the earliest abundant fossils we find anywhere in Britain.'

In August 1831, Darwin received tuition from Sedgwick in field geology. They took a three week expedition in Wales, calling at Llangollen, Conway, Bangor, Capel Curig and Cwm Idwal.[11] This geological tour coincided with the time that Sedgwick was undertaking nationally important studies. Toghill[18] writes that in the 1830's Sir Roderick Impey Murchison, Director of the Geological Survey, was studying rocks of Shropshire and Welsh Borders and Professor Adam Sedgwick of North Wales. Sedgwick worked out the order of the rock succession in North Wales and in 1835 named them all the Cambrian System. Murchison published works on the Silurian System in 1839. However when fossils of the two systems were compared there was much similarity between the Lower Silurian and the Upper Cambrian. The rocks differed but the fossils were the same. After their deaths, Charles Lapworth later named the 'overlap' the Ordovician System in 1879.

But did they explore Shropshire as part of this tour? On the third and fourth August, Sedgwick's notes 'describe forays to the south-west of Shrewsbury, looking mostly at Carboniferous strata, including the Cardeston limestone. He also visited some 'transition' limestone outcrops above Pontesbury...He climbed Pontesford Hill, and regarded these volcanic rocks as younger than the New Red Sandstone, although they were later recognised as Pre-Cambrian.'[11] It is presumed that Darwin was with him on these dates.

Darwin wrote[19]: 'On this tour I had a striking instance of how easy it is to overlook phenomena, however conspicuous, before they have been observed by anyone. We spent many hours...examining all the rocks with extreme care...but neither of us saw a trace of the wonderful glacial phenomena all around us.' Darwin said that the 'tour was of decided use in teaching me a little how to make out the geology of a country.'[20] Roberts states that 'Darwin rapidly progressed under Sedgwick's tuition.'[21] Later in 1837-8 Darwin: 'looked at glacial deposits around Shrewsbury and went to Wenlock Edge.'[22]

Toghill[23] writes: '...it was noticed that the Cambrian fossils of north west Scotland were slightly different from those of Wales and Shropshire. Although the trilobite Olenellus occurs in both areas, there are slight differences in the species...These...differences were discussed in great detail by Darwin, who suggested the idea of faunal provinces – closely related animals evolving in isolation, and thus appearing different from each other.'

'*Principles of Geology*' was published in 1830 by Charles Lyell. Lyell asked Robert FitzRoy, captain of *HMS Beagle*, to search for erratic boulders on the survey voyage. FitzRoy gave Darwin Volume 1 of the book as a welcoming gift. Lyell's interpretation of geological change as the steady accumulation of minute changes over enormously long spans of time was a powerful influence on Darwin.[24] Darwin later wrote:[25] 'Without the principles there would have been no Origin'. Lyell was eager to meet Darwin after his return from *The Beagle* voyage. They became life-long friends. Darwin wrote[26] that from 1837–9 Darwin: 'acted as one of the honorary secretaries of the Geological Society. I saw a great deal of Lyell.' Although Lyell did not publicly accept descent with modification at the time of writing the Principles, Lyell wrote in his notebook after hearing the Darwin–Wallace papers: May 3, 1860: 'Mr. Darwin has written a work which will constitute an era in geology & natural history to show that...the descendants of common parents may become in the course of ages so unlike each other as to be entitled to rank as a distinct species, from each other or from some of their progenitors'.[27] In the five years of the voyage, Darwin wrote 1,383 pages of notes about geology – compared to 368 pages of notes on plants and animals.[28]

Geology had become such an important part of Darwin's life that it even featured in his 1837–8[29] 'This is the Question' note:

'If not marry travel? Europe – Yes? America??? If travel it must be exclusively geological – United States – Mexico. Depend upon health and vigour and how far I become zoological. If I don't travel – work at transmission of species – microscope – simplest forms of life –Geology? Oldest formations? Some experiments – physiological observations on lower animal. Live in London – for where else possible – in small home near Regent's Park – keep horses – take summer tours collect specimen some line of Zoolog: speculations of Geograph: range and geological general works – systemic and study affinities. If marry Cambridge Professorship either Geolog or Zoolog…I could not indolently take country house and do nothing – Could I live in London like a prisoner?…In country – experiment and observations on lower animals – more space'.

Darwin's interest in geology continued well into his later life. After moving to Downe, Darwin wrote the following about the area:[30] 'In most countries the roads and footpaths ascend along the bottoms of valleys, but here this is scarcely ever the case. All the villages and most of the ancient houses are on the platforms or narrow strips of flat land between the parallel valleys. Is this owing to the summits having existed from the most ancient times as open downs and the valleys having been filled up with brushwood? I have no evidence of this, but it is certain that most of the farmhouses on the flat land are very ancient. There is one peculiarity which would help to determine the footpaths to run along the summits instead of the bottom of the valleys, in that these latter in the middle are generally covered, even far more thickly than the general surface, with broken flints. This bed of flints, which gradually thins away on each side, can be seen from a long distance in a newly ploughed or fallow field as a whitish band. Every stone which ever rolls after heavy rain or from the kick of an animal, ever so little, all tend to the bottom of the valleys; but whether this is sufficient to account for their number I have sometimes doubted, and have been inclined to apply to the case Lyell's theory of solution by rain-water, etc., etc.

The flat summit-land is covered with a bed of stiff red clay, from a few feet in thickness to as much, I believe, as twenty feet: this [bed], though lying immediately on the chalk, and abounding with great, irregularly shaped, unrolled flints, often with the colour and appearance of huge bones, which were originally embedded in the chalk, contains not a particle of carbonate of lime. This bed of red clay lies on a very irregular surface, and often descends into deep round wells, the origin of which has been explained by Lyell. In these cavities are patches of sand like sea-sand, and like the sand which alternates with the great beds of small pebbles derived from the wear-and-tear of chalk-flints, which form Keston, Hayes and Addington Commons. Near Down a rounded chalk-flint is a rarity, though some few do occur; and I have not yet seen a stone of distant origin, which makes a difference-at least to geological eyes-in the very aspect of the country, compared with all the northern counties.

The chalk-flints decay externally, which...is owing to the flints containing a small proportion of alkali; but, besides this external decay, the whole body is affected by exposure of a few years, so that they will not break with clean faces for building.

This bed of red clay, which renders the country very slippery in the winter months from October to April, does not cover the sides of the valleys; these, when ploughed, show the white chalk, which tint shades away lower in the valley, as insensibly as a colour laid on by a painter's brush.'

Darwin provided an explanation for the valleys around Downe. He wrote[31]: 'These valleys are in all probability ancient sea-bays, and I have sometimes speculated whether this sudden steepening of the sides does not mark the edges of vertical cliffs formed when these valleys were filled with sea-water, as would naturally happen in strata such as chalk'. The 2009 Darwin's Landscape Laboratory Nomination Document[32] states: 'Later, when he learnt about geologists' developing understanding of surface erosion by rain and surface water, he came to see how the two valleys had been carved by river action during the recent Ice Ages. He understood how the sea had advanced and retreated over the land and how during extreme climatic changes a pattern of Quaternary deposits had been left on the high ground and alluvium along the valley bottoms...'

In July 1880, Darwin writes to Professor James Geikie[33] 'Here I live on a chalk platform gently sloping down from the edge of the escarpment to the south (which is about 800 feet in height) to beneath the Tertiary beds to the north. The beds of the large and broad valleys...are covered with an immense mass of closely packed broken and angular flints...' Toghill[34] highlights that in Shropshire '...a large interval of time from about 190 million years ago to about only 100,000 years ago...[there are] no rocks in Shropshire which belong to the Cretaceous or Tertiary periods...The next sediments we find are...unconsolidated sediments...superficial or drift deposits.....and only the lowest part of the Jurassic system...the next sediments we find...[were]... formed during the 'Ice Age' of the present Quarternary period...' Perhaps this is why Darwin took such an interest in the geology around Downe, where both Cretaceous and Tertiary deposits[35] are present.

The North Downs Way skirts the southern boundary of the London Borough of Bromley and this lies just a few miles from Down House. It is from here in particular you gain an appreciation of the fact that the valleys either side of Down House (two of five in the Borough) form the dip slope of the North Downs and that there is a sudden drop of the scarp slope, where views extend towards Kent and Sussex. In thinking about the enormity of time for the transmutation of species, Darwin wrote in the Origin of Species (1859)[36]: 'The consideration of [the time-scale of geological formations] impresses my mind almost in the same manner as does the vain endeavour to grapple with the idea of eternity...It is an admirable lesson to stand on the North Downs and to look at the distant South Downs; for, remembering that at no great distance to the west the northern and southern escarpments meet and close, one can safely picture to oneself the great dome of rocks which must have covered up the Weald within so limited a period as since that latter part of the Chalk formation...I have made these few remarks because it is highly important for us to gain some notion, however imperfect, of the lapse of years. During each of these years, over the whole world, the land and the water have been peopled by hosts of living forms. What an infinite number of generations, which the mind cannot grasp, must have succeeded each other in the long roll of years!'

In 1859, Darwin hadn't forgotten about Shropshire's geology. After hearing about evidence of life in 'Barrande's premordial zone'[37] he writes to C.R. Ramsay: 'Is it certain that traces of organic remains have been found in the Longmynd Beds?'[38] Ramsay responds: 'I believe it is certain about the worm holes in the Longmynd. I do not doubt it having often seen them.' [39] Biodiversity in such old rocks is significant. Natural England[40] writes: 'The oldest rocks in the County, and in England, are the Pre-Cambrian and Cambrian marine sediments and volcanics that form the 'whaleback' ridge of the Long Mynd and the other distinctive, steep-sided hills running north-east from the Stretton area up to The Wrekin.'

In the first edition of the Origin of Species, Darwin wrote: 'On the sudden appearance of groups of Allied Species in the lowest known fossiliferous strata.—There is another and allied difficulty, which is much graver. I allude to the manner in which numbers of species of the same group, suddenly appear in the lowest known fossiliferous rocks. Most of the arguments which have convinced me that all the existing species of the same group have descended from one progenitor, apply with nearly equal force to the earliest known species. For instance, I cannot doubt that all the Silurian trilobites have descended from some one crustacean, which must have lived long before the Silurian age, and which probably differed greatly from any known animal. If, moreover, they had been the progenitors of these orders, they would almost certainly have been long ago supplanted and exterminated by their numerous and improved descendants.

Consequently, if my theory be true, it is indisputable that before the lowest Silurian stratum was deposited, long periods elapsed, as long as, or probably far longer than, the whole interval from the Silurian age to the present day; and that during these vast, yet quite unknown, periods of time, the world swarmed with living creatures. To the question why we do not find records of these vast primordial periods, I can give no satisfactory answer. Several of the most eminent geologists, with Sir R. Murchison at their head, are convinced that we see in the organic remains of the lowest Silurian stratum the dawn of life on this planet. Other highly competent judges, as Lyell and the late E. Forbes, dispute this conclusion. We should not forget that only a small portion of the world is known with accuracy. M. Barrande has lately added another and lower stage to the Silurian system, abounding with new and peculiar species. Traces of life have been detected in the Longmynd beds beneath Barrande's so-called primordial zone.'

In the 5th Edition of the Origin of Species, Darwin amends his comments: 'Not long ago M. Barrande added another and lower stage, abounding with new and peculiar species beneath the old Silurian system. Remnants of several forms have also been detected beneath Barrandes so-called primordial zone in the Longmynd group, now divided into two stages, and constituting the Lower Cambrian system. Still more recently, the remarkable discovery has been made by Torell of the remains of monocoty-ledonous plants in a Swedish formation, corresponding with the Longmynd group; so that terrestrial or freshwater plants existed several great stages lower down in the series than has hitherto been supposed.'

Darwin also adds these poignant thoughts on the fossil record:

'I look at the natural geological record, as a history of the world imperfectly kept, and written in a changing dialect; of this history we possess the last volume alone, relating only to two or three countries. Of this volume, only here and there a short chapter has been preserved; and of each page, only here and there a few lines. Each word of the slowly-changing language, in which the history is supposed to be written, being more or less different in the interrupted succession of chapters, may represent the apparently abruptly changed forms of life, entombed in our consecutive, but widely separated, formations.'

Time also has a great role to play in the creation of soil, of course. Soil is miraculous. A complex mix of physical, chemical and biological factors creates it from a variety of geologies. One of the biological factors responsible for its formation is the humble earthworm.

After Darwin's travels abroad, at Maer, Josiah Wedgwood, pointed out to Darwin how a field:[41] 'upon which had been scattered fifteen years earlier, a mass of lime, cinders and burnt marble, the detritus of his Etruria pottery works...had...been covered by a layer of earth...Wedgwood suggested...that perhaps worms had done the job'. This, and the writings of Gilbert White of Selborne (Hampshire) were to influence Darwin. The last book Darwin ever wrote was 'On the Formation of Vegetative Mould by the Action of Earth Worms'. Darwin wrote:[42] 'I have now (May 1881) sent to the printers...a little book...this is a subject of but small importance; and I know not whether it will interest any readers, but it has interested me'. Through this work he showed how the very smallest of creatures has a great influence on our environs. He ended his book: 'It may be doubted whether there are many other animals which have played so important a part in the history of the world, as have these lowly organised creatures..'[43]

I remember reading through the book in preparation for a bespoke talk I was giving. Studies involved everything from the analysis of worm casts to testing whether earthworms could hear to seeing whether they were intelligent enough to pull pieces of paper of different shapes into their burrows. Darwin wrote regarding their senses[44]: 'Worms do not possess any sense of hearing. They took not the least notice of the shrill notes from a metal whistles, whiuch was repeatedly sounded near them; nor did they of the deepest and loudest tones of a bassoon. They were indifferent to shouts... When placed on a table close to the keys of a piano, which was played as loudly as possible, they remained perfectly quiet. Although they are indifferent to undulations in the air audible by use, they are extremely sensitive to vibrations in any solid object'. '...Worms are poorly provided with sense-organs, for they cannot be said to see, although they can just distinguish between light and darkness; they are completely deaf, and have only a feeble power of smell; the sense of touch alone is well developed...'

Darwin wrote of the formation and lining of earthworm burrows[45]:

'Every morning during certain seasons of the year, the thrushes and blackbirds on all the lawns throughout the country draw out of their holes an astonishing number of worms; and this they could not do, unless they lay close to the surface. It is not probable that worms behave in this manner for the sake of breathing fresh air...I believe that they lie near the surface for the sake of warmth...and...they often coat the mouths of their burrows with leaves, apparently to prevent their bodies from coming into close contact with the cold damp earth'...they...apparently exhibit some degree of intelligence...in their manner of plugging up the mouths of their burrows...with different kinds of leaves...'

A detailed study[46] around Downe was undertaken by the Earthworm Research Group, to find out which species occurred around Downe. This uncovered nineteen of the twenty-eight found in Britain.

Allolobophora chlorotica (green)

Allolobophora chlorotica (pink)

Aporrectodea caliginosa Grey worm

Aporrectodea longa

Aporrectodea rosea Rosy-tipped worm

Dendrobaena attemsi

Dendrodrilus octaedra Octagonal-tailed worm

Dendrodrilus rubidus

Eisenia andrei

Eisenia fetida Brandling worm

Lumbricus castaneus Chestnut worm

Lumbricus eiseni

Lumbricus festivus

Lumbricus friendi

Lumbricus rubellus Redhead worm

Lumbricus terrestris Lobworm

Murchieona minuscula

Octolasion cyaneium Blue-grey worm

Octolasion tyrtaeum

Satchellius mammalis

N.B. In the hectad in which The Mount occurs nowadays, the following species of earthworm has been found to date: *Dendrobaena veneta*, as well as those asterixed above.[47]

Darwin went so far as to conduct a twenty-nine year experiment to ascertain the pace at which earthworms could move soil[48]: 'A quantity of broken chalk was spread on December 20, 1842, over a part of a field near my house, which had existed as pasture certainly for 30, probably for twice or thrice as many years...At the end of November 1871...a trench was dug across this part of the field; and a line of white nodules could be traced on both sides of the trench, at a depth of 7 inches from the surface. The mould, therefore (excluding the turf) had here been thrown up at an average rate of .22 inches per year...'

This study helped to prove how even larger objects could become covered in 'mould' over time. Darwin wrote[49]: 'Archaeologists are probably not aware how much they owe to worms for the preservation of many ancient objects...many years ago a grass-field was ploughed on the northern side of the Severn, not far from Shrewsbury; and a surprising number of iron arrow-heads were found at the bottom of the furrows, which, as Mr. Blakeway, a local antiquary, believed, were relics of the battle of Shrewsbury in the year 1403, and no doubt had been originally left strewed on the battle-field...not only implements...are thus preserved, but that the floors and remains of many ancient buildings in England [Wroxeter, the old Roman city] have been buried...in large part through the actions of worms...' Archaeologists ought to be grateful to worms, as they protect and preserve for an indefinitely long period every object, not liable to decay, which is dropped on the surface of the land, by burying it beneath their castings...'

Darwin wrote on the benefits of worms[50]: 'In almost all humid countries they are extraordinarily numerous, and for their size possess great muscular power. In many parts of England a weight of more than ten tons (10,516kg) of dry earth annually passes through their bodies is it brought to the surface on each acre of land...the particules of...softer rocks suffer some amount of mechanical trituration in the muscular gizzards of worms...Worms prepare the ground in an excellent manner for the growth of fibrous–rooted plants and for seedlings of all kinds. They periodically expose the mould to air, and sift it so that not stones larger than the particles which they can swallow are left in it...burrows...allow the air to penetrate deeply into the ground. They also greatly facilitate the downward passage of roots of moderate size; and these will be nourished by the humus with which the burrows are lined...The plough is one of the most anicent and most valuable of man's inventions; but long before he existed the land was in fact regularly ploughed, and still continues to be thus ploughed by earthworms.'

Darwin's study of earthworms around Downe helped to show how the movement of worm casts could help to shape the landscape . He wrote [51]: 'Visited Grass-Field with Game Keeper's cottage...I cd see no signs in steep slope of castings blown upwind by late storms – plenty of old subsided ones...This blowing up the slopes wd occur only during very violent storms...The wind is chiefly important for local surfaces' and again[52] 'Visited steepish slope on Stony Field & Game Keeper's field after late storms... Many of the castings have flowed like semi-fluid mortar (better simile than honey) over to rather coarse grass, & was about 5 inches in length in line of slope...No doubt finer matter washed down lower...In part of the slope where wind had acted sideways the matter had flowed obliquely down the slope'.

One of his key pieces of work in relation to earthworms was on the heathland at Keston Common, near Downe. Here he showed how soil type could influence the presence of worms[53]: 'On Keston Common in the triangle between the Hayes & Keston-Mark roads, & north of the path that runs across from the Holwood [&] wicket is a high bit of land covered with heath the ground amongst the heath being quite covered with lichen; I walked carefully over this place & pulled up the heath & looked among the roots, saw no trace of worms. The Holwood path divides the lower part of this bit of common into two regions, the S being chiefly gone & fern with grass & having worm castings, the north part region being the pure heath & lichen region. There is gras[s] on both borders of the path in this part, & worm castings on both borders. But higher up the heath vegetation is on both sides of the path & here there are no worms on the grass edging. In another place there where the there is gorse-fern-grass vegetation in the damp bottom of the valley, & heath on the sides of the valley, & a little gully glade 20–25 yards...long went cutting running up into the heath; this glade had grass, fern, broom, gorse brambles a few flowers & very little heath & was about a yard wide. It was a little tongue of the worm-producing vegetation land which ought to have yielded worms running up into the worm-less vegetation. I hunted it carefully & found no castings but found them directly in the towards bottom of the valley at the base of the glade.'

The lowland dry heathland communities at Keston Common, near Downe, where Darwin studied earthworms were much more extensive in his lifetime, but still occupy some of the higher ground on the dry, infertile, acid soils of the Blackheath Pebble Beds. The heathland is characterised[54] by *Calluna vulgaris* (Heather), and is also notable for the occurrence of *Erica cinerea* (Bell heather) with *Vaccinium myrtillus* (Bilberry) in one of its only two London localities. *Melampyrum pratense* (Common cow-wheat) and small amounts of *Ulex minor* (Dwarf gorse) also occur. *Sarothamnus scoparius* (Broom), and *Ulex europaeus* (Gorse) still grow there. Restoration work is currently focusing on extending the habitat through tree and scrub clearance. The dry acid grassland occurs interspersed within the heather and has a value of its own. Grasses found here include *Deschampsia flexuosa* (Wavy hair grass), *Festuca ovina* (Sheep's fescue) and *Sieglingia decumbens* (Heath grass) and are characteristic of the community, as are the herb species, *Rumex acetosella* (Sheep's sorrel), *Potentilla erecta* (tormentil) and *Juncus squarrosus* (Heath rush). Other species present which are locally restricted in London include *Ornithopus perpusillus* (Bird's foot), and *Carex pilulifera* (Pill sedge). *Moenchia erecta* (Upright chickweed) and *Trifolium striatum* (knotted clover).

BRINK OF EXTINCTION

The impact of 20th century man has often made the greatest headlines when it comes to biodiversity loss. In my delving into old references it was interesting for me, as a conservationist, to find reference[1] to the impact of man in Darwin's time in Shropshire. 'There are a few instances in which agricultural improvements have destroyed the old habitats, and other instances in which recent investigation has failed to detect the plants put down for them'. Soon after reading this, I read the 'State of Nature' Report,[2] produced by 25 UK conservation and research organisations in 2013. This states that of: 'quantitative assessments of the population or distribution trends of 3148 species...60%...have declined over the last 50 years and 31% have strongly declined...species with specific habitat requirements are faring worse than generalist species that are better able to adapt to a changing environment...Of more than 6000 species that have been assessed using modern Red List criteria, more than one in ten are thought to be under threat of extinction in the UK' with destruction of valuable habitat, or its degradation, and climate change posing some of the greatest threats. What examples of 'near extinction' can be found in Darwin's two landscapes?

One butterfly that has historically only been listed in a few locations in Shropshire is the Small Blue (*Cupido minimus*)[3]. This is a species that flies along 'The Terrace', and associated banks, just at the edge of Darwin's grounds at Down House. West Kent Golf Course Nature Reserve represents the last recorded colony in the London Borough of Bromley. As this is a sedentary butterfly it must be presumed that it has been present for some time in this location, including in Darwin's day. Had Darwin known more about it (no records show that he took a particular interest in the species), the Small Blue would have been one that Darwin would have been intrigued by due to its interdependence on other species, namely the Kidney Vetch, *Anthyllis vulneraria* (the caterpillar's only foodplant) and the ant.

The Small Blue is in flight from late May to the end of June. It likes sheltered conditions and sunny nooks where soil is thin. It is often associated with ungrazed or very irregularly grazed sites. The adults tend to drink from birds foot trefoil, horseshoe vetch or kidney vetch and so the correct composition of grassland plants is necessary for their sustenance. Their eggs are laid singly in the flower heads of Kidney Vetch. The species has weak flight with few females flying more than 40m from their emergent spot (though there is evidence that excursions of up to 5km can be made to colonise new sites)[4]. The Small Blue is therefore a species highly affected by fragmentation of habitat.

For the butterfly to flourish and expand its population at any particular location, management on the sites where it occurs should be tailored to increase the abundance of Kidney Vetch. Kidney vetch is a short lived perennial (3–4 years) and thrives on areas of bare soil. Competition from dense neighbouring vegetation can limit its vigour and spread. One approach to managing for Kidney Vetch is more generic; to prevent scrub encroachment of the grassland on which the butterfly occurs. A more intensive approach can be to encourage an increase in plant numbers through sensitive scraping in and around existing plants, in the hope that this will promote germination of seeds. Despite this, there is a twist in the tale of the Small Blue; the caterpillars actually feed on the vetch anthers and seed and therefore as a species puts its own foodplant seedbank under pressure.[4] Yet another complication in the story of their vulnerability as a species is that the caterpillars do not tolerate fellow caterpillars in the same location and that they can even be canabilistic.

The caterpillars are also thought to need ants. There are a handful of locations around Downe that yellow meadow anthills (*Lasias flavius*). – normally representative of long-established meadows – occur, and one consolation is that West Kent Golf Course Nature Reserve has an exceptionally high number. At their final stage in development the caterpillars possess ant-attracting organs[4] During feeding they are occasionally tended by ants.[5] The caterpillars settle in crevices under soil or moss where they lie dormant over winter[4]. In the Spring, they seek a pupation site. It is assumed that the pupa is buried by ants[6].

Recent surveys have shown numbers of Small Blues at the Nature Reserve[7] to be very low, indicating a population that's probably 'on its way out'. This is despite a general rotational cut of the grassland and strimming in key kidney vetch areas having been implemented by London Wildlife Trust and local volunteer groups, including one I lead. Active propogation of plants is perhaps the only remaining step that could be taken.

In Shropshire, records of Small Blues were noted in the west of the county and in central Shropshire in the 1980's and viewed as 'Very scarce'.[8] No recent records for the Small Blue exist[9] and therefore it is likely to be extinct in the County. Action plans[10] for butterfly species in Shropshire have focussed on a number of other threatened species: the Wood White (occurring at Bury Ditches, Radnor Wood and Purslow Wood), Pearl Bordered Fritillary (occurring at Wyre Forest), Silver Studded Blue (occurring at Prees Heath), Small Pearl Bordered Fritillary (occurring at Wyre Forest and Llynclys Common), Dingy Skipper (occurring at Telford & Wrekin, Oswestry Uplands, Wyre Forest and the Stiperstones) and Grizzled Skipper (occurring at Oswestry Uplands and the Wyre Forest). The Shropshire Biodiversity Action Plan states the following to be threats to these species: overgrazing and undergrazing; lack of appropriate woodland management; conifer planting; changes in bracken management; lack of management of unimproved grassland and scrub; redevelopment and quarrying; fragmentation and isolation of habitats.

Let's now look a plant on the edge of local extinction. Blackbush Shaw, near Downe, was purchased by the Woodland Trust some years ago, with backing from Plantlife. One driving factor for the acquisition was the fact that it was the recent location of the rare Kentish Milkwort (*Polygala amara* ssp *austriaca*). In such an isolated location, in the glade of a secondary woodland, it is likely to have been present there for some time, including in Darwin's day.

The plant is 'vulnerable' in the UK according to the Vascular Plant Red Data book (1999) and is being considered as IUCN 'Critically Endangered' category[11]. It has 'suffered a catastrophic decline which is not fully understood and whose causes have almost certainly not ceased' with the species forming 'critically small population sizes' and 'highly fragmented distributions'.[11] 'The lowland southern populations...have occurred along the scarp slope of the North Downs, from the Wye and Crundale Downs in the east, where first reported in 1871, to near Caterham in the west, where first found in 1888...Localities elsewhere on the North Downs...[are] scattered...several...lost due to agricultural improvements'.[11] Blackbush Shaw is one of these 'scattered' localities and the Kentish Milkwort was discovered there in 1964.

Plant numbers at Blackbush Shaw have fluctuated over the years. 31 plants were recorded in 1985, 218 in 1986 and 50 in 1989; numbers have lessened thereafter.[11] Unfortunately, the plant has not been recorded at the site over the last few years, despite efforts to enlarge the woodland glade in which it grew. The glade had been maintained by local volunteers of the Orpington Field Club for many years through strimming and I carried on this work with conservation volunteers before and whilst the site was grazed with stock from 2008.

Southern plants of this species are 'functionally annual'.[11] Continued management of the grassland sward supplemented by monitoring has endeavoured to seek the reappearance of the species from the seedbank. Intensive management has also been undertaken, including soil scraping and tight strimming to create a short turf. Another option that has been considered is its reintroduction from the nearest available seed source, which would probably have genetic similarities to those that have grown at Blackbush Shaw. The problem is that donor sites themselves have few individuals from which to harvest seed. The Millenium Seed Bank at Wakehurst Place also only holds one accession of the species.[11] 'Bulking up' numbers through off-site cultivation: 'in the absence of predation and competition', has been mooted, though trials have shown this to be difficult.[11] In the meantime, we wait to see if the plant is to return of its own accord. The difficulty in distinguishing it from other species of milkwort that grow at the site makes it all the more awkward to spot.

In a very different location, at nearby Keston Common, Darwin studied an insectivorous plant, *Drosera rotundifolia* and took home, to Down House, samples of the species to pot on and experiment with. It is a plant that famously has sticky glands on which insects are captured and digested by the plant.

Darwin looked at how these plants could supplement their diet in a nutrient-poor environment as well as their ability to move. Darwin wrote:[12] 'Is it not curious that a plant should be far more sensitive to a touch than any nerve in the human body!' His fascination with the plant is further revealed when he wrote:[13] 'The fact that a plant should secrete, when properly excited, a fluid containing an acid and ferment, closely analagous to the digestive fluid of an animal, was certainly a remarkable discovery'. Darwin returned to his 'mad chemist' days in testing out the plant's reaction to various chemicals and 'treatments'. A report by William Baxter in the Bromley and District Times outlines his encounter with Darwin[14].

'My father had been accustomed in his business as pharmaceutical chemist to supply Mr Darwin with nearly all his requirements in the shape of drugs and chemicals for his experiments on plants...Being fond of botany...I was attracted by some experiments Mr Darwin was then making with Drosera rotundifolia (the Sundew), which is a flesh-eating plant and easily obtained from the sphagnum-moss bed near Keston Ponds. So one day I went up there with my vasculum to get specimens and was busy collecting the plant when I espied a shaggy pony wandering about, and instantly I though Mr Darwin must be there! Not seeing him, however, I went on with my job. Presently I was conscious of someone standing over me and a quiet voice said, " Well, young man, what are you doing here?" I got up and there facing me was the grand old man, wrapped in his well-known cape.

After recovering myself I replied, "I am collecting some Drosera to reproduce some of your experiments, Mr Darwin". Mr Darwin then asked me what I was doing with the Drosera and I told him I was not feeding it on flies, &c., but on sulphur and poisonous alkaloids. I told him I found it absorbed sulphur. "How interesting," he remarked, "for that corroborates my experience; but I envy you your access to that mysterious cupboard you have, full of interesting poisons." I told him that of course we could send him any he might wish for. "I know! I know!" he said, "but I should like to try everything." After a few words of encouragement, and some enquiries about my examinations, he shook hands with me, caught his pony and rode away.'

Darwin noted the sundew's adaptation to temperature[15]: 'it is a remarkable fact that the leaves of *Drosera rotundifolia*, which flourishes on bleak upland moors throughout Great Britain, and exists (Hooker) within the Arctic Circle, should be able to withstand for even a short time immersion in water heated to a temperature of 145°...It appears that cold-blooded animals are, as might have been expected, far more sensitive to an increase of temperature than is *Drosera*...It may be worth adding that immersion in cold water does not cause any inflection: I suddenly placed four leaves, taken from plants which had been kept for several days at a high temperature, generally about 75° Fahr. (23°.8 Cent.), in water at 45° (7°.2 Cent.)...

We know that 'Keston Bog' became a regular spot for Victorian collectors to visit, from an article in the Saturday Half-Holiday Guide 'The London Microscopist's Collecting Grounds' (1873)[16] which described: 'Keston Common...A most choice resort for the botanist and the lover of primeval nature.' This, no doubt with the demise of regular grazing that would have been traditional on the common, and the resulting build up of scrub alongside the drying out of the bog, has led to the loss of *Drosera rotundifolia*. Active conservation work which has aimed to grub out *Molinia*, remove trees and improve water levels, hopes to give 'time-capsuled' sundew seeds a chance to appear. In reality, its reintroduction is likely when conditions appear suitable, but its establishment will be no easy task.

Whilst in Shropshire I came across *Drosera rotundifolia* at Crammer Gutter and in wet flushes on the Stiperstones. Leighton[17] lists three species of *Drosera* in Shropshire in Darwin's time. These are: *Drosera rotundifolia,* Round leaved sundew, described as being on 'bogs and moist ground; frequent'; *Drosera longifolia,* described as being on 'bogs and wet mossy places; not common'; *Drosera anglica,* described as being 'on bogs not common...covered with red pedunculated glands, exuding a viscous liquid which retains insects'. The 'Rare Plants of Shropshire'[18] cites 'succession to scrub and ultimately to dense woodland within reserves', as probably the main cause of the extinction of the sundews *Drosera anglica* and *Drosera intermedia*' in Shropshire. It also lists *D. obovata* as extinct in 1965 (Hybrid sundew *D. anglica x rotundifolia*) but lists *Drosera rotundifolia* and *D. longifolia* as: 'habitat indicator species in Shropshire' for quality heathland and mire habitat. This teaches us that we can't take the presence of a species for granted.

One of the birds I would regularly marvel at when traveling along the M40 towards Oxford, was the Red kite, *Milvus milvus,* with its distinctive silhouette and striking chestnut red colour. With a wingspan of nearly two metres, and a relatively small body weight of two-three Ibs, they are agile and are able to stay in the air for many hours.[19] I was delighted to find it doing well in Shropshire, with an estimated thirty pairs breeding in the county[20]. The British Red Kite population almost became extinct in the 1930s in England, with individuals only remaining in Wales. Reintroduction programmes in various parts of Britain started in 1989. I read that the first pair to nest since 1876 in Shropshire, fledged young in 2006.[21] The Red Kite remains on the Amber List of Birds of Conservation Concern in Britain, with only 1500 pairs occurring.[22] Their conservation status, including across Europe, has been shaped by changes in land-use, poisoning from pesticides and persecution.

Red Kites breed for the first time when two or three years old and usually pair for life. For established pairs, courtship and nest-building starts during March, about two to four weeks before the first egg is laid.[23] Novices may delay breeding until April. Stick nests are normally built in trees, such as oaks. Eggs are normally laid at three-day intervals. Normally two eggs are laid, but the clutch can be as high as four. Each egg hatches between 31 and 35 days. The majority of nests only successfully fledge one young and many of these die in their first year. An estimated 40% of Red Kites are believed to survive to breeding age.[24] Adult Kites eat carrion and earthworms but can also take small mammals, rabbits, rats, amphibians and birds (mainly crows and magpies), especially when feeding young.

Recovery of the species has been helped by the establishment of feeding stations. One was established at Gigrin Farm, Rhayader in 1995. In 2013, the proposal to establish a Red Kite Feeding Station in Craven Arms had mixed reactions. On the positive side it was felt that a feeding station would increase public knowledge of Kites, and generate support for their conservation and other conservation activities. It was also believed by some that this would help to disperse the population, encouraging Red Kites to 'move in' from Wales. The alternative view was that there was no conservation case for having a feeding station as the birds were expanding their range anyway; that 'the need to feed' wild animals was not the right message to pass on to the public; that the 'attraction' might devalue a 'genuine' wildlife experience that was already possible. Even in nature conservation there is never one answer!

When Forrest[25] wrote his book in 1899 he said of the Pine Marten, *Martes martes*, 'This beautiful animal is now extinct in Shropshire... Eyton...1838...mentions two taken near Stapleton. Mr Henry Gray saw a pair at Ludlow in 1837, that had been killed in Stokes Wood, near Onibury...A male and a female were killed on Wenlock Edge, about 1840... The latest record is one killed in Bucknell Wood, in 1862.' On my arrival in Shropshire, the Shropshire Mammal Society had just actively started to survey for evidence of pine martin in the county as there had been some unconfirmed sightings of them. Darwin refers to the presence of this mammal in the area when he wrote to W. D. Fox:[26] 'I think it is probable we shall get for you both the common & Pine Marten, the latter alive, which I should think you would like, as they are very interesting animals to keep tame, so an Irish gentleman tells me.' A letter thereafter reveals that Darwin does send them, but that both had been stuffed! The pine marten had actually been sourced from Wales in the end.

Let's now turn to a threatened mollusc. English Nature reported that the freshwater pearl mussel, *Margaritifera margaritifera*, 'has been exploited in Britain since pre-Roman times. Indeed, its occurrence here may have been an important factor ininducing the first Roman invasion of Britain in 55BC. Scottish pearls were traded in Europe during the 12th century, and commercial exploitation on a much larger scale developed during the 16th century across Britain and Ireland, when river bailiffs were employed to ensure that all valuable pearls were kept for the King. Many people worked in the industry during the 19th Century, but this level of exploitation was apparently unsustainable and the fishery declined sharply. There was a constant but small-scale pearl fishery, traditionally plied by travelling people, until the mussel was afforded complete legal protection in 1998.'[27] The 'State of Nature' reports that the species is now threatened with global extinction[28].

What would Darwin have thought of the Freshwater Pearl Mussels which live in the Clun catchment? There is nothing to suggest that he knew of their occurrence in Shropshire but I think he would have been fascinated in the complex life history of this lowly species. In the last six months of Darwin's life, Darwin published six scientific communications, one of these was on 'The Dispersal of Freshwater Bivalve Molluscs'[29].

The Freshwater Pearl Mussel life cycle runs as follows. Adults reach re-productive maturity at 10–15 years. Male adults release sperm which are inhaled into the female inhalant siphon and fertilisation occurs in brood chambers. These develop into larvae, called cochlidia (about 0.07 mm in length) over a month, and are then released in a synchronised event over a period of one to two days, sometime between June and September. A small percentage are drawn into the oxygen-rich gills of trout and salmon where they clamp onto the gills and encyst. They remain there for 9–11 months then drop off and bury themselves in the gravel-rich beds of the river, surviving only where the substrate is suitable. Sufficient oxygen is required in the interstial spaces of the bed. As they grow they come closer to the surface of the river bed and use their 'foot' to keep a grip on the gravels. They become exposed to river flows from the age of five to ten. As bivalves they filter water for fine particles of detritus. They can move, but normally for short distances. The species is believed to have a lifespan of at least 100 years – so perhaps those in the Clun river in present times are two generations away from when Darwin lived in Shropshire!

So what are the threats to them? Extremes of flooding, now more frequent due to climate change, can dislodge them from the river. The dry summers, leading to low water regimes, can cause the mussels to dry out. Sediment running in from diffuse and point sources, such as fords and poached riverbanks disrupts their feeding regime. The widening of rivers, on account of a less-treed landscape, has resulted in the slowing down of water and deposition of sediment. Warmer water, on account of loss of riverside trees and increasingly warmer summers, creates sub-optimum temperatures for survival. There has been a loss of riffles, which help to oxygenate the water in which they live. The existence of weirs can limit the migration of fish upstream, so creating a gap in lifecycle; 0+ and 1+ age groups of salmon or trout are required. Mussels also require nutrient poor waters, with low conductivity, low calcium levels and a pH of 7.5 or less[30]. The demise of the species is representative of the demise in environmental quality of the rivers and catchments in which they lie.

One can get an idea of sensitivity , or some might say 'fussiness', of the species when looking at the favourable target conditions that have been devised by various agencies. Scandanavian water target conditions for the mussel are as follows[31]: Inorganic aluminium 30 micrograms/l (maximum); total phosphorus <5-15 micrograms/l (average); nitrate <125 micrograms/l (median); turbidity <1FNU (average, spring flood); water temperature <25o (maximum); fine grain (<1mm) substrate <25% (share of particles, maximum); Redox potential <300mV. Water quality status required of the River Clun key mussel locations has been identified as[32]: orthophosphate target 0.01mg/l; suspended solid concentrations <10mg/l;

nitrogen <1.5mg/l; pH <=7.5 Conductivity < 100-120 µS cm-1; biochemi-
cal oxygen demand BOD <1 mg/l 25c; dissolved oxygen of 90-110%.[32] The
Environment Agency has also indicated the following requirements[33]: Minimum of 15-20cm depth of water at lowest levels (ideal being 50cm deep);
moderately flowing water with ideal flow velocity of 0.25-0.75 m/s; shade
60-100% (ideally from trees that extend away from the river, rather than
forming a narrow, linear nature); patches of clean sand or fine gravel (which
may be under or between larger substrate); patches of sand surrounded by
larger, stable substrate (cobbles or boulders); stability of substrate indicated
by presence of moss (eg. *Fontinalis*) on boulders and cobbles; flow defined
as glide or run; sinous or meandering river; minimum of 5/100m[2] juvenile
salmonids present.

With such a combination of problems surrounding the conservation of
the mussel – is their conservation a losing battle? In England, most populations are considered 'functionally extinct' in that 'they consist of a relatively small number of old specimens with no substantial evidence of recent
recruitment' in the wild.[35] During the period I was in Shropshire, numbers
in the Clun River were found to have dropped by an average of 50% between
2008-13,[36] so leaving less than 1500 mussels in the river. In 2013, the mussels
were described as 'in extremely poor condition', this being gauged by the
fact that 'very few were well buried' with many 'almost fully out of the substrate with their foot retracted rather than the normal situation with the foot
anchoring the mussels into the substrate.' The report continued: 'A retracted
foot can be caused by high stress levels leading to muscle deterioration. They
displayed a very poor level of filtration, and most were covered in mud and
diatom growth'.[36]

A report[35] was written highlighting a list of measures that would need
to occur to restore freshwater pearl mussel habitat to favourable condition.
These measures included: reductions or cessation of fertiliser use; reductions
or cessation of slurry application; reductions or cessation of application of
battery chicken waste; implementation of nutrient management plans;
reductions or cessation of ploughing; reductions or cessation of drainage
and drainage maintenance; reductions in grazing intensity or livestock units;

reductions in land use intensity such as conversion to native woodland; cessation of liming of land; containment of sheep dip and its removal from the catchment; fencing off of drains, streams or rivers where there is significant bed or bank erosion; establishment of appropriate, site-specific buffer zones of native woodland or semi-natural vegetation around drains, streams, rivers and lakes; floodplain and wetland restoration or creation of artificial wetlands or filter beds; installation of appropriately-sized sediment traps; implementation of measures to increase infiltration or slow surface run-off of land drains; modification of voluntary agri-environmental schemes to include freshwater pearl mussel measures; cessation of water abstraction using tankers; cessation of the use of rivers to wash tankers; fencing of grazing animals away from potential pearl mussel habitat; provision of suitable watering troughs to limit reliance on river water; non-modification of riverbed or banks; non-use of vehicular fords across the riverbed; improvement in the efficiency of septic tanks and small effluent systems.

It is plain to see that implementing these measures is an uphill task and arguably unachievable. I, along with other colleagues from the Shropshire Hills Area of Oustanding Natural Beauty Partnership, Environment Agency and Natural England, directed effort into implementing some of these measures with landowners. Despite this, the urge for conservation of the species was so strong that the Freshwater Biological Association took the ultimate route – to take around seventy individuals into captivity to save the population. An 'Ark' in Cumbria has literally been tasked with the responsibility of 'holding the babies', whilst suitable translocation sites in the catchment are found.

What would Darwin's view be of all the 'near-extinctions' raised above. Would Darwin have said that we should accept circumstances and that nature is taking its course through the principle of 'survival of the fittest' or would he have realised the impact humans have had on these species and supported the need to conserve them at whatever cost? Certainly, nowadays, as a 'conservationist' the desire is often to 'do what we can' to help species. There is another view point of conservationists too, that perhaps too much effort is put into conserving 'niche species'.

De Beer stated[37] that in Victorian times: 'To admit that species of plants or animals could become extinct involved the admission that the protection of divine providence had been withheld from such species', something Darwin aimed to challenge by showing that species were mutable. Darwin wrote[38]: 'The more I think, the more convinced I am, that extinction plays greater part than transmutation' in the development of species.

What did Darwin write about extinction? One extract of his works shows how he recognised that rarity was a precursor to local extinction. Darwin writes in the Origin of Species:

'I believe in no fixed law of development, causing all the inhabitants of a country to change abruptly, or simultaneously, or to an equal degree. The process of modification must be extremely slow. The variability of each species is quite independent of that of all others. Whether such variability be taken advantage of by natural selection, and whether the variations be accumulated to a greater or lesser amount, thus causing a greater or lesser amount of modification in the varying species, depends on many complex contingencies,—on the variability being of a beneficial nature, on the power of intercrossing, on the rate of breeding, on the slowly changing physical conditions of the country, and more especially on the nature of the other inhabitants with which the varying species comes into competition.[39]

We can clearly understand why a species when once lost should never reappear, even if the very same conditions of life, organic and inorganic, should recur. For though the offspring of one species might be adapted (and no doubt this has occurred in innumerable instances) to fill the exact place of another species in the economy of nature, and thus supplant it; yet the two forms—the old and the new—would not be identically the same; for both would almost certainly inherit different characters from their distinct progenitors.[40]

On Extinction.—We have as yet spoken only incidentally of the disappearance of species and of groups of species. On the theory of natural selection the extinction of old forms and the production of new and improved forms are intimately connected together. The old notion of all the inhabitants of the earth having been swept away at successive periods by catastrophes, is very generally given up, even by those geologists, as Elie de Beaumont, Murchison, Barrande, &c., whose general views would naturally lead them to this conclusion. On the contrary, we have every reason to believe, from the study of the tertiary formations, that species and groups of species gradually disappear, one after another, first from one spot, then from another, and finally from the world.[41]

The whole subject of the extinction of species has been involved in the most gratuitous mystery. Some authors have even supposed that as the individual has a definite length of life, so have species a definite duration. No one I think can have marvelled more at the extinction of species, than I have done.[42]

It is most difficult always to remember that the increase of every living being is constantly being checked by unperceived injurious agencies; and that these same unperceived agencies are amply sufficient to cause rarity, and finally extinction. We see in many cases in the more recent tertiary formations, that rarity precedes extinction; and we know that this has been the progress of events with those animals which have been exterminated, either locally or wholly, through man's agency. I may repeat what I published in 1845, namely, that to admit that species generally become rare before they become extinct—to feel no surprise at the rarity of a species, and yet to marvel greatly when it ceases to exist, is much the same as to admit that sickness in the individual is the forerunner of death—to feel no surprise at sickness, but when the sick man dies, to wonder and to suspect that he died by some unknown deed of violence.[43]

The theory of natural selection is grounded on the belief that each new variety, and ultimately each new species, is produced and maintained by having some advantage over those with which it comes into competition; and the consequent extinction of less-favoured forms almost inevitably follows.'[44]

DARWIN'S LAST YEARS

Alphonse de Candolle (1806–1893), a Swiss botanist wrote about his visit to Darwin in 1880[1]. From it, we can get a sense of Darwin's well-being a couple of years before Darwin's death. 'I longed to converse once more with Darwin, whom I had seen in 1839, and with whom I kept up a most interesting correspondence. It was on a fine autumn morning in 1880 that I arrived at Orpington station, where my illustrious friend's break met me. I will not here speak of the kind reception given to me at Down, and of the pleasure I felt in chatting familiarly with Mr and Mrs Darwin and their son Francis. I note only that Darwin at seventy was more animated and appeared happier than when I had seen him forty-one years before. His eye was bright and his expression cheerful, whilst his photographs show rather the shape of his head, like that of an ancient philosopher. His varied, frank, gracious conversation, entirely that of a gentleman, reminded me of that of Oxford and Cambridge savants. The general tone was like his books, as is the case with sincere men, devoid of every trace of charlatanism. He expressed himself in English easily understood by a foreigner,...Darwin had more firmness in his opinions, whether from temperament, or because he had published nothing without prolonged reflection. Around the house no trace appeared to remain of the former labours of the owner. Darwin used simple means. He was not one who would have demanded to have palaces built in order to accommodate laboratories. I looked for the greenhouse in which such beautiful experiments on hybrid plants had been made. It contained only a vine. One thing struck me, although it is not rare in England, where animals are loved. A heifer and a colt were feeding close to us with the tranquillity which tells of good masters, and I heard the joyful barking of dogs. 'Truly,' I said to myself, 'the history of the variations of animals was written here, and observations must be going on, for Darwin is never idle.' I did not suspect that I was walking above the dwellings of those lowly beings called earthworms, the subject of his last work, in which Darwin showed once more how little causes in the long run produce great effects. He had been studying them for thirty years, but I did not know it. Returning to the house, Darwin showed me his library, a large room on the ground floor, very convenient for a studious man; many books on the shelves; windows on two sides; a writing-table and another for apparatus for his experiments. Those on the movements of stems and roots were still in progress. The hours passed like minutes. I had to leave. Precious memories of that visit remain.'

Atkins[2] writes that in June 1881, in a letter to Wallace, from Ullswater Darwin wrote: 'everything tires me, even the scenery...life has become very wearisome to me'. In a letter to Hooker at around the same time, Darwin wrote: '...idleness is downright misery for me; as I find here, as I cannot forget my discomfort for an hour. I have not the heart or strength at my age to begin any investigation lasting years, which is the only thing I enjoy; and I have no little jobs which I can do. So I must look forwards to Down graveyard as the sweetest place on earth. This place is magnificently beautiful, and I enjoy the scenery though weary of it'.[3]

After Darwin's seventy-third birthday in 1882, Darwin wrote to a friend: 'my course is nearly run'.[4] Emma reports[5] of Darwin's last few months: Mar. 3. [1882] His state was now more languid, walking short distances very slowly. (I remember one walk with him to the Terrace on a beautiful, still, bright day, I suppose in Feb.)...A peaceful time without much suffering – exquisite weather – often loitering out with him.'

After Darwin's death on 19 April 1882, *The Shrewsbury Journal*[6] reported on April 26 1882 that: 'All who knew anything of Mr Darwin know that, massive as he seemed, it was only by the greatest care and the simplest habits that he was able to maintain a moderate amount of health and strength. Mr. Darwin had been suffering for some time past from weakness of the heart, but had continued to do a slight amount of experimental work up to the last. He was taken ill on the night of 11 April 1882 when he had an attack of pain in the chest, with faintness and nausea. The latter lasted, with more or less intermission, during next days, and culminated in his death, which took place about four o'clock on Wednesday 19 April. He remained fully conscious to within a quarter of an hour of his death. His wife and several of his children were present at the closing scene'. It seems that as a 'celebrity', his final hours were for all to know.

Darwin wrote[7] '...my father lived to his eighty-third year with his mind as lively as ever it was, and all his faculties undimmed; and I hope that I may die before my mind fails to a sensible extent!' It seems that his wish came true. For his own death, Darwin had spoken with John Lewis, the carpenter at Downe, and had given him instructions about how his coffin was to be made. It had been planned that Darwin was to be buried at St. Mary the Virgin Church, Downe, but his friend and neighbour, Sir John Lubbock and others petitioned to have him buried at Westminster Abbey. The funeral took place on Wednesday 26 April. The pall bearers at Darwin's funeral were:

George Campbell	The 9th Duke of Argyll
William Cavendish	The 7th Duke of Devonshire
Edward Henry Stanley	The 15th Earl of Derby
James Russell Lowell	The American Ambassador to Britain
William Spottiswoode	Mathematician, physicist, the Queen's Printer, and friend of Darwin
Joseph Dalton Hooker	Darwin's close friend and champion of his Theory of Evolution
Thomas Henry Huxley	Darwin's close friend and champion of his Theory of Evolution
Alfred Russel Wallace	Darwin's friend and the co-founder of Natural Selection
Sir John Lubbock	The 1st Baron of Avebury, Darwin's next door neighbour and close friend[8]

What of Darwin's epitaph? By 1850, Darwin is not listed under 'The Eminent Natives of Shrewsbury' by his friend Leighton.[9] By the time of his death, he was however, well known. The Shropshire Archaeological & Natural History Society[10] wrote: 'Mr Darwin is looked upon by many as a very Shakespeare among the naturalists, and is probably the greatest man that has ever been born here [Shropshire]...Mr Darwin lived long enough to see the truth he had found out on the way to general acceptance. Now he has left his clay-chrysalis of a body, let us honour his memory. His bones will lie with the good and great Englishmen in Westminster Abbey. It is a meet recognition of the man, yet it would have been fitter that grass and flowers should have covered the grave of this great lover of Nature...'

Emma wrote[11] about Darwin earlier in his life: 'He is the most open transparent man I ever saw, and every word expresses his real thoughts... He is particularly affectionate, and very nice to his father and sisters, and perfectly sweet-tempered, and possesses some minor qualities that add particularly to one's happiness, such as not being fastidious, and being humane to animals.' He was fond of talking, and scarcely ever out of spirits; even when he was unwell, he continued sociable, and was 'not like the rest of the Darwins, who will not say how they really are'.

Robert Lowe, Viscount Sherbrooke, later recollects of Darwin, 'He was making a geological tour in Wales, and carried with him, in addition to his other burdens, a hammer of 14 lbs. weight. I remember he was full of modesty, and was always lamenting his bad memory for languages and inability to quote. I am proud to remember that though quite ignorant of physical science, I saw a something in him which marked him out as superior to anyone I had ever met...I walked twenty-two miles with him...'[12]

The Daily News[13] wrote on 24 April 1882:
'Little children, who have a quick instinct for a kind and gentle nature, would run to open a gate when they saw Mr Darwin coming, encouraged thereto by a smile and a kind word. Downe folk, by whom he was much beloved, like now to dwell upon these trifles, and to speak of his considerate kindness to all about him.'

Lord Derby, of Holwood House near Downe, wrote[14] of Darwin 'He was one of the greatest scientific discoverers of our age, [yet] free from envy, jealousy or vanity in any form.'

Sir John Lubbock, of High Elms in Downe, wrote[15]: 'An hour with him...proved a wonderful cordial and brushed away the cobwebs of the imagination like a breath of fresh air'.

Scientist G.J. Romanes wrote the following poem as a memorial to Darwin:[16]

I loved him with a strength of love
Which man to man can only bear
When one in station far above
The rest of men, yet deigns to share
A friendship true with those far down
The ranks: as though a mighty king,
Girt with his armies of renown,
Should call within his narrow ring
Of counsellors and chosen friends
Some youth who scarce can understand
How it began or how it ends
That he should grasp the monarch's hand.

Bettany[17] wrote of Darwin's 'gradual exhaustion' in 1882 and said of him that he was: '...a marvellously patient and successful revolutioniser of thought; a noble and beloved man...'. He talked of Darwin's legacy: 'The botanist looked down on the varieties, races and strains, raised with so much pride by the patient skill of the florist as on things unworthy of his notice and study. The horticulturalist, on his side, knowing how very imperfectly plants can...be studied from the mummified specimens of herbaria, which...constituted in most cases all the material that the botanist of this country considered necessary for the study of plants, naturally looked on the botanist somewhat in the light of a laborious trifler...Darwin altered all this. He made the dry bones live; he invested plants and animals with a history, a biography, a geneology, which at once confessed an interest and dignity on them. Before, they were as the stuffed skin of a beast in the glass case of a museum; now they are living beings, each in their degree affected by the same circumstances that affect ourselves and swayed...by like feelings and like passions...The apparently trifling variations, the very which it was once the fashion for botanists to overlook, have become, as it were, the keystone of a great theory...The belief that every generation is a step in progress to a higher and fuller life contains within it the promise of a glorious evolution which is no longer a faint hope, but a reasoned faith... The discovery of intermediate fossils forms of animals...The break between vertebrate and invertebrate animals, between flowering and non-flowering plants...is now bridged over by discoveries in the life histories of animals and plants which exist today...Embryo animals and plants are now known to go through stages which repeat and condense the upward ascent of life; and they give us information of the greatest value as to the lost stages in the path'

The *Shropshire Journal*[18] reported: 'All Mr Darwin's subsequent work [following the '*Origin of Species*'] were developments in difficult directions of the great principles applied in the *Origin of Species*'...'when we consider Mr. Darwin's always feeble health and his deliberately slow method of work, never hasting but rarely resting, the result seems marvellous.'

LANDSCAPE CONSERVATIONISTS

What I have always found endearing about Darwin, is how he did not observe the rare in his locality, but rather tried to explain the ordinary – perhaps so that people could identify with his outputs. This makes his work 'accessible'. Darwin's last paragraph of the *Origin of Species*, for example, very simply embraces the essence of our understanding of ecology.[1] 'It is interesting to contemplate a tangled bank, clothed with many plants of many kinds,with birds singing on the bushes, with various insects flitting about, and with worms crawling through the damp earth, and to reflect that these elaborately constructed forms, so different from each other, and dependent upon each other in so complex a manner, have all been produced by laws acting around us'. This was a conclusion he reached after years of observation of nature. Nowadays, observations of amateur naturalists and professionals is always, in my view, something to be valued. As long as records are shared, and not 'lost', everyone can be in a better position to understand and appreciate the natural world around them. Without records, we would not have some faint picture of Darwin's Shropshire and Downe.

Records can help us to: establish the location or distribution of habitats and species; determine the quality and condition of a habitat; assess the abundance and viability of populations; understand species behaviour and ethology and help monitor environmental change. But this is not enough on its own; it needs to be translated into positive action in order that our landscapes and their biodiversity can be conserved well into the future. Through the action of conservationists, observations can influence decisions on management techniques for landholdings, inform the designation of sites, enable the protection of nature conservation on development sites, guide approaches to species reintroduction and habitat restoration, help raise the profile of the natural world amongst the public, support funding bids and fuel further survey work.

As the number of people able to identify various species continues to fall, the focus on conservation has evolved from only protecting well-studied nature reserves, to taking action for specific species and habitats to looking at generic improvements on a much wider landscape scale. There has also been a shift to justifying the conservation of the natural environment by emphasising its multiple uses and benefits to people; it does not seem to be enough to just conserve biodiversity for its own sake any more. Perhaps one could say it has 'gone full circle' and we now take the Victorian attitude that other species exist for our pleasure and purposes. Though I have difficulty with this approach I can see that in many ways it's the strongest argument for justifying the cost and effort of conservation work to most people, and therefore must be embraced.

There are numerous landscape scale projects, led by various organisations and partnerships, that are active in Shropshire and Greater London these days. Those involved, including many volunteers, are passionate about these special places, just as Darwin was. In each of these areas many of the elements of the landscape which Darwin would have treasured remain and many individuals devote their time to conserving them for the future. What is involved in a landscape scale approach? It involves: Improving the quality of existing patches of wildlife habitat; enhancing connectivity between them through the creation of 'green corridors'; creating new sites that can support a range of species; making existing wildlife sites bigger; reducing pressure on wildlife areas by maintaining or creating buffer zones; reducing pressure on sites by enhancing the wider environment for wildlife. Conservation of the built heritage is also important in retaining the character of the landscape Darwin knew.

Whatever the justification for conservation, life is too short not to explore and appreciate areas as beautiful as those I have been lucky enough to have enjoyed in Shropshire and around Downe, and to understand something of their history. These landscapes are influenced by so many factors and though precious are by no means free of detrimental change. For example, I discovered, from a report by Edwards of the 'Bromley Local History Society'[2] that in 1898, sixteen years after Darwin's death, a railway line was proposed from Orpington Station up to Biggin Hill, following the passing of the Light Railway Act in 1896. This was to cut straight through Cudham valley, through Darwin's precious Hang Grove and Orchis Bank. Though approved at an inquiry on 2 March 1899, the organisers ran out of time to come up with the necessary funds to enable its construction. We very nearly came to losing a significant piece of Darwin's heritage all in the name of progress.

It brought a smile to my face when writing this book, to come across an unexpected connection with Downe at the very front of the the book by Forrest[3] on *The Fauna of Shropshire* (1899); a paragraph taken from the book '*The Beauties of Nature*'[4] by Sir John Lubbock, Darwin's friend and neighbour at Downe. It can be used in a moment of uplifting reflection: 'Happy indeed is the naturalist: to him the season comes round like old friends; to him the birds sing: as he walks along, the flowers stretch out from the hedges, or look up from the ground; and as each year fades away, he looks back on a fresh store of happy memories'. This compliments Darwin's comment in his *Journal of Researches* (1839)[5]: 'In England any person fond of natural history enjoys in his walks a great advantage, by always having something to attract his attention.'

REFERENCES

PREFACE

1 Darwin's Landscape Laboratory Nominated World Heritage Property Nomination Document, London Borough of Bromley and the Department for Culture, Media and Sport on behalf of the Darwin's Landscape Laboratory Partnership, 2009

Sourcing of a number of letters and Darwin manuscripts has been possible due to http://darwin-online.org.uk and http://www.darwinproject.ac.uk

AN EXCEPTIONAL OBSERVATIONIST

1 Barlow, Nora ed. 1945. Charles Darwin and the voyage of *The Beagle*. London: Pilot Press

2 Darwin, Francis ed. 1887. The life and letters of Charles Darwin, including an autobiographical chapter. vol. 1. London: John Murray

3 Huxley, Leonard. 1921. Charles Darwin. London: Watts

4 The Autobiography of Charles Darwin 1809–1882 The First Complete Edition Edited by his grand-daughter Nora Barlow, Collins, 1958

5 CUL-DAR26.1-121 Draft: [1876.00.00–1882.04.00] 'Recollections of the development of my mind and character' [autobiography] author's fair copy, Darwin

6 CUL-DAR26.1-121 Draft: [1876.00.00–1882.04.00] 'Recollections of the development of my mind and character' [autobiography] author's fair copy, Darwin

7 Report to Natural England on Childhood & Nature: A Survey on Changing Relationships with Nature Across Generations, England Marketing, March 2009

8 Transactions of the Shropshire Archaeological & Natural History Society (established 1877), Volume VIII, 1885

9 Darwin, C. R. 1958. The autobiography of Charles Darwin 1809-1882. With the original omissions restored. Edited and with appendix and notes by his grand-daughter Nora Barlow. London: Collins

10 CUL-DAR26.1-121 Draft: [1876.00.00–1882.04.00] 'Recollections of the development of my mind and character' [autobiography] author's fair copy

11 Bowlby, John Charles Darwin, A New Biography Century Hutchinson Ltd, London 1990

12 Darwin, C. R. 1958. The autobiography of Charles Darwin 1809–1882. With the original omissions restored. Edited and with appendix and notes by his grand-daughter Nora Barlow. London: Collins

13 Children & Nature Network: Research & Studies Volume 5 'Benefits to children from contact with nature; children's experience of nature'. Review of papers from 2009-2011 & Childhood Development and Access to Nature (Strife & Downey, University of Colorado, 2009)

14 Darwin, Francis ed. 1887. The life and letters of Charles Darwin, including an autobiographical chapter. vol. 1. London: John Murray

15 Darwin, Francis ed. 1887. The life and letters of Charles Darwin, including an autobiographical chapter. vol. 1. London: John Murray

16 Darwin's Illness by Ralph Colp Jr., University Press of Florida, 2008

17 Darwin – The Child & the Man, Randal Keynes, Charles Darwin Memorial Lecture, The Friends of Shrewsbury Museum, 10 February 2002

18 Examples include: 'The Descent of Genius: Charles Darwin's Brilliant Career', Roy Porter, History Today Volume: 32 Issue 7 and Richard Dawkins in introduction to 'Origin of Species and the Voyage of The Beagle' by Charles Darwin, 2003, Everyman's Library, Random House

19 Darwin, Francis ed. 1887. The life and letters of Charles Darwin, including an autobiographical chapter. vol. 1. London: John Murray

20 Letter from Charles Darwin to A. Gunther, March 23 1870

21 Letter from Charles Darwin to Hooker, February 4 1861 in The Life & Letters of Charles Darwin including an autobiographical chapter by Francis Darwin, Volume 2, John Murray, London 1887

22 Letter from Charles Darwin to G.J. Romanes (undated) in The Life & Letters of George John Romanes, Longman, Green & Co. 1908

23 Transactions of the Shropshire Archaeological & Natural History Society (established 1877), Volume VIII, 1885

24 'Dealing with the impact of perfectionism on pupil's mental health', Optimus Education, 31 May 2013

25 Darwin, Francis ed. 1887. The life and letters of Charles Darwin, including an autobiographical chapter. vol. 1. London: John Murray

26 Darwin's Illness by Ralph Colp Jr., University Press of Florida, 2008

27 Charles Darwin's Mitochondria by John Hayman, Genetics, May 1 2013 Volume 194 No. 1 21-25

28 Down:The Home Of The Darwins,The Story of a House and the People who lived there by Sir Hedley Atkins Kbe, Phillimore for

The Royal College of Surgeons of England, Lincoln's Inn Fields London,1974

29 Was the Darwin/Wedgwood Dynasty Adversely Affected by Consanguinity? By M. Berra, G. Alvarez & F. Ceballos, Bioscience, May 2010, Volume 60 No. 5

30 The Life & Letters of Charles Darwin including an autobiographical chapter, Volume 3 by Francis Darwin, John Murray, London, 1887

31 Darwin, C. R. to Hooker, J. D. 28 Mar 1849

32 Driven: How Human Nature Shapes Our Choices, P.R. Lawrence & I Nohria, Jossey Bass, 2001

33 Take 5 for Play – An Induction Course for Playworks, A Helpful Guide to Practical Playwork, Editors Clare Hein, Hilary Smith, Leonie Labistour and Karen Benjamin, Playwork Partnerships 2012

34 The Autobiography of Charles Darwin 1809-1882 The First Complete Edition Edited by his grand-daughter Nora Barlow, Collins, 1958

35 The American Museum of Natural History website, October 2013

36 Professor Huxley lecture on "The Coming of Age of the Origin of Species" in 1880 cited in The Times, Friday, Apr 21, 1882; Issue 30487; pg. 5; col E — Charles Robert Darwin

DARWIN'S PLAY SETTINGS

1 Official Darwin Shrewsbury Tour, Tourist Information Shrewsbury, 2013

2 Darwin, Francis ed. 1887. The life and letters of Charles Darwin, including an autobiographical chapter. vol. 1. London: John Murray

3 Peter D. A. Boyd, The Darwin Garden Research Project, 'The Sale of The Mount in 1866'; Web version of BOYD, P.D.A. 2000(b). Darwin Garden Project Part 2 Shropshire Parks and Gardens Trust Newsletter

4 Peter D. A. Boyd, 'Pteridomania - the Victorian passion for ferns'; Web version of BOYD, P.D.A. 1993(a). Pteridomania - the Victorian passion for ferns. Antique Collecting 28, 6, 9-12

5 A Guide to the Botany, Ornithology and Geology of Shrewsbury and its Vicinity edited by W. Phillips, Bunny & Davies 1878

6 The Young Charles Darwin, Keith Thomson, Yale University Press, 2009

7 The Young Charles Darwin, Keith Thomson, Yale University Press, 2009

8 Darwin, Francis ed. 1887. The life and letters of Charles Darwin, including an autobiographical chapter. vol. 1. London: John Murray

9 CUL-DAR26.1-121 Draft: [1876.00.00–1882.04.00] 'Recollections of the development of my mind and character' [autobiography] author's fair copy, Darwin

10 CUL-DAR26.1-121 Draft: [1876.00.00–1882.04.00] 'Recollections of the development of my mind and character' [autobiography] author's fair copy, Darwin

11 CUL-DAR26.1-121 Draft: [1876.00.00–1882.04.00] 'Recollections of the development of my mind and character' [autobiography] author's fair copy, Darwin

12 Letter from Susannah Darwin to Josiah Wedgwood II on June 1813 referenced in Bowlby, John Charles Darwin, A New Biography Century Hutchinson Ltd, London 1990

13 Barlow, Nora ed. 1945. Charles Darwin and the voyage of The Beagle. London: Pilot Press

14 Letter to Darwin from Caroline Darwin on 22nd March 1826

15 Letter from Catherine Darwin and Caroline Darwin to Darwin, April 1826

16 Barlow, Nora ed. 1945. Charles Darwin and the voyage of *The Beagle*. London: Pilot Press

17 Darwin, Francis ed. 1887. The life and letters of Charles Darwin, including an autobiographical chapter. vol. 1. London: John Murray

18 Letter from Emily Darwin to Darwin from Maer in June 1823

19 Countryside Recreation - Glyptis, Sue, Institute of Leisure & Amenity Management 1991

20 The Autobiography of Charles Darwin 1809–1882 The First Complete Edition Edited by his grand-daughter Nora Barlow, Collins, 1958

21 Darwin, Francis ed. 1887. The life and letters of Charles Darwin, including an autobiographical chapter. vol. 1. London: John Murray

22 Litchfield, H. E. ed. 1904. Emma Darwin, wife of Charles Darwin. A century of family letters. Cambridge: University Press printed. Volume 1

23 History, Gazetteer and Directory of Shropshire by Bagshaw, 1851

24 Darwin, C. R. to Fox, W. D. Oct 1828

25 Personal communication with Natural History Museum, 2013

26 Personal communication with Ludlow Museum Resources, 2013

27 CUL-DAR91.56-63 Draft: 1838.08.00 [An autobiographical fragment] [of `Life'] My earliest recollection the date of which I can approximately tell

28 Letter from Caroline Darwin to Sarah Wedgwood October 5 1836 in Correspondence 1: 304-5 cited in Charles Darwin: A New Biography by John Bowlby, Hutchinson 1990

29 John van Wyhe ed., Darwin's 'Journal' (1809-1881). CUL-DAR158.1-76 (Darwin Online, http://darwin-online.org.uk/)

30 CUL-DAR158.1-76 Note: [1838.08.00–1881.00.00] Personal 'Journal' 1809-1881

31 Charles Darwin & The Voyage of *The Beagle* by Nora Barlow, London Pilot Press, 1945

32 A Most Glorious Country: Charles Darwin and North Wales, especially his 1831 Geological Tour by Peter Lucas, Archives of Natural History 29 (1):1-26, 2002

33 Freeman, R. B. 1978. Charles Darwin: A companion. Folkstone: Dawson

34 Letter from Darwin, C. R. to Darwin, C. S., 9 Nov 1836

35 Letter from Darwin, C. R. to Lyell, Charles 6 [July 1841]

36 Freeman, R. B. 1978. Charles Darwin: A companion. Folkstone: Dawson

37 Letter from Darwin, S. E. to Darwin, C. R. , 12 Feb 1832

38 CUL-DAR26.1-121 Draft: [1876.00.00–1882.04.00] 'Recollections of the development of my mind and character' [autobiography] author's fair copy

39 Darwin, Francis ed. 1887. The life and letters of Charles Darwin, including an autobiographical chapter. vol. 1. London: John Murray

40 Moore, Richard Shropshire Doctors & Quacks, Amberley Publishing, Gloucestershire 2011

41 Shropshire Wildlife Trust Tour of Darwin's Gardens, 16th February 2013

42 CUL-DAR26.1-121 Draft: [1876.00.00–1882.04.00] 'Recollections of the development of my mind and character' [autobiography] author's fair copy, Darwin

43 Darwin, Francis ed. 1887. The life and letters of Charles Darwin, including an autobiographical chapter. vol. 1. London: John Murray

44 Darwin, Francis ed. 1887. The life and letters of Charles Darwin, including an autobiographical chapter. vol. 1. London: John Murray

45 CUL-DAR26.1-121 Draft: [1876.00.00–1882.04.00] 'Recollections of the development of my mind and character' [autobiography] author's fair copy, Darwin

46 Chancellor, John Great Lives: Charles Darwin George Weidenfeld and Nicolson Limited and Book Club Associates, London 1973

47 Darwin, Francis ed. 1887. The life and letters of Charles Darwin, including an autobiographical chapter. vol. 1. London: John Murray

48 CUL-DAR26.1-121 Draft: [1876.00.00--1882.04.00] 'Recollections of the development of my mind and character' [autobiography] author's fair copy

49 The Young Charles Darwin, Keith Thomson, Yale University Press, 2009

50 Barlow, Nora ed. 1945. Charles Darwin and the Voyage of *The Beagle*. London: Pilot Press.

51 Letter from Darwin to his father, Robert Darwin on 31st August 1831

52 Darwin, Francis ed. 1887. The life and letters of Charles Darwin, including an autobiographical chapter. vol. 1. London: John Murray

53 Letter from Frederic Watkins to Darwin 18 September 1831

54 Salopian Shreds and Patches Volume 5 1882-3, The Shrewsbury Journal, April 26 1882

55 Letter from C. Darwin to R. Fitz-Roy (Shrewsbury, Thursday morning, October 6 1836) in Darwin, Francis ed. 1887. The life and letters of Charles Darwin, including an autobiographical chapter. vol. 1. London: John Murray

56 The Young Charles Darwin, Keith Thomson, Yale University Press, 2009

57 CUL-DAR26.1-121 Draft: [1876.00.00–1882.04.00] 'Recollections of the development of my mind and character' [autobiography] author's fair copy

58 Emma Darwin, notes on Down House and neighbourhood, CUL DAR 251, September 1842

59 Darwin's Landscape Laboratory Nominated World Heritage Property Nomination Document, London Borough of Bromley and the Department for Culture, Media and Sport on behalf of the Darwin's Landscape Laboratory Partnership, 2009

60 Official Darwin Shrewsbury Tour, Tourist Information Centre, Shrewsbury, 2013

61 The Sand Walk, Randal Keynes (paper as part of personal communication, November 2013)

62 Darwin, Francis ed. 1887. The life and letters of Charles Darwin, including an autobiographical chapter. vol. 1. London: John Murray

63 George Darwin, reminiscences for Francis Darwin, 'Life and letters' (1887), CUL DAR 112 [Folio 30]

64 Transactions of the Shropshire Archaeological & Natural History Society (established 1877), Volume VIII, 1885

65 LETTER NO. 17 From Darwin to Caroline Darwin from Buenos Ayres, September 20 1833 in Barlow, Nora ed. 1945. Charles Darwin and the voyage of *The Beagle*. London: Pilot Press

66 The Life And Letters Of Charles Darwin, Including An Autobiographical Chapter. Edited By His Son, Francis Darwin

GENERAL ASPECTS

1 Letter from Darwin to W.D. Fox on 30 June 1828 and letter from Darwin to W.D. Fox on 26th February 1829

2 Letter from Darwin to W. D. Fox 12 March 1837 (Burkhardt, 1996: 55)

3 Darwin, Francis ed. 1887. The life and letters of Charles Darwin, including an autobiographical chapter. vol. 1. London: John Murray

4 Letter from Darwin to W.D. Fox in October 1839 in Darwin, Francis ed. 1887. The life and letters of Charles Darwin, including an autobiographical chapter. vol. 1. London: John Murray

5 Emma Darwin: A Century of Family Letters by H. E. Litchfield, Cambridge University Press, Volume 2, 1904

6 Darwin, Francis ed. 1887. The life and letters of Charles Darwin, including an autobiographical chapter. vol. 1. London: John Murray

7 Darwin, Francis ed. 1887. The life and letters of Charles Darwin, including an autobiographical chapter. vol. 1. London: John Murray

8 Letter from Darwin to W.D. Fox, December 1842 in Darwin, Francis ed. 1892. Charles Darwin: his life told in an autobiographical chapter, and in a selected series of his published letters [abridged edition]. London: John Murray

9 Darwin, Francis ed. 1887. The life and letters of Charles Darwin, including an autobiographical chapter. vol. 1. London: John Murray

10 Letter from Darwin to Captain Fitzroy in October, 1846 in Darwin, Francis ed. 1887. The life and letters of Charles Darwin, including an autobiographical chapter. vol. 1. London: John Murray

11 Letter from Darwin to Catherine Darwin on Sunday July 1842 in

Darwin, Francis & Seward, A. C. eds. 1903. More letters of Charles Darwin. A record of his work in a series of hitherto unpublished letters. London: John Murray. Volume 1

12 'Account of Downe' in Darwin, Francis & Seward, A. C. eds. 1903. More letters of Charles Darwin. A record of his work in a series of hitherto unpublished letters. London: John Murray. Volume 1

13 Letter from Darwin to Mr. Fox on March 28th, 1843 in Darwin, Francis ed. 1887. The life and letters of Charles Darwin, including an autobiographical chapter. vol. 1. London: John Murray

14 Period Piece – A Cambridge Childhood by Gwen Raverat, 1952

15 From Darwin to Caroline Darwin, from Approaching Ascencion on July 18th. 1836 in Barlow, Nora ed. 1945. Charles Darwin and the voyage of *The Beagle*. London: Pilot Press

16 Forrest, H. Edward The Fauna of Shropshire being an account of all the mammals, birds, reptiles and fishes found in the county of Salop by, L. Wilding, Castle Street, Shrewsbury, 1899

17 WW Watts The Geography of the County of Salop, Wilding & Son Ltd Shrewsbury, 1939

Sourcing of a number of letters and Darwin manuscripts has been possible due to http://darwin-online.org.uk and http://www.darwinproject.ac.uk

SIX-LEGGED CURIOSITIES

1 The Autobiography of Charles Darwin The First Complete Version, Nora Barlow, Collins 1958

2 The Aurelian's Fireside Companion: An Entomological Anthology by Michael Salmon & Peter Edwards, Paphia Publishing Ltd, 2005

3 A History of Shropshire volume I. (The Victoria history of the counties of England), xxv, 497p illus, maps; Geology; Palaeontology; Mosses, Natural history; Lichens 1908 with additions from Riley, Adrian A Natural History of the Butterflies and Moths of Shropshire, Swan Hill Press, Shrewsbury 1991

4 Extract from Shropshire Ecological Data Network (SEDN), tetrad SJ41W

5 Pamphlet: de Beer, Gavin ed. 1960. Darwin's notebooks on transmutation of species. Part III. Third notebook [D] (July 15 to October 2nd 1838). Bulletin of the British Museum (Natural History). Historical Series 2 (4) (July):119–150

6 Darwin, C. R. 1859. On the origin of species by means of natural selection, or the preservation of favoured races in the struggle for life. London: John Murray. 1st edition, 1st issue

7 The Autobiography of Charles Darwin 1809–1882 The First Complete Edition Edited by his grand-daughter Nora Barlow, Collins, 1958

8 Letter from Darwin to W.D. Fox, 12th June 1828, from Shrewsbury

9 Bowlby, John Charles Darwin, A New Biography Century Hutchinson Ltd, London 1990

10 Letter from Darwin to W.D. Fox on 29th October 1828

11 Letter from Darwin to W.D.. Fox on 25 August 1830

12 Darwin, George. 5.1882. [Recollections of Charles Darwin]. CUL-DAR112.B9-B23 (Darwin Online, http://darwin-online.org.uk/)

13 Sourced from National Biodiversity Network (NBN) for hectad TQ46

14 Periodical contribution: Smith, K.G.V. 1987. Darwin's insects: Charles Darwin's entomological notes, with an introduction and comments by Kenneth G. V. Smith. Bulletin of the British Museum (Natural History) Historical Series. Vol. 14(1): 1-143

15 A History of Shropshire volume I. (The Victoria history of the counties of England), xxv, 497p illus, maps; Geology; Palaeontology; Mosses, Natural history; Lichens 1908. Updated species names provided by Maxwell Barclay, Natural History Museum in 2014 (personal communication)

16 Personal communication with Natural History Museum, May 2013

17 Personal communication with Natural History Museum, May 2013

18 Personal communication with Ludlow Museum Resource Centre, June 2013

19 The Autobiography of Charles Darwin 1809–1882 The First Complete Edition Edited by his grand-daughter Nora Barlow, Collins, 1958

20 Letter from Darwin to W.D. Fox

21 National Biodiversity Network, hectad SJ41

22 Extract from Shropshire Ecological Data Network (SEDN), tetrad SJ41W

23 Personal communication with Mr. Boardman, Preston Montford Field Studies Council Centre, September 2013

24 Coope, R. (1984). A Beetle's Eye View of the Ice Age, p.7–8 from Proceedings of the Shropshire Geological Society No.4 (1984)

25 David R. Maddison, Coleoptera Beetles, September 2000 http://tolweb.org

26 South Shropshire – Find out how you can help save our wonderful butterflies', Butterfly Conservation leaflet, 2011

27 A History of Shropshire volume I. (The Victoria history of the counties of England), xxv, 497p illus, maps; Geology; Palaeontology; Mosses, Natural history; Lichens 1908 with additions from Riley, Adrian A Natural History of the Butterflies and Moths of Shropshire, Swan Hill Press, Shrewsbury 1991

28 Records from personal surveys undertaken in the area; Purple emperor and White Admiral reported by High Elms Country Park staff and Fred O'Hare

29 Shropshire Ecological Database Network, tetrad SJ41W

30 A Guide To The Butterflies Of Llanymynech Hill, Montgomeryshire Wildlife Trust

31 Letter from Darwin to W.D. Fox in October 1828

32 Darwin, C. R. 1874. The descent of man, and selection in relation to sex. London: John Murray. 2d edition; tenth thousand

33 Darwin, C. R. 1874. The descent of man, and selection in relation to sex. London: John Murray. 2d edition; tenth thousand

34 'June 25th' in Darwin, Francis & Seward, A. C. eds. 1903. More letters of Charles Darwin. A record of his work in a series of hitherto unpublished letters. London: John Murray. Volume 1

35 Periodical contribution: Freeman, R. B. ed. 1968. Charles Darwin on the routes of male humble bees. Bulletin of the British Museum (Natural History). Historical Series Vol. 3, pp. 177–189, one plate. Contains a [second] edition of no. 1580, with transcript of Darwin's original field notes

36 Periodical contribution: Freeman, R. B. ed. 1968. Charles Darwin on the routes of male humble bees. Bulletin of the British Museum (Natural History). Historical Series Vol. 3, pp. 177-189, one plate. Contains a [second] edition of no. 1580, with transcript of Darwin's original field notes

37 Darwin, C. R. 1859. On the origin of species by means of natural selection, or the preservation of favoured races in the struggle for life. London: John Murray. 1st edition, 1st issue

38 Darwin scientific papers, April 1st 1863

39 Darwin scientific papers, April 15th 1863

40 Information sourced from: Hang Grove and Musk Orchid Bank Invertebrate Appraisal (Colin Plant Associates UK, November 2009); West Kent Golf Course Grasslands Invertebrate Appraisal (Colin Plant Associates UK, November 2009); Invertebrate Survey at Downe Scout Activity Centre, Downe (ECOSA Ltd, October 2009); Invertebrate Survey at Shaws Camp Site (ECOSA Ltd, October 2009); Invertebrate Survey at Primrose Bank (ECOSA Ltd, October 2009); personal communication from Geoff Allen from Kent Field Club, January 2013

(Sourcing of a number of letters and Darwin manuscripts has been possible due to www.darwin-online.org.uk and www.darwinproject.ac.uk)

FLIGHT FANTASTIC

1 CUL-DAR26.1-121 Draft: [1876.00.00--1882.04.00] 'Recollections of the development of my mind and character' [autobiography] author's fair copy, Darwin

2 Forrest, H. Edward The Fauna of Shropshire being an account of all the mammals, birds, reptiles and fishes found in the county of Salop by, L. Wilding, Castle Street, Shrewsbury, 1899

3 WW Watts The Geography of the County of Salop Wilding & Son Ltd Shrewsbury, 1939

4 CUL-DAR26.1-121 Draft: [1876.00.00–1882.04.00] 'Recollections of the development of my mind and character' [autobiography] author's fair copy

5 The Young Charles Darwin, Keith Thomson, Yale University Press, 2009

6 Darwin's Diary 1826 (William Darwin Fox factbites website)

7 Game & Wildlife Conservation Trust: Grey Partridge (website)

8 Farming for Birds: Grey Partridge Factsheet, RSPB and Game Conservancy Trust

9 Forrest, H. Edward The Fauna of Shropshire being an account of all the mammals, birds, reptiles and fishes found in the county of Salop by, L. Wilding, Castle Street, Shrewsbury, 1899

10 Letter from Darwin to WD Fox on 26th February 1829

11 CUL-DAR26.1-121 Draft: [1876.00.00–1882.04.00] 'Recollections of the development of my mind and character' [autobiography] author's fair copy

12 Personal communication with Ludlow Museum Resources, 2013

13 Personal communication with Natural History Museum, 2013

14 Letter from C. R. Darwin to Fox W. D. October 1828

15 Darwin's The Edinburgh Ladies & Gentlemans Pocket Souvenir for 1826

16 Forrest, H. Edward The Fauna of Shropshire being an account of all the mammals, birds, reptiles and fishes found in the county of Salop by, L. Wilding, Castle Street, Shrewsbury, 1899

17 Guide Through the Town of Shrewsbury, Reverend W.A. Leighton, John Davies, Shrewsbury, 1850

18 A Guide to the Botany, Ornithology & Geology of Shrewsbury & its Vicinity, edited by W. Philips, Bunny & Davies 1878

19 Guide Through The Town of Shrewsbury, WA Leighton, John Davies, Shrewsbury, 1850 'Birds seen in the neighbourhood of Shrewsbury'

20 A Guide to the Botany, Ornithology & Geology of Shrewsbury & its Vicinity, edited by W. Philips, Bunny & Davies 1878

21 Personal communication with Dr. Rob Robinson of British Trust for Ornithology, November 2013

22 Personal communication with Robert Francis, December 2013 (records by himself and Ros Sim)

23 National Biodiversity Network (NBN) tetrad

24 Darwin, Francis ed. 1887. The life and letters of Charles Darwin, including an autobiographical chapter. vol. 1. London: John Murray

25 CUL-DAR26.1-121 Draft: [1876.00.00–1882.04.00] 'Recollections of the development of my mind and character' [autobiography] author's fair copy

26 J Bunting: Charles Darwin (undated) pages 106–107 (the childhood recollections of a sixty-nine-year-old farmworker who met Darwin in 1871)

27 On Natural Selection, completed March 31, 1857 in Stauffer, R. C. ed. 1975. Charles Darwin's Natural Selection; being the second part of his big species book written from 1856 to 1858. Cambridge: Cambridge University Press

28 Transactions of the Shropshire Archaeological & Natural History Society (established 1877), Volume VIII, 1885

29 Darwin, C. R. [1868]. The variation of animals and plants under domestication. With a preface by Asa Gray. New York: Orange Judd and Co. Volume 1

30 Personal communication with Joanne Cooper, Birds Curation Group, Natural History Museum, Tring, Hertfordshire, May 2013

Sourcing of a number of letters and Darwin manuscripts has been possible due to http://darwin-online.org.uk and http://www.darwinproject.ac.uk

IN THE THICK OF IT

1 Transactions of the Shropshire Archaeological & Natural History Society (established 1877), Volume VIII, 1885

2 Stauffer, R. C. ed. 1975. Charles Darwin's Natural Selection; being the second part of his big species book written from 1856 to 1858. Cambridge: Cambridge University Press

3 Darwin, Francis ed. 1887. The life and letters of Charles Darwin, including an autobiographical chapter. vol. 1. London: John Murray

4 Down:The Home Of The Darwins,The Story of a House and the People who lived there by Sir Hedley Atkins Kbe, Phillimore for The Royal College of Surgeons of England, Lincoln's Inn Fields London,1974

5 Emma Darwin: A Century Of Family Letters 1792–1896 Edited By Her Daughter Henrietta Litchfield

6 Emma Darwin: A Century Of Family Letters 1792–1896 Edited By Her Daughter Henrietta Litchfield

7 Emma Darwin: A Century Of Family Letters 1792–1896 Edited By Her Daughter Henrietta Litchfield

8 Sourced from 'Magic', DEFRA mapping website

9 Letter from Darwin to Emma Darwin on 13th March 1842

10 Darwin, C. R. to Darwin, Emma [12–24 Oct 1843]

11 WW Watts The Geography of the County of Salop Wilding & Son Ltd Shrewsbury, 1939

12 Leighton, W.A. 1841. A Flora of Shropshire. John van Voorst, London, and John Davies, Shrewsbury

13 A Guide to the Botany, Ornithology & Geology of Shrewsbury and its Vicinity, edited by W. Philips, Bunny & Davies, 1878

14 Sinker, C. A., Packham, J. R., Trueman, I. C., Oswald, P. H., Perring, F. H. and Prestwood, W. V., 1985; Ecological Flora of the Shropshire Region; Shropshire Trust for Nature Conservation

15 A Guide to the Botany, Ornithology & Geology of Shrewsbury and its Vicinity, edited by W. Philips, Bunny & Davies, 1878

16 Personal communication with Mr. Spencer of Natural History Museum, London, October 2013

17 Semi-Natural Broadleaved Woodland 2009, Shropshire Biodiversity Action Plan, Shropshire County Council

18 Darwin, Francis & Seward, A. C. eds. 1903. More letters of Charles Darwin. A record of his work in a series of hitherto unpublished letters. London: John Murray. Volume 1

20 Litchfield, H. E. ed. 1904. Emma Darwin, wife of Charles Darwin. A century of family letters. Cambridge: University Press printed. Volume 2

16 Letter from Emma Darwin to daughter Henrietta Litchfield in Litchfield, H. E. ed. 1904. Emma Darwin, wife of Charles Darwin. A century of family letters. Cambridge: University Press printed. Volume 2

21 Darwin, C. R. 1884. The different forms of flowers on plants of the

same species. 3d thousand. Preface by Francis Darwin. London: John Murray

22 Darwin, C. R. 1877. The different forms of flowers on plants of the same species. London: John Murray

23 Ancient Woodland Indicators in Shropshire Botanical Society Newsletter No. 8, Spring 2003, with addition of cow-wheat (personal communication with Sarah Whild, Manchester Metropolitan University, December 2013)

24 Ancient Woodland Indicator list specifically for Kent drawn up by local experts in consultation with Francis Rose and included in Kent Wildlife Trust's 'Criteria for the Selection and Delineation of Local Wildlife Sites', Personal communication from Anne Waite, Conservation Officer, Kent Wildlife Trust

25 Sir John Lubbock IV, note for a lecture referenced in High Elms Country Park Local Nature Reserve Management Plan 2008-2012, London Borough of Bromley

26 Darwin's note on March 25th 1844 in Litchfield, H. E. ed. 1904. Emma Darwin, wife of Charles Darwin. A century of family letters. Cambridge: University Press printed. Volume 2

27 Darwin, C. R. 1880. The power of movement in plants. London: John Murray

28 Darwin, C. R. 1880. The power of movement in plants. London: John Murray

29 Darwin, C. R. 1880. The power of movement in plants. London: John Murray

30 Leighton, W.A. 1841. A Flora of Shropshire. John van Voorst, London, and John Davies, Shrewsbury

31 Lichen Survey of Selected Sites Within the Proposed World Heritage Site, Ishpi Blatchley for the London Borough of Bromley, March 2009

32 Letter from Darwin to Joseph Hooker dated May 1860, CUL DAR 115.1.57

33 Cambridge University Library (CUL) Darwin Archive (DAR 48:A16 May 1860)

34 Leighton, W.A. 1841. A Flora of Shropshire. John van Voorst, London, and John Davies, Shrewsbury

35 Rare Plants of Shropshire, 3rd edition, by Alex Lockton & Sarah Whild, 2005

36 Darwin, Francis ed. 1887. The life and letters of Charles Darwin, including an autobiographical chapter. vol. 1. London: John Murray

37 Shropshire Biodiversity Action Plan, Shropshire Biodiversity Partnership, 2009

38 Personal communication with Kate Thorne, Churton Ecology, 2013

38a Personal communication with Fiona Gomersall, Shropshire Wildlife Trust 2013

39 Peterken, G.F. 1981 Woodland conservation and management. London: Chapman & Hall

40 Sinker, C. A., Packham, J. R., Trueman, I. C., Oswald, P. H., Perring, F. H. and Prestwood, W. V., 1985; Ecological Flora of the Shropshire Region; Shropshire Trust for Nature Conservation

41 Strettons Area Community Wildlife Group Annual Report 2012

42 Account of Downe' in Darwin, Francis & Seward, A. C. eds. 1903. More letters of Charles Darwin. A record of his work in a series of hitherto unpublished letters. London: John Murray. Volume 1

43 Emma Darwin: notes on Down House and neighbourhood, CUL DAR 251

44 Darwin's Hedgerows, London Borough of Bromley, 2009

45 Darwin's papers

46 Leighton, W.A. 1841. A Flora of Shropshire. John van Voorst, London, and John Davies, Shrewsbury

47 Darwin, C. R. 1865. On the movements and habits of climbing plants. London: Longman, Green, Longman, Roberts & Green and Williams & Norgate

48 Periodical contribution: Darwin, C. R. 1865. On the movements and habits of climbing plants. [Read 2 February] Journal of the Linnean Society of London (Botany) 9: 1-118, 13 text figures

49 Darwin, C. R. 1875. The movements and habits of climbing plants. 2d edition. London: John Murray

50 Darwin, C. R. 1865. On the movements and habits of climbing plants.

London: Longman, Green, Longman, Roberts & Green and Williams & Norgate

51 Darwin, C. R. 1865. On the movements and habits of climbing plants. London: Longman, Green, Longman, Roberts & Green and Williams & Norgate

52 Darwin, C. R. 1865. On the movements and habits of climbing plants. London: Longman, Green, Longman, Roberts & Green and Williams & Norgate

53 Darwin, C. R. 1865. On the movements and habits of climbing plants. London: Longman, Green, Longman, Roberts & Green and Williams & Norgate

54 Darwin, C. R. 1865. On the movements and habits of climbing plants. London: Longman, Green, Longman, Roberts & Green and Williams & Norgate

55 Darwin, C. R. 1865. On the movements and habits of climbing plants. London: Longman, Green, Longman, Roberts & Green and Williams & Norgate

56 Stauffer, R. C. ed. 1975. Charles Darwin's Natural Selection; being the second part of his big species book written from 1856 to 1858. Cambridge: Cambridge University Press

Sourcing of a number of letters and Darwin manuscripts has been possible due to http://darwin-online.org.uk and http://www.darwinproject.ac.uk

A BIT OF BOTANISING

1 Correspondence between Charles Darwin & Hooker in 1845.

2 A Guide to the Botany, Ornithology & Geology of Shrewsbury and its Vicinity Edited by W. Phillips, Bunny & Davies 1878

3 Personal communication with Mr. Spencer of the Natural History Museum, London, October 2013

4 A Flora of Shrewsbury by Whild, Godfrey & Lockton, Shropshire Botanical Society & University of Birmingham, 2011

5 Leighton, W.A. 1841. A Flora of Shropshire. John van Voorst, London, and John Davies, Shrewsbury

6 Darwin, C. R. 1868. The variation of animals and plants under domestication. London: John Murray. 1st edition, first issue. Volume 2

7 Letter from Darwin, C. R. to Leighton, W. A. [1–23 July 1841]

8 A botanical record by Charles Darwin in Shropshire Botanical Society Newsletter No. 10, Spring 2004

9 A botanical record by Charles Darwin in Shropshire Botanical Society Newsletter No. 10, Spring 2004

10 'Mutual Checks on Increase' in Darwin, C. R. 1859. On the origin of species by means of natural selection, or the preservation of favoured races in the struggle for life. London: John Murray. 1st edition, 1st issue

11 Stauffer, R. C. ed. 1975. Charles Darwin's Natural Selection; being the second part of his big species book written from 1856 to 1858. Cambridge: Cambridge University Press

12 Darwin, C. R. 1859. On the origin of species by means of natural selection, or the preservation of favoured races in the struggle for life. London: John Murray. 1st edition, 1st issue

13 Lowland Species Rich Grassland Habitat Action Plan, Shropshire Biodiversity Action Plan, Shropshire Biodiversity Partnership, 2009

14 Down:The Home Of The Darwins,The Story of a House and the People who lived there by Sir Hedley Atkins Kbe, Phillimore for The Royal College of Surgeons of England, Lincoln's Inn Fields London, 1974

15 Darwin, Francis. 1917. Rustic sounds and other studies in literature and natural history. London: John Murray. [Darwin family recollections only]

16 Following Darwin's Footsteps shows Changing Landscape Press Release, Natural History Museum, 2006

17 Darwin, Francis ed. 1887. The life and letters of Charles Darwin, including an autobiographical chapter. vol. 1. London: John Murray

18 Plants of Shropshire, 3rd edition, by Alex Lockton & Sarah Whild, 2005

19 Litchfield, H. E. ed. 1904. Emma Darwin, wife of Charles Darwin. A century of family letters. Cambridge: University Press printed. Volume 2

20 Stauffer, R. C. ed. 1975. Charles Darwin's Natural Selection; being the second part of his big species book written from 1856 to 1858.

Cambridge: Cambridge University Press

21 Butterfly Transect Surveys by Jan Wilson, Bob Fisher and Elaine Cocks

22 Hang Grove and Musk Orchid Bank Invertebrate Appraisal Report number BS/2473/09 November 2009 Prepared by Colin Plant Associates (UK) Consultant Entomologists for the London Borough of Bromley

23 Letter from C. Darwin to J. D. Hooker, Down, June 3rd 1857 in Darwin, Francis ed. 1887. The life and letters of Charles Darwin, including an autobiographical chapter. vol. 2. London: John Murray

24 Darwin, C. R. 1860. On the origin of species by means of natural selection, or the preservation of favoured races in the struggle for life. London: John Murray. 2d edition, second issue

25 Darwin, C. R. 1859. On the origin of species by means of natural selection, or the preservation of favoured races in the struggle for life. London: John Murray. 1st edition, 1st issue

26 Sinker, C. A., Packham, J. R., Trueman, I. C., Oswald, P. H., Perring, F. H. and Prestwood, W. V., 1985; Ecological Flora of the Shropshire Region; Shropshire Trust for Nature Conservation

27 Leighton, W.A. 1841. A Flora of Shropshire. John van Voorst, London, and John Davies, Shrewsbury

28 Periodical contribution: Darwin, C. R. 1862. On the two forms, or dimorphic condition, in the species of Primula, and on their remarkable sexual relations. [Read 21 November 1861] Journal of the Proceedings of the Linnean Society of London (Botany) 6: 77–96

29 On the Difference between Primula veris...P. vulgaris...and P. elatior... and on the Hybrid Nature of the Common Oxlip...by Charles Darwin, March 19 1868

30 Darwin, C. R. 1877. The various contrivances by which orchids are fertilised by insects. London: John Murray. 2d ed

31 Letter from Darwin to Hooker, 12 July 1860

32 Darwin C. R. 1862 On the various contrivances by which British and Foreign orchids are fertilised by Insects and on the good effects of intercrossing, John Murray, London, 1st Edition

33 Darwin, C. R. 1877. The various contrivances by which orchids are fertilised by insects. London: John Murray. 2d ed

34 Comparatives of Orchids and Pollinators in Darwin's Time, compiled by Ian Ferguson for Kent Wildlife Trust

35 Periodical contribution: Darwin, C. R. 1861. Fertilisation of British orchids by insect agency. Gardeners' Chronicle and Agricultural Gazette no. 6 (9 February): 122

36 Darwin, Francis ed. 1887. The life and letters of Charles Darwin, including an autobiographical chapter. vol. 3. London: John Murray

37 Leighton, W.A. 1841. A Flora of Shropshire. John van Voorst, London, and John Davies, Shrewsbury

38 List 1V Flowering Plants of the Bromley District, Bromley Naturalist's Society, Reverend J.J. Scargill, 1895–98

39 A Guide to the Botany, Ornithology & Geology of Shrewsbury and its Vicinity Edited by W. Phillips, Bunny & Davies 1878

40 Rare Plants of Shropshire, 3rd edition, by Alex Lockton & Sarah Whild, 2005

41 Sinker, C. A., Packham, J. R., Trueman, I. C., Oswald, P. H., Perring, F. H. and Prestwood, W. V., 1985; Ecological Flora of the Shropshire Region; Shropshire Trust for Nature Conservation

42 Leighton, W.A. 1841. A Flora of Shropshire. John van Voorst, London, and John Davies, Shrewsbury

43 Letter 601.from Darwin To J.D. Hooker September 28th 1861 in Darwin, Francis & Seward, A. C. eds. 1903. More letters of Charles Darwin. A record of his work in a series of hitherto unpublished letters. London: John Murray. Volume 2

44 Letter from Darwin to Hooker, October 1862

45 Sinker, C. A., Packham, J. R., Trueman, I. C., Oswald, P. H., Perring, F. H. and Prestwood, W. V., 1985; Ecological Flora of the Shropshire Region; Shropshire Trust for Nature Conservation

46 Leighton, W.A. 1841. A Flora of Shropshire. John van Voorst, London, and John Davies, Shrewsbury

47 Double Flowers – Their Origin, Gardener's Chronicle, No. 36, September 1843, page 628

48 Periodical contribution: Darwin, C. R. 1843. Double flowers-their origin. Gardeners' Chronicle no. 36 (9 September): 628

49 Letter from C. Darwin to J. D. Hooker June 5th, 1855 in Darwin, Francis ed. 1887. The life and letters of Charles Darwin, including an autobiographical chapter. vol. 2. London: John Murray

50 Draft: [1884] 'Reminiscences of My Father's Everyday Life' (partial fair copy)

51 Stauffer, R. C. ed. 1975. Charles Darwin's Natural Selection; being the second part of his big species book written from 1856 to 1858. Cambridge: Cambridge University Press

52 Darwin, C. R. [1857] [Abstract of species theory sent to Asa Gray]. CUL-DAR6.51 Transcribed by John van Wyhe

53 Leighton, W.A. 1841. A Flora of Shropshire. John van Voorst, London, and John Davies, Shrewsbury

54 A Guide to the Botany, Ornithology & Geology of Shrewsbury and its Vicinity Edited by W. Phillips, Bunny & Davies 1878

WATERY INVESTIGATIONS

1 Life And Letters Of Charles Darwin Including An Autobiographical Chapter Edited By His Son, Francis Darwin In Three Volumes:—Vol. I. London: John Murray, Albemarle Street.

2 Forrest, H. Edward The Fauna of Shropshire being an account of all the mammals, birds, reptiles and fishes found in the county of Salop by, L. Wilding, Castle Street, Shrewsbury, 1899

3 The Geography of the County of Salop by WW Watts (1939 Wilding & Son Ltd Shrewsbury)

4 EHBeagleDiary Note: 1831.00.00--1836.00.00 Beagle diary

5 EHBeagleDiary Note: 1831.00.00--1836.00.00 Beagle diary

6 Keynes, Richard Darwin ed. 2001. Charles Darwin's Beagle Diary. Cambridge: Cambridge University Press

7 Himalayan Balsam, Impatiens glandulifera, GB Non-Native Species Secretariat (website)

8 Darwin's St Helena July 1836 notes in Keynes, Richard Darwin ed. 2001. Charles Darwin's Beagle Diary. Cambridge: Cambridge University Press

9 Barlow, Nora ed. 1945. Charles Darwin and the voyage of *The Beagle*. London: Pilot Press

10 http://en.m.wikipedia.org/wiki/The_Quarry_(park)

11 Guide Through the Town of Shrewsbury, Reverend W.A. Leighton, John Davies, Shrewsbury, MDCCCL

12 Forrest, H. Edward The Fauna of Shropshire being an account of all the mammals, birds, reptiles and fishes found in the county of Salop by, L. Wilding, Castle Street, Shrewsbury, 1899

13 WW Watts The Geography of the County of Salop Wilding & Son Ltd Shrewsbury, 1939

14 Personal communication with Mrs. Leach, July 2013

15 Shropshire Ecological Data Network (SEDN), tetrad SJ41W

16 Darwin, C. R. 1871. The descent of man, and selection in relation to sex. London: John Murray. Volume 2 [Huxley, T.H.] 1860. Darwin on the origin of Species. Westminster Review 17 (n.s.): 541–70

17 Shropshire Biodiversity Action Plan, Shropshire Biodiversity Partnership, 2002

18 A survey of glacial pools in Shropshire by Whild Associates for Shropshire County Council, 2010

19 Invertebrate Survey of Glacial Pools in Shropshire undertaken by Richard Wright (RWEcology) September to November 2010, commissioned by Shropshire Council with funding supplied by Natural England

20 Odonata at Bomere Pool, 2012 by Sue McLamb, September 2012 and Odonata at Shomere Pool, 2012 by Sue McLamb, September 2012

21 Shropshire Ecological Data Network (SEDN), tetrad SJ41W

22 Letter from McLachlan, Robert to Darwin, C. R. 21 Feb 1868

23 Litchfield, H. E. ed. 1904. Emma Darwin, wife of Charles Darwin. A century of family letters. Cambridge: University Press printed. Volume 2

24 Darwin, C. R. 1859. On the origin of species by means of natural

selection, or the preservation of favoured races in the struggle for life. London: John Murray. 1st edition, 1st issue

25 Darwin's Landscape Laboratory Nominated World Heritage Property Nomination Document, Darwin's Landscape Laboratory Partnership, 2009

26 Darwin, C. R. 1859. On the origin of species by means of natural selection, or the preservation of favoured races in the struggle for life. London: John Murray. 1st edition, 1st issue

27 1856, held in the Cambridge University Darwin archive (DAR 157a)

28 Periodical contribution: Darwin, C. R. 1855. Does sea-water kill seeds? Gardeners' Chronicle and Agricultural Gazette no. 15 (14 April): 242

29 Darwin, C. R. 1876. The origin of species by means of natural selection, or the preservation of favoured races in the struggle for life. London: John Murray. 6th edition, with additions and corrections. [First issue of final definitive text]

30 Periodical contribution: Darwin, C. R. 1857. On the action of sea-water on the germination of seeds. [Read 6 May 1856] Journal of the Proceedings of the Linnean Society of London (Botany) 1: 130–140

31 DAR 157a Experiment Book leaf 78

32 Darwin's Landscape Laboratory Project, Aquatic Invertebrate Survey Of The Keston Common Ponds And Bog, Bromley, March 2010, by ECOSA Ltd for the London Borough of Bromley

Sourcing of a number of letters and Darwin manuscripts has been possible due to http://darwin-online.org.uk and http://www.darwinproject.ac.uk

MAMMALIAN AND REPTILIAN ENCOUNTERS

1 WW Watts The Geography of the County of Salop Wilding & Son Ltd Shrewsbury, 1939

2 Shropshire Biodiversity Action Plan, Shropshire Biodiversity Partnership, 2009

3 Personal communication with Mr. Leach, Darwin's Gardens, 2013

4 Personal communication with Shropshire Bat Group, September 2013

5 Forrest, H. Edward The Fauna of Shropshire being an account of all the mammals, birds, reptiles and fishes found in the county of Salop by, L. Wilding, Castle Street, Shrewsbury, 1899

6 'Bat Survey of Down House Estate: May–September 2003', Ishpi Blatchley for the London Borough of Bromley and English Heritage, November 2003

7 Personal communication with Mr Leach, Darwin's Gardens, 2013

8 Shropshire Ecological Data Network (SEDN), tetrad SJ41W

9 Personal communication with Shropshire Bat Group, September 2013

10 Forrest, H. Edward The Fauna of Shropshire being an account of all the mammals, birds, reptiles and fishes found in the county of Salop by, L. Wilding, Castle Street, Shrewsbury, 1899

11 Darwin, C. R. 1859. On the origin of species by means of natural selection, or the preservation of favoured races in the struggle for life. London: John Murray. 1st edition, 1st issue

12 Darwin, C. R. 1859. On the origin of species by means of natural selection, or the preservation of favoured races in the struggle for life. London: John Murray. 1st edition, 1st issue

13 Darwin, C. R. 1859. On the origin of species by means of natural selection, or the preservation of favoured races in the struggle for life. London: John Murray. 1st edition, 1st issue

14 Forrest, H. Edward The Fauna of Shropshire being an account of all the mammals, birds, reptiles and fishes found in the county of Salop by, L. Wilding, Castle Street, Shrewsbury, 1899

15 Periodical contribution: Darwin, C. R. 1867. Hedgehogs. Hardwicke's Science Gossip 3 (36) (1 December): 280

16 Conversation with Alison Scimia, 2013

17 Shropshire Mammal Group Map of Sightings (webpages)

18 Charles Darwin: Evolution of a Naturalist by Richard Milner, Fact on File Series, 1994

19 Forrest, H. Edward The Fauna of Shropshire being an account of all the mammals, birds, reptiles and fishes found in the county of Salop by, L. Wilding, Castle Street, Shrewsbury, 1899

20 'Variation Under Nature' by Darwin in Stauffer, R. C. ed. 1975. Charles Darwin's Natural Selection; being the second part of his big species book written from 1856 to 1858. Cambridge: Cambridge University Press

21 Darwin, C. R. 1859. On the origin of species by means of natural selection, or the preservation of favoured races in the struggle for life. London: John Murray. 1st edition, 1st issue

22 Personal communication with Mr. Leach, 2013

23 Forrest, H. Edward The Fauna of Shropshire being an account of all the mammals, birds, reptiles and fishes found in the county of Salop by, L. Wilding, Castle Street, Shrewsbury, 1899

24 Salopian Shreds and Patches Volume 5 1882-3, The Shrewsbury Journal, April 26 1882

25 Darwin, Francis ed. 1887. The life and letters of Charles Darwin, including an autobiographical chapter. vol. 1. London: John Murray

26 Darwin, Francis ed. 1887. The life and letters of Charles Darwin, including an autobiographical chapter. vol. 1. London: John Murray

27 Forrest, H. Edward The Fauna of Shropshire being an account of all the mammals, birds, reptiles and fishes found in the county of Salop by, L. Wilding, Castle Street, Shrewsbury, 1899

28 Letter from Darwin to H. Falconer dated 26th December 1863, in Darwin F. & Seward, A.C. Eds, (1903) More letters of Charles Darwin. Chapter3. John Murray, London

29 Shropshire Wildlife Trust tour of Darwin's Gardens, Shrewsbury 2013

30 Forrest, H. Edward The Fauna of Shropshire being an account of all the mammals, birds, reptiles and fishes found in the county of Salop by, L. Wilding, Castle Street, Shrewsbury, 1899

30a Personal communication with Mike Kelly, 2013

31 Forrest, H. Edward The Fauna of Shropshire being an account of all the mammals, birds, reptiles and fishes found in the county of Salop by, L. Wilding, Castle Street, Shrewsbury, 1899

32 Personal communication with Mr. Leach, 2013

33 Forrest, H. Edward The Fauna of Shropshire being an account of all the mammals, birds, reptiles and fishes found in the county of Salop by, L. Wilding, Castle Street, Shrewsbury, 1899

34 'Difficulties on the Theory' by Darwin in Stauffer, R. C. ed. 1975. Charles Darwin's Natural Selection; being the second part of his big species book written from 1856 to 1858. Cambridge: Cambridge University Press

35 Forrest, H. Edward The Fauna of Shropshire being an account of all the mammals, birds, reptiles and fishes found in the county of Salop by, L. Wilding, Castle Street, Shrewsbury, 1899

36 CUL DAR 140.3.1-159 Draft 1884 Reminiscences of my Father's Everyday Life (partial fair copy), Francis Darwin

37 Letter from Darwin C.R to Jenyns, Leonard 17th October 1846

38 Forrest, H. Edward The Fauna of Shropshire being an account of all the mammals, birds, reptiles and fishes found in the county of Salop by, L. Wilding, Castle Street, Shrewsbury, 1899

39 Periodical contribution: Darwin, C. R. 1875. [Letter on animal tails.] in R. L. Tait, The uses of tails in animals. Hardwicke's Science Gossip 11, no. 126 (1 June): 126-127, p. 127

40 Forrest, H. Edward The Fauna of Shropshire being an account of all the mammals, birds, reptiles and fishes found in the county of Salop by, L. Wilding, Castle Street, Shrewsbury, 1899

41 Darwin, C. R. 1872. The origin of species by means of natural selection, or the preservation of favoured races in the struggle for life. London: John Murray. 6th edition; with additions and corrections. Eleventh thousand

42 Personal communication with Mr. Leach, 2013

43 Forrest, H. Edward The Fauna of Shropshire being an account of all the mammals, birds, reptiles and fishes found in the county of Salop by, L. Wilding, Castle Street, Shrewsbury, 1899

44 Darwin, C. R. 1860. On the origin of species by means of natural selection, or the preservation of favoured races in the struggle for life. London: John Murray. 2d edition, second issue

45 Forrest, H. Edward The Fauna of Shropshire being an account of all the mammals, birds, reptiles and fishes found in the county of Salop by, L. Wilding, Castle Street, Shrewsbury, 1899

46 Darwin, C. R. 1871. The descent of man, and selection in relation to sex. London: John Murray. Volume 2

47 Shropshire Ecological Data Network (SEDN), tetrad SJ41W

48 Darwin, Francis ed. 1887. The life and letters of Charles Darwin, including an autobiographical chapter. vol. 1. London: John Murray

49 Shropshire Ecological Data Network (SEDN)

50 Forrest, H. Edward The Fauna of Shropshire being an account of all the mammals, birds, reptiles and fishes found in the county of Salop by, L. Wilding, Castle Street, Shrewsbury, 1899

51 Brown Hare (*Lepus europaeus*) 2009, Shropshire Biodiversity Action Plan

52 Forrest, H. Edward The Fauna of Shropshire being an account of all the mammals, birds, reptiles and fishes found in the county of Salop by, L. Wilding, Castle Street, Shrewsbury, 1899

53 Darwin, C. R. 1868. The variation of animals and plants under domestication. London: John Murray. 1st edition, second issue. Volume 1

54 Darwin, C. R. 1875. The variation of animals and plants under domestication. London: John Murray. 2d edition. Volume 1

55 Personal communication with Daphne Hills c/o Mammal Group, Natural History Museum, May 2013

56 Forrest, H. Edward The Fauna of Shropshire being an account of all the mammals, birds, reptiles and fishes found in the county of Salop by, L. Wilding, Castle Street, Shrewsbury, 1899

57 WW Watts The Geography of the County of Salop Wilding & Son Ltd Shrewsbury, 1939

58 Shropshire Ecological Data Network (SEDN), tetrad SJ41W

59 CUL-DAR91.56–63 Draft: 1838.08.00 [An autobiographical fragment] [of `Life'] My earliest recollection the date of which I can approximately tell

60 CUL-DAR129. – Note: 1826.00.00 diary: with entries about birds, beasts and flowers seen on walks

Sourcing of a number of letters and Darwin manuscripts has been possible due to http://darwin-online.org.uk and http://www.darwinproject.ac.uk

UNDER OUR FEET

1 Shropshire Geodiversity Action Plan Consultation Draft – May 2007, Shropshire County Council, Shropshire Wildlife Trust, Natural England & Shropshire Geological Society

2 Shropshire Geodiversity Action Plan - Consultation Draft – May 2007, Shropshire County Council, Shropshire Wildlife Trust, Natural England and Shropshire Geological Society

3 The Autobiography of Charles Darwin 1809-1882 The First Complete Edition Edited by his grand-daughter Nora Barlow, Collins, 1958

4 Letter from Erasmus to Darwin on 14th March 1822

5 Letter from Erasmus to Darwin on 25th October 1822

6 Official Darwin Shrewsbury Tour, Tourist Information Office, Shrewsbury, 2013

7 The Autobiography of Charles Darwin 1809-1882 The First Complete Edition Edited by his grand-daughter Nora Barlow, Collins, 1958

8 CUL-DAR26.1-121 Draft: [1876.00.00–1882.04.00] 'Recollections of the development of my mind and character' [autobiography] author's fair copy

9 Darwin, Francis ed. 1887. The life and letters of Charles Darwin, including an autobiographical chapter. vol. 1. London: John Murray

10 Letter from Darwin to Caroline Darwin on 28th April 1831

11 Just Before *The Beagle*: Charles Darwin's Geological Fieldwork in Wales, Summer 1831 by Michael Roberts in Endeavour Volume 25 (1) 2001

12 Letter from Darwin to W.D. Fox in June 1831

13 I Coloured a Map: Darwin's Attempts at Geological Mapping in 1831 by Michael Roberts, Archives of Natural History, 27 (1): 69–79, 2000

14 Darwin at Llanymynech: The Evolution of a Geologist, British Journal for the History of Science 29, 1996 by Michael B. Roberts

15 A study of Limestone Quarrying at Llanymynech by Harvey Kynaston, 1984

16 Where I live Shropshire, Nature Features: Llanymynech Rock, BBC (webpage)

17 Darwin at Llanymynech: The Evolution of a Geologist by Michael Roberts, BJHS, 1996, 29, 469–78

18 Toghill, Peter Geology in Shropshire The Crowood Press, Wiltshire 2004

19 The Autobiography of Charles Darwin 1809-1882 The First Complete Edition Edited by his grand-daughter Nora Barlow, Collins, 1958

20 Draft: [1876.00.00–1882.04.00] 'Recollections of the development of my mind and character' [autobiography] author's fair copy

21 Darwin's Dog Leg:The Last Stages of Darwin's Welsh Field Trip of 1831 by Michael Roberts, Archives of Natural History 1998, 25 (1): 59–73

22 Personal communication with Michael Roberts, November 2013

23 Toghill, Peter Geology in Shropshire The Crowood Press, Wiltshire 2004

24 Principles of Geology, Wikipedia (webpage)

25 Boulter, Michael Darwin's Garden: Down House and the Origin of Species, Constable & Robinson Ltd, London 2008

26 Darwin, Francis ed. 1887. The life and letters of Charles Darwin, including an autobiographical chapter. vol. 1. London: John Murray

27 May 3, 1860, Charles Lyell's notebook

28 History of Geology (webpages) Darwin the Geologist by David Bressan

29 Darwin's 1837-8 'This is the Question' note in 'The Autobiography of Charles Darwin 1809-1882 Edited by Nora Barlow, Collins, London 1958

30 "Account of Down" 1843. May 15th by Darwin in Darwin, Francis & Seward, A. C. eds. 1903. More letters of Charles Darwin. A record of his work in a series of hitherto unpublished letters. London: John Murray. Volume 1

31 "Account of Down" 1843. May 15th by Darwin in Darwin, Francis & Seward, A. C. eds. 1903. More letters of Charles Darwin. A record of his work in a series of hitherto unpublished letters. London: John Murray. Volume 1

32 Darwin's Landscape Laboratory Nomination Document 2009, London Borough of Bromley

33 Letter from Darwin to Professor James Geikie in July 1880

34 Toghill, Peter Geology in Shropshire The Crowood Press, Wiltshire 2004

35 Personal communication with Mr. Robin Cocks, former geologist for the Natural History Museum, 2013

36 Darwin, C. R. 1859. On the origin of species by means of natural selection, or the preservation of favoured races in the struggle for life. London: John Murray. 1st edition, 1st issue

37 Origin of Species, Charles Darwin, 1859

38 Letter from Darwin, C.R. to Ramsay, A.C. 26 June 1859

39 Letter from Ramsay, A.C. to Darwin, C.R. 27–30 June 1859

40 Natural England (website)

41 Darwin's Island: The Galapagos in the Garden of England by Steve Jones, Little Brown Book Group, 2009

42 Darwin, Francis ed. 1887. The life and letters of Charles Darwin, including an autobiographical chapter. vol. 1. London: John Murray

43 The Formation of Vegetable Mould Through the Action of Worms with Observations of Their Habits, Charles Darwin, The International Scientific Series, Appletone & Company, 1882

44 The Formation of Vegetable Mould Through the Action of Worms with Observations of Their Habits, Charles Darwin, The International Scientific Series, Appletone & Company, 1882

45 The Formation of Vegetable Mould Through the Action of Worms with Observations of Their Habits, Charles Darwin, The International Scientific Series, Appletone & Company, 1882

46 Darwin's Earthworms Revisited by Butt, Lowe, Beasley, Hanson & Keynes, (University of Central Lancashire, English Heritage, Bournemouth University & Charles Darwin Trust), European Journal of Soil Biology, April 2008

47 National Biodiversity Network (NBN), hectad SJ41; recordings sourced from Earthworm Records for England collected by Citizen Scientists in the OPAL Soil and Earthworm Survey (March 2009 to November 2012)

48 The Formation of Vegetable Mould Through the Action of Worms with Observations of Their Habits, Charles Darwin, The International Scientific Series, Appletone & Company, 1882

49 The Formation of Vegetable Mould Through the Action of Worms with Observations of Their Habits, Charles Darwin, The International Scientific Series, Appletone & Company, 1882

50 The Formation of Vegetable Mould Through the Action of Worms with Observations of Their Habits, Charles Darwin, The International Scientific Series, Appletone & Company, 1882

51 Cambridge University Library 21 January 1872, DAR 63:18

52 Cambridge University Library 25 January 1872, DAR 63:20

53 Cambridge University Library; DAR 64.1: 511 Notes of 15th October 1880

54 Notes by Dr. Judith John, Keston Common Management Plan, London Borough of Bromley, 2009

Sourcing of a number of letters and Darwin manuscripts has been possible due to http://darwin-online.org.uk and http://www.darwinproject.ac.uk

BRINK OF EXTINCTION

1 'A guide to the Botany, Ornithology and Geology of Shrewsbury and its vicinity' Edited by W. Phillips, Bunny & Davies 1878 check

2 The State of Nature in the UK and its Overseas Territories, 22 May 2013, The State of Nature Partnership

3 Riley, Adrian A Natural History of the Butterflies and Moths of Shropshire, Swan Hill Press, Shrewsbury 1991

4 The Butterflies of Britain & Ireland, Jeremy Thomas & Richard Lewington, British Wildlife Publishing, 2010

5 Small Blue Butterfly Conservation Factsheet (website)

6 Personal communication with John Tilt, Butterfly Conservation West Midlands Branch, 2013

7 West Kent Golf Course Grasslands Invertebrate Appraisal, Colin Plant Associates (UK), November 2009

8 Riley, Adrian A Natural History of the Butterflies and Moths of

Shropshire, Swan Hill Press, Shrewsbury 1991

9 Personal communication with John Tilt, Butterfly Conservation West Midlands Branch, 2013

10 Shropshire Biodiversity Action Plan, 2009

11 A Survey of Kentish Milkwort (Polygala amarelle subspecies austriaca) with Recommendations for Management, Revised Draft, F.J. Rumsey, Angela Marmont Centre for UK Biodiversity, Natural History Museum, London, May 2010

12 Letter from Darwin to Lyell, November 1860 in Darwin, Francis ed. 1887. The life and letters of Charles Darwin, including an autobiographical chapter. vol. 3. London: John Murray

13 Draft: [1876.00.00–1882.04.00] 'Recollections of the development of my mind and character' [autobiography] author's fair copy

14 in the Bromley and District Times on 13 September 1929 by William Baxter

15 Darwin, C. R. 1875. Insectivorous plants. London: John Murray

16 Saturday Half-Holiday Guide 'The London Microscopist's Collecting Grounds' (1873)

17 Leighton, W.A. 1841. A Flora of Shropshire. John van Voorst, London, and John Davies, Shrewsbury

18 Rare Plants of Shropshire, 3rd edition, by Alex Lockton & Sarah Whild, 2005

19 www.redkites.org.uk

20 Personal communication with Mr. Smith, Shropshire Ornithological Society

21 Proposal For A Red Kite Feeding Station In The South-West Shropshire Hills Public Consultation by Leo Smith, Ornithological Surveys & Consultancy, 2013

22 Proposal For A Red Kite Feeding Station In The South-West Shropshire Hills Public Consultation by Leo Smith, Ornithological Surveys & Consultancy, 2013

23 www.redkites.org.uk

24 Proposal For A Red Kite Feeding Station In The South-West Shropshire Hills Public Consultation by Leo Smith, Ornithological Surveys & Consultancy, 2013

25 Forrest, H. Edward The Fauna of Shropshire being an account of all the mammals, birds, reptiles and fishes found in the county of Salop by, L. Wilding, Castle Street, Shrewsbury, 1899

26 Darwin, C. R. to Fox, W. D. [25–9 Jan 1829]

27 Ecology of the Freshwater Pearl Mussel, Conserving Natura 2000 Rivers, Ecology Series No.2 by Skinner, Young & Hastie, English Nature, Peterborough, 2003

28 The State of Nature in the UK and its Overseas Territories, 22 May 2013, The State of Nature Partnership

29 Darwin, C. R. 1882. On the dispersal of freshwater bivalves. Nature. A Weekly Illustrated Journal of Science 25 (6 April): 529-530

30 Ecology of the Freshwater Pearl Mussel, Conserving Natura 2000 Rivers, Ecology Series No.2 by Skinner, Young & Hastie, English Nature, Peterborough, 2003

31 Restoration of Freshwater Pearl Mussel Streams, World Wildlife Fund Sweden, 2009

32 Draft River Clun SAC Nutrient Management Plan, Atkins, Environment Agency and Natural England, 2 October 2013

33 Identifying Potential Freshwater Pearl Mussel Habitat in the Clun and Teme Catchments, Liz Etheridge, Environment Agency, 2013

35 An Assessment Of The Potential For The Restoration Of The Freshwater Pearl Mussel Margaritifera Margaritifera (L., 1758) Population In The

River Clun, Shropshire Malacological Services, Ian Killeen, March 2009

36 Summary of Work Carried Out in the River Clun and Teme Tributaries in [Relation to the Freshwater Pearl Mussel], Ian Killeen, 14th June 2013

37 Pamphlet: de Beer, Gavin ed. 1960. Darwin's notebooks on transmutation of species. Part I. First notebook [B] (July 1837–February 1838). Bulletin of the British Museum (Natural History). Historical Series 2 (2) (January): 23–73.

38 CUL-DAR124.- Note: 1838.00.00–1839.00.00 Notebook E: [Transmutation of species]

39 Darwin, C. R. 1859. On the origin of species by means of natural selection, or the preservation of favoured races in the struggle for life. London: John Murray. 1st edition, 1st issue

40 Darwin, C. R. 1859. On the origin of species by means of natural selection, or the preservation of favoured races in the struggle for life. London: John Murray. 1st edition, 1st issue

41 Darwin, C. R. 1860. On the origin of species by means of natural selection, or the preservation of favoured races in the struggle for life. London: John Murray. 2d edition, second issue

42 Darwin, C. R. 1859. On the origin of species by means of natural selection, or the preservation of favoured races in the struggle for life. London: John Murray. 1st edition, 1st issue

43 Darwin, C. R. 1859. On the origin of species by means of natural selection, or the preservation of favoured races in the struggle for life. London: John Murray. 1st edition, 1st issue

44 Darwin, C. R. 1859. On the origin of species by means of natural selection, or the preservation of favoured races in the struggle for life. London: John Murray. 1st edition, 1st issue

Sourcing of a number of letters and Darwin manuscripts has been possible due to http://darwin-online.org.uk and http://www.darwinproject.ac.uk

DARWIN'S LAST YEARS

1 Candolle, Alphonse de. 1882. [Recollection of Darwin]. In Bettany, G. T. 1887. Life of Charles Darwin. London: Walter Scott, pp. 148-150

2 Down:The Home Of The Darwins,The Story of a House and the People who lived there by Sir Hedley Atkins Kbe, Phillimore for The Royal College of Surgeons of England, Lincoln's Inn Fields London, 1974

3 Darwin Revalued by Sir Arthur Keith, Watts & Co. 1955

4 Charles Darwin and His World by Huxley and Kettlewell, Thames and Hudson, 1965

5 Litchfield, H. E. ed. 1904. Emma Darwin, wife of Charles Darwin. A century of family letters. Cambridge: University Press printed. Volume 2

6 Salopian Shreds and Patches Volume 5 1882–3, The Shrewsbury Journal, April 26 1882

7 Darwin, Francis ed. 1887. The life and letters of Charles Darwin, including an autobiographical chapter. vol. 1. London: John Murray

8 www.aboutdarwin.com

9 Guide Through the Town of Shrewsbury, Reverend W.A. Leighton, John Davies, Shrewsbury, 1850

10 Transactions of the Shropshire Archaeological & Natural History Society (established 1877), Volume VIII, 1885

11 Barlow, Nora ed. 1945. Charles Darwin and the voyage of The Beagle. London: Pilot Press

12 Martin, A. Patchett. 1893. Life and letters of the Right Honourable Robert Lowe, Viscount Sherbrooke, G.C.B., D.C.L., etc., with a memoir of Sir John Coape Sherbrooke, G.C.B. sometimes Governor-General of Canada. London: Longmans, Green and Co. 2 vols. [Darwin recollections only, vol. 1, pp. 19-20; vol. 2, pp. 198-207.]

13 The Daily News, 24 April 1882

14 Keston Common, Ravensbourne Meadows & Padmal Wood Management Plan, 2006-9, London Borough of Bromley

15 High Elms Country Park Management Plan, 2006-9, London Borough of Bromley

16 'Charles Darwin: A Memorial Poem' in Macmillan cited in The Life & Letters of George John Romanes by Romanes, 6th impression, Longmans, London, 1908

17 'Darwin: Great Writers' by G T Bettany, 1887, Walter Scott

18 The Shrewsbury Journal Shreds and Patches, April 26 1882

LANDSCAPE CONSERVATIONISTS

1 Darwin, C. R. 1869. On the origin of species by means of natural selection, or the preservation of favoured races in the struggle for life. London: John Murray. 5th edition

2 By Rail to Biggin Hill by John Edwards, Bromley Local History Publication

3 Forrest, H. Edward The Fauna of Shropshire being an account of all the mammals, birds, reptiles and fishes found in the county of Salop by, L. Wilding, Castle Street, Shrewsbury, 1899

4 The Beauties of Nature by Sir John Lubbock 1892

5 Darwin, C.R. 1845. Journal of researches into the natural history and geology of the countries visited during the voyage of H.M.S. Beagle round the world, under the Comman of Capt. Fitz Roy, R. N. 2d edition. London: John Murray